Ancient Law

Law & Society Series

Ancient Law
Henry Sumner Maine
with an introduction by Dante J. Scala

An Introduction to the Sociology of Law
Nicholas S. Timascheff
with an introduction by A. Javier Treviño

Critique of the Legal Order
Richard Quinney
with an introduction by Randall G. Shelder

Fundamental Principles of the Sociology of Law
Eugen Ehrlich
with a new introduction by Klaus A. Ziegert

Penal Philosophy
Gabriel Tarde
with a new introduction by Piers Beirne

Sociology of Law
Georges Gurvitch
with a new introduction by Alan Hunt

The General Theory of Law and Marxism
Evgeny Bronislavovich Pashukanis
with a new introduction by Dragan Milovanovic

The Social Reality of Crime
Richard Quinney
with a new introduction by A. Javier Treviño

with a new introduction by
Dante J. Scala

Henry Sumner Maine

Ancient Law

Transaction Publishers
New Brunswick (U.S.A.) and London (U.K.)

New material this edition copyright © 2002 by Transaction Publishers, New Brunswick, New Jersey 08903. Originally published in 1866 by J. Murray.

This book is printed on acid-free paper that meets the American National Standard for Permanence of Paper for Printed Library Materials.

Library of Congress Catalog Number: 2001034712
ISBN: 0-7658-0795-5
Printed in the United States of America

Library of Congress Cataloging-in-Publication Data

Maine, Henry Sumner, Sir, 1822-1888.
    Ancient law / Henry Sumner Maine ; with a new introduction by Dante J. Scala.
        p. cm.
    Originally published: 3rd ed. London : J. Murray, 1866.
    Includes bibliographical references and index.
    ISBN 0-7658-0795-5 (paper : acid-free paper)
        1. Law, Ancient. 2. Law, Primitive. 3. Comparative law. I. Title

K190 .M35 2001
340.5' 3—dc21   2001034712

CONTENTS.

Introduction to the Transaction Edition   vii

Preface to the First Edition   xli

Preface to the Third Edition   xliii

I.   Ancient Codes   1

II.   Legal Fictions   21

III.   Law of Nature and Equity   44

IV.   The Modern History of the Law of Nature   73

V.   Primitive Society and Ancient Law   113

VI.   The Early History of Testamentary Succession   171

VII.   Ancient and Modern Ideas Respecting Wills and Successions   215

VIII.   The Early History of Property   244

IX.   The Early History of Contract   304

X.   The Early History of Delict and Crime   367

INTRODUCTION

TO

THE TRANSACTION EDITION.

ANCIENT Law, the most famous work of the nine-teenth-century legal historian Henry Sumner Maine, is known as a history of progress, and its reputation as such is perhaps an obstacle to its appreciation by today's readers. The danger is that first-time readers of the book may think they already know how Maine's argument is going to end before they begin reading it.

For those with a background in the social sciences, but who never have read *Ancient Law*, Maine's famous phrase "from status to contract" may still sound a familiar note about the progress of society. Maine's narrative of change spans the ancient world, in which individuals were tightly bound to traditional groups such as the Roman patriarchal family, and the modern one, in which individuals are viewed as autonomous beings, free to make contracts and form associations with whomever they see fit. It is part and parcel of a larger tradition in the social sciences. The dichotomy Maine drew between status-based societies and contract-based societies is a variation on a theme that has dominated the social sciences for a century: the distinction between *Gemeinschaft* (community) and *Gesellschaft* (society), elaborated upon by such scholars as Tönnies, Durkheim, Weber, Simmel, and Parsons.[1] All of these great minds, and many lesser ones, have considered the question of what we gained and what we lost when we left behind a social world held together by communal, primordial bonds, and adopted one allegedly held together by impersonal, temporary agreements among individuals. The analytical dichotomy between *Gemeinschaft* and *Gesellschaft* as a description of historical evolution, the sociologist Edward Shils observed, was an example of what he aptly termed "the tyranny of tradition."[2] What was in Maine's day a fresh and interesting idea—that law was now no more than a "mere surface-stratum," thinly covering the "ever-changing assemblage of contractual rules" that actually governed social arrangements[3]—has become in our day a rather hackneyed concept in the social sciences. Thus one of the problems confronting Maine's readers, who today live with daily tales of

the all-encompassing power of markets and global-
ization, is resisting the lull of a too-familiar analysis of Progress and Modern Society.

One of the dangers of knowing (or presuming)
the ending of Maine's history is bypassing the more
interesting question of how we got from there to
here. If human progress was the end, was the end
inevitable? Or, was there an indispensable means
toward this end? What was the vehicle of
progress?[4] For Maine, the means toward the end
of Progress was Empire: an unsurprising conclusion, perhaps, for a Victorian Englishman.

The empire Maine had in mind, however, was
one not composed of troops and commerce, garri-
sons and administrations, but rather one of words
and ideas, those compiled under the formidable
array of Roman law. The law of the Roman Empire was the winning contender in what Maine
variously described as "the empire of ideas"[5] and
"the empire of primitive notions;"[6] the achievement
of Roman law should not only be measured in words
on paper, or laws enforced, but in its effects on the
Western imagination. Such effects could be measured as physical empires are sometimes measured, in terms of time and space; consider, for example, Maine's assertion of the "known social law"
that "the larger the space over which a particular
set of institutions is diffused, the greater is its tenacity and vitality."[7] How did an empire of words

and ideas gain "tenacity and vitality?" What were the mechanics of innovation and diffusion that led to the success of this empire of the Western mind? These are the questions which should guide today's reader of Maine's *Ancient Law* beyond the well-traveled roads of the distinction between status and contract, into the open, unsettled country of how societies innovate and how knowledge is diffused.

In Maine's own day (a quite fruitful period of legal historiography in Europe, from Savigny to Maitland), he warned that the study of jurisprudence had failed to answer these questions about the nature of progress. He regarded *Ancient Law* as an attempt to supply the defects of previous studies and to increase knowledge of the internal mechanics of progressive societies. One of the major problems in this field of scholarship, Maine argued, was the lack of understanding of how law develops over time. This failure to understand temporal processes, in relation to legal development, had led to the creation of false dichotomies. The most preeminent of these is the alleged division between the ancient and the modern, which Maine described as an "imaginary barrier" at which modern scholars felt they must stop and go no further in their study of the ancient world.[8] Maine's desire to breach this barrier led him to present a much more complicated and nuanced analysis of legal evolution than is captured by the signature phrase, "from status to contract."

This barrier between ancients and moderns was created in part, Maine argued, by his contemporaries' overreliance on functionalism: This scholarly error was "the mistake of supposing that every wheel and bolt in the modern social machine had its counterpart in more rudimentary societies."[9] Progress, according to Maine, did not consist of some ongoing process of replacing old, worn-out parts of social machinery with newer, more efficient cogs, while the design of the machine itself remained basically the same. Such a vision of social progress made the faulty assumption that all societies performed more or less equivalent functions, and thus could be judged along a continuum according to how well they performed those functions. In actuality, Maine argued, some ancient institutions had performed functions that had no modern equivalents:

> ... the warning can never be too often repeated, that the grand source of mistake in questions of jurisprudence is the impression that those reasons which actuate us at the present moment, in the maintenance of an existing institution, have necessarily anything in common with the sentiment in which the institution originated.[10]

The achievement (and ascertainment) of progress in legal development is difficult to accomplish, Maine argued, in part because of the complicated relationship in which the ancient and the modern, the old and the new, both converge and diverge. A measuring stick for progress is difficult to devise because the utility of law is not a sufficient explanation for its formation and development: "Nothing in law springs entirely from a sense of convenience."[11] A society's sense of convenience, of what is more or less useful or beneficial, is shaped by the ideas that came before it. Options and alternatives are constructed out of the materials of the past, which were in turn created with far different intentions in mind. Only in this way, Maine argued, can it be said that ancient ideas are part of our modern "every-day mental stock."[12]

For example, in opening a chapter on the early history of testamentary succession, Maine attested to the following difficulties in explaining the development of the will as a legal instrument. The scholar's dilemmas are manifold. At the beginning of this particular line of legal development, one finds oneself "surrounded by conceptions which it requires some effort of mind to realise in their ancient form." At the end of the line, one is stuck "in the midst of legal notions which are nothing more than those same conceptions disguised by the phraseology and by the habits of thought which belong to modern times."[13] For the historian, understanding how this development unfolded means divorcing oneself from the notion of progress. In other words, the historian must resist the urge to view the ancient world as mere prelude to the modern one, in order to understand the past on its own terms, rather than in the idiom of the current day. Maine was determined that legal history should not take the shape of a "search for origins," assimilating past events in order to explain the present in an arbitrary fashion.[14] How Maine fashioned a superior kind of historiography will be clarified by an overview of his historical narrative of the development of ancient Roman law.

The Importance of Roman Law

If one associates the modern mind with progress and a society's self-consciousness of that progress, then according to Maine, the Romans were the first moderns. In *Ancient Law*, the Roman legal code emerges as the linchpin to the development of progressive societies in the West - an accomplishment of great significance, given the paucity of such societies in a world where inertia has tended to govern. Part and parcel of social progress, Maine argued, is the improvement of the law of society. Such improvement is similarly rare. One finds cases of sudden, violent change in which one set of laws is upended in favor of another, as well as instances in which a code of apparently divine origin grows "into the most surprising forms, by the perversity of sacerdotal commentators." Only a small part of the world, however, has been graced with gradualism, that is, with a legal system which underwent slow, steady improvement over time. "There has been material civilisation," Maine declared, "but, instead of the civilisation expanding the law, the law has limited the civilisation."[15]

The paradigm of a legal system beating such long odds, the exception to the rule of failure, is the Roman system of law, which displayed a long, continuous, recorded history of successful improvement:

> The Roman jurisprudence has the longest known history of any set of human institutions. The character of all the changes which it underwent is tolerably well ascertained. From its commencement to its close, it was progressively modified for the better, or for what the authors of the modification conceived to be the better, and the course of improvement was continued through periods at which all the rest of human thought and action materially slackened its pace, and repeatedly threatened to settle down into stagnation.[16]

The success of Roman law, however, had implications far beyond the institution of a legal code. For not only did the expansion of the Roman Empire expand the sphere governed by the Roman code; in turn, the Roman law expanded the sphere of the Western mind itself. For Maine, Roman law was the *lingua franca* of the West: "To the cultivated citizen of Africa, of Spain, of Gaul, and of

Northern Italy, it was jurisprudence, and jurisprudence only, which stood in the place of poetry and history, of philosophy and science."[17] The Roman law became the language of the Western intellect, providing a common grammar for various courses of thought: "I know nothing more wonderful," Maine declared, "than the variety of sciences to which Roman law, Roman Contract-law more particularly, has contributed modes of thought, courses of reasoning, and a technical language."[18] Such tools were necessary before advanced thought could even begin on a particular subject, and so in this way Roman law provided the architectonics of the Western mind: "Politics, Moral Philosophy, and even Theology, found in Roman law not only a vehicle of expression, but a nidus in which some of their profoundest enquiries were nourished into maturity."[19]

As an example of the far-reaching effects of Roman law on the thought of the West, Maine offered the development of Western theology as a stream of thought separate from its older source in the East. To be sure, this separation was prompted by causes beyond the reach of the law, such as the founding of Constantinople and the division of the Roman Empire into two parts. The separation of East and West left the latter not only politically autonomous, but intellectually independent for the first time from the venerated Greeks.

For at least three centuries, philosophy and science were without a home in the West; and though metaphysics and metaphysical theology were engrossing the mental energies of multitudes of Roman subjects, the phraseology employed in these ardent enquiries was exclusively Greek, and their theatre was the Eastern half of the Empire.[20]

The separation of East from West, however, did not leave a complete vacuum in the latter, more backward part of the Empire. While the Latin of the common folk was deteriorating into various vernacular dialects, a Latin worthy of use for the endeavors of the greatest minds in the West had been retained in the Roman law codes. The jurisprudence of Roman law filled the gap left behind by the departure of Eastern influences, remaining the "one department of enquiry, difficult enough for the most laborious, deep enough for the most subtile, delicate enough for the most refined, [which] had never lost its attractions for the educated classes of the Western provinces."[21]

As such, Roman law became both midwife and nurse to the new intellectuals of the West, and left an indelible mark on their birth and development, especially on the ultimate subject of theology.[22] (In Max Weber's terms, the Roman code provided a means toward the routinization of charisma: the institutionalization of the personal charism of a divine figure in the corporate body of a church.) As the Middle Ages began, Christian theologians in the East remained devoted to the study of the nature and substance of the divine: How many persons was God? How could God be simultaneously fully divine and fully human? Such studies were undertaken in the idiom of Greek metaphysics. In regard to these deliberations, the Western members of the Christian Church had remained respectful but quiet spectators. As the halves of the Roman Empire diverged, however, Western theologians began to emerge from the shadow of their more mystical Eastern brethren, making over problems of the divine in their own image: that is, the image of Roman law and its particular mode of jurisprudence. It was no accident, Maine noted, that intellectuals who were imbued with the theoretical categories of Roman law (such as the theory of obligations created under Contract, or of the acquisition and removal of debt, or the continued legal existence of the individual through the principle of Universal Succession) would turn to a whole new set of theological questions: How can humans acquire original sin by means of inheritance from their predecessors? What was the nature of the debt owed by human beings, that it required divine atonement? How can free will coexist with an omnipotent God? When the Romans "ceased to sit at the feet of the Greeks and began to ponder out a theology of their own," Maine argued, "the theology proved to be permeated with

longer is law regarded as the result of divine fiat,
a gift (*Themis*) of the gods given to a king, a series
of "separate, isolated judgments" unconnected by
comprehensive principle.[25] Even after aristocracy
replaced monarchy as the governing body, the law
remained the province of a few, a collection of customs reposited in the memory of "a caste, an aristocracy, a priestly tribe, or a sacerdotal college."[26]
The creation of a code of law such as Rome's Twelve
Tables, however, marked a legal and political
breakthrough: written, published tablets replaced
the recollections of the elite as the carrier of law.[27]
This great step forward in legal development might
be attributed by some observers to democratic
movements in the West, and Maine did admit that
aristocracies' tight control over legal knowledge
may have posed a serious obstacle to democratiza-
tion. Maine stressed, however, that in the case of
ancient Rome, as in other cases, a wave of progress
in legal development was the result of several
crosscurrents acting simultaneously. In this case,
the crosscurrent was a technological innovation,
the creation of writing, and its application to the
law:

> Inscribed tablets were seen to be a better deposi-
> tary of law, and a better security for its accurate
> preservation, than the memory of a number of per-
> sons however strengthened by habitual exercise...
> [The legal codes'] value did not consist in any ap-

proach to symmetrical classifications, or to terseness and clearness of expression, but in their publicity, and in the knowledge which they furnished
to everybody, as to what he was to do, and what
not to do.[28]

The widespread dissemination of the law was a
catalyst to the development of the young Roman
nation. Before this period, Maine argued, the law
developed spontaneously—that is, with hardly an
inkling of purpose or deliberation; after the legal
codes were made available, development was
linked to "the conscious desire of improvement," or
at the least, a widening of the goals of that development.[29] Maine went to great lengths to make
clear that the development of law was the result of
considerable exertion in practice, not merely in
theory,[30] even offering a rough formula for measuring progress in legal development: the amount
of the intellectual force in the nation devoted to
the project must be measured, as well as how much
time that force was devoted to the particular task.[31]

The elaboration of a legal code was an intellectual task equal to the inquiry into the First Things
of metaphysics, yet an eminently practical project:
"As soon as the mind makes its first conscious efforts towards generalisation, the concerns of every-day life are the first to press for inclusion
within general rules and comprehensive formulas."[32] In Maine's mind, the everyday things with

which the law is concerned present as difficult a challenge as the First Things of metaphysics. This challenge springs from the age-old dilemma of governing and regulating the great variety of everyday human situations by means of "general rules and comprehensive formulas:" How may a society apply abstract ideals of justice to the specific idiosyncrasies and irregularities of everyday situations, without either failing to do justice in the specific, or betraying the ideals in the abstract? Furthermore, how may the law respond to factors such as "social necessities" and "social opinion," which Maine argued is necessary for a progressive society, while still retaining the stability that is a hallmark of the law? The capacity to work out these sorts of questions in practice, Maine argued, is the peculiar genius of the Romans:

> One of the rarest qualities of national character is the capacity for applying and working out the law, as such, at the cost of constant miscarriages of abstract justice, without at the same time losing the hope or the wish that law may be conformed to a higher ideal.[33]

Progress as Recovery

As the author of a book that celebrates the achievements of progressive societies, Maine nonetheless was sometimes rather ambivalent and circumspect about progress—more specifically, he was cautious about the promise, or prospect, of progress. For all of his insistence that progressive societies belong among the few, great elite in human history, elevated to a station far above the rest, he also insisted that the select elite faced their share of dangers from the temptations of progress. The paradox here is that a society which devotes itself to such an ideal in its laws loses the flexibility which a system of laws needs to act as a means toward the end of progress.

A fine example of the dangers of progress emerges in Maine's discussion of the influence of Equity, or "justice," on the development of a nation's laws. Equity is a set of rules which exerts influence on the development of a nation's laws by acting as their foil. In England, for example, Equity became a distinct body of law created to address the shortcomings of the precedent-laden common law courts in supplying remedies for any and all injuries. Equity, in short, is a parallel, or shadow, system of jurisprudence. Its authority does not come from within the nation, it cannot claim the prerogative of an executive or the law-making capability of a legislature as its source of power. Nor is Equity like a legal fiction, a judicial tool which smuggles in new legal principles under old legal conceptions and categories. Instead, Equity is a foreign (even otherworldly) body of law, "founded on distinct principles and claiming incidentally to supersede the civil law in virtue of a superior sanctity inherent in those principles."[34] Equity does not claim its authority on the basis of consent, but rather demands that its authority be respected (and implemented into a nation's law) on the basis of "the special nature of its principles, to which it is alleged that all law ought to conform."[35]

On the one hand, Equity provides a plethora of tools to the jurist for making wholesale innovations to the legal code of the nation.   With the use of Equity, the jurist is well-stocked for all the steps in a project of renovating the laws of a nation: the means of elaborating on first principles, making generalizations, drawing interpretations of the law, and providing "that great mass of limiting rules which are rarely interfered with by the legislator, but which seriously control the application of every legislative act."[36]   For example, under the employment of the Roman Praetor, who was both the chief equity judge and the great common law magistrate,[37] no part of Roman jurisprudence was left untouched by the influence of Equity.   Thus Equity appears essential to a progressive society's development of law to aid its evolution.

At some point, however, Equity outlives its usefulness, and threatens to become a hindrance to legal development rather than a help:

A time always comes at which the moral principles originally adopted have been carried out to all their legitimate consequences, and then the system founded on them becomes as rigid, as unexpansive, and as liable to fall behind moral progress as the sternest code of rules avowedly legal.[38]

Maine's warning on the dangers of Equity eventually hamstringing progressive societies is reminiscent of his discussion of the danger of adherence to customs in less advanced nations. A society in the earlier stages of development takes on particular usages and customs, which tend in practice to be positive means to the development of the fledgling community; these usages, though unconsciously followed by the masses of a particular society, are in fact reasonable and well-suited toward development. Inevitably, however, "usage which is reasonable generates usage which is unreasonable."[39] Popular belief converts a generally salutary and expedient adherence to custom into widespread superstition:

Prohibitions and ordinances, originally confined, for good reasons, to a simple description of acts, are made to apply to all acts of the same class, because a man menaced with the anger of the gods for doing one thing, feels a natural terror in doing any other thing which is remotely like it. After one kind of food has been interdicted for sanitary reasons, the prohibition is extended to all food resembling it, though the resemblance occasionally depends on analogies the most fanciful.[40]

The use of analogy in legal reasoning, while a useful tool for sophisticated cultures, is an onerous trap for a young society which unwittingly uses it to impede progressive development. Other sorts of dangers, however, await maturing, progressive societies: just as primitive societies blindly adhere to custom and allow "irrational imitation" to attach to the law "an immense apparatus of cruel absurdities,"[41] so mature societies might irrationally follow the demands of Equity without considering how to integrate these higher principles with their own system of jurisprudence.

A main reason why progressive societies are vulnerable to the attractions of higher-law jurisprudence is their own ambivalence toward their progress as a society.

Human beings, whether individually or collectively, are modest, even somewhat ashamed, of the notion that they are somehow an improvement over what came before them: "Nothing is more distasteful to men, either as individuals or as masses, than the admission of their moral progress as a substantive reality."[42] Human beings' psychological resistance to the acceptance of their own progress is such that when progress does occur, they tend to describe it not as a step forward, but as a recovery of what once belonged to the society, a return to a lost state of grace: "the recovery of a lost perfection—the gradual return to a state from which the

race has lapsed."[43] Thus, despite the dichotomy
Maine drew between the few progressive societies
and the many backward ones, he did note that "advanced" peoples persist in some of the same habits
as "backwards" peoples, especially a proclivity to
adhere to the ways of old. Maine elaborated on this
odd persistence of progressive societies in his discussion of the Romans' treatment of one of the most
prominent examples of Equity, the natural law.

The Romans and the Natural Law

The gradual incorporation of natural-law jurisprudence into the framework of Roman law was
another example of the eccentric steps which
progress takes, and of the odd crosscurrents which
propel progress within a nation's code of laws.
Maine began his discussion of Roman natural-law
jurisprudence with a quotation from the Institutional Treatise published under the Emperor Justinian:

> All nations who are ruled by laws and customs,
> are governed partly by their own particular laws,
> and partly by those laws which are common to all
> mankind. The law which a people enacts is called
> the Civil Law of that people, but that which natu-
> ral reason appoints for all mankind is called the
> Law of Nations, because all nations use it.[44]

The first odd twist in the Roman chapter of the
history of natural law is that the above descrip-

tion—"that which natural reason appoints for all mankind is called the Law of Nations, because all nations use it"—sounds as if the Romans placed this type of law above all others; but, in fact, the law of nations, or *jus gentium*, began as a mere bow to expediency. In short, according to Maine, the *jus gentium* did not begin as a matter of principle drawn from the dictates of natural reason. Rather, it began as a matter of expediency in coping with the difficulties of maintaining an increasingly diverse political society, by creating a set of laws that would serve as the least common denominator among the various nations that made up the expanding empire. Faced with the basic governmental problems of maintaining police and ensuring commerce, made all the more difficult by the threat of instability which plagued all ancient governments, the Roman state began to extend its jurisdiction beyond the domestic sphere, to situations in which one or both parties were foreigners. Using the already-established Civil Law was not an option, because foreigners had been excluded from such privileges from the early days of the Roman republic. Employing the law of the foreigner's nation on Roman soil was considered a disgraceful option. The solution which Roman jurists chose was to paste together a compendium of laws which these foreigners shared, "a system answering to the primitive and literal meaning of Jus Gentium, that is, Law common to all Nations... the sum of the common ingredients in the customs of the old Italian tribes."[45] Thus the *jus gentium* took its place alongside the civil law of the Romans as an "ignoble appendage."[46] The lowly, inferior nature of the *jus gentium* cannot be overstated to the modern ear, Maine warned. We moderns, with our taste for discovering universality beneath diversity, tend to view the Roman creation of the *jus gentium* as a great work of legal excavation, or a distillation of largely irrelevant ceremony and ritual which reveals the simple essence of the primitive law of the Italian nations. The Romans who created the *jus gentium* would have none of that:

> ... the results to which modern ideas conduct the observer are, as nearly as possible, the reverse of those which were instinctively brought home to the primitive Roman. What we respect or admire, he disliked or regarded with jealous dread. The parts of jurisprudence which he looked upon with affection were exactly those which a modern theorist leaves out of consideration as accidental and transitory; the solemn gestures of the mancipation; the nicely adjusted questions and answers of the verbal contract; the endless formalities of pleading and procedure.[47]

The desire for simplicity, for a return to basic principles, was actually the result of innovation; the old Roman law actually was quite complicated and ritualistic. It took the importation of another foreign element, Greek philosophy—a byproduct of Roman conquest—to effect in Roman jurisprudence the transformation of the *jus gentium* into the *jus naturale*, or law of nature. This "progress" in jurisprudence, however, was actually viewed by Romans as *regress*, as a return to first principles; this perception was a product of the influence of Greek philosophy. Nature, according to the earliest Greek philosophers, was wonderful in its simplicity, and reducible to one single principle, be it "movement, fire, moisture, or generation."[48] Later generations of Greek thinkers extended this conception of Nature to the moral realm:

> ... just as the oldest Greek theorists supposed that the sports of chance had changed the material universe from its simple primitive form into its present heterogeneous condition, so their intellectual descendants imagined that but for untoward accident the human race would have conformed itself to simpler rules of conduct and a less tempestuous life.[49]

Thus the epistemological efforts of early Greek philosophy acquired a moral component in its later manifestation (most prominently in the thinking of the Stoics), namely, to live according to nature: specifically, to cast aside bad habits and vulgar indulgences in favor of self-control and faithful observation of the "higher laws of action."[50] It was this philosophical injunction to simplicity, amidst the "unbounded profligacy" of imperial Rome, that caught the attention of part of the ruling class—most importantly, Maine argued, Stoicism captured the imagination of the Roman lawyers. These lawyers composed one of the two main factions of Rome's ruling class. On the one hand, the leaders of the military, immediately responsible for the development of Rome from a simple republic to the head of a vast empire, headed the "party of movement." On the other, lawyers took the lead of the "party of resistance"[51] in the Roman regime, though their mode of resistance in fact led to considerable innovation.

The Roman lawyers' subsequent, and substantial, innovations in their nation's jurisprudence, then, were the result of a fundamentally conservative movement.   Of what did this resistance movement consist? Maine argued that the innovations of the Roman lawyers should not be measured by such a crude yardstick as the number of laws that may be directly connected to the dogmas of Stoicism. Rather, the influence of Stoicism on Roman jurisprudence had to be considered in terms of the effects of its "great though vague" animating principle, "resistance to passion."[52] In reaction to a Rome awash in the throes of empire, the Stoics preached a return to a golden era of simplicity, and it was that spirit of calm asceticism that informed the innovations of the Roman lawyers.

Progress was measured in terms of the amount recovered from the past, and the *jus gentium* became the vessel which the Roman lawyers filled with their interpretation of the past. After Nature "had become a household word in the mouths of the Romans," Roman lawyers slowly but surely became convinced that the *jus gentium*, that unfortunately necessary appendix to the civil code, was actually "the lost code of Nature," and thus belonged at the core of all Roman jurisprudence. It followed, then, that the Praetor should use his Edicts (annual proclamations) as means toward the end of this program of recovery, "to supersede the Civil Law as much as possible by the Edict, to revive as far as might be the institutions by which Nature had governed man in the primitive state."[53]

Again, however, Maine stressed that recovery of the lost code of Nature was as much a matter of style as of substance. Stoicism, according to Maine, refined the palate of the Roman lawyers. Just as the early Greek philosophers had stressed "simplification and generalisation" in their understanding of Nature, so Roman lawyers were motivated to scrape off all the excesses from their code, like barnacles off the side of a ship: "simplicity, symmetry, and intelligibility came therefore to be regarded as the characteristics of a good legal system, and the taste for involved language, multiplied ceremonials, and useless difficulties disap-

well.　The criteria employed to separate what belonged to the law of nature from "the gross ingredients" mixed in with this original code over time
were "simplicity" and "harmony," the qualities
which attracted the Stoic-influenced jurists.　Yet
the ultimate reasons for the deference accorded to
the natural law were not said to be these qualities,
but rather its origins in "the aboriginal reign of
Nature." These inconsistencies and difficulties in
defending the sovereignty of the law of nature
were serious, but Maine stressed that the confusion of the ancients over this matter actually
was less severe than that of the moderns, who
"betray much more indistinctness of perception
and are vitiated by much more hopeless ambiguity of language" than the Roman jurists.
Modern interpreters of the law of nature, for instance, sometimes tried to avoid the problem of
time altogether by casting the placement of the
law of nature far into the future, conceiving it as a
goal which all human laws aim to reach in time.
This attempt Maine dismissed as an unwitting
turning of natural-law theory on its head, influenced by the Christian expectation of perfection
in the future; the ancients held no such hope or
expectation that things would improve in the full-
ness of time.[55]

In addition to this confusion over the correct
placement of natural law in human history, the

Roman mode of implementing natural-law jurisprudence possessed a subtlety easily lost on the
modern mind, which in Maine's opinion had become enamored with the apparent possibilities of
natural-law jurisprudence as a tool for social and
political change. For the Romans, the function of
natural law was "remedial, not revolutionary or
anarchical."[56]   Unlike the ancient Greeks, whose
leading minds were always inclined to allow speculation over matters of "pure law" to trump adherence to legal rules, the Roman jurists refused to
surrender the primacy of their home-grown civil
law to the purity of the natural law. Instead, they
sought to maintain a balance between the two. For
example, existing civil law retained its authority,
even in the presence of higher natural law, unless
it was specifically repealed; the system of natural
law would only gradually be combined with civil
law, rather than suddenly replacing it. For the
Roman jurists, the equity of the natural-law system became a standard to be aspired to, rather
than a superstition to be blindly followed.

> The value and serviceableness of the conception
> [of Natural Law] arose from its keeping before the
> mental vision a type of perfect law, and from its
> inspiring the hope of an indefinite approximation
> to it, at the same time that it never tempted the
> practitioner or the citizen to deny the obligation
> of existing laws which had not yet been adjusted
> to the theory.[57]

Maine's admiration for the Roman jurists' ability to integrate civil law with higher law reflects the priorities that he held highest as a legal historian. In dealing with the question of progress, he recognized that progress over time could not be properly understood in the abstract, without an appreciation of the concrete details of practical legal activity.   Maine might well have agreed with Michael Oakeshott's reflection that "Activities emerge naively, like games that children invent for themselves.   Each appears, first, not in response to a premeditated achievement, but as a direction of attention pursued without premonition of what it will lead to."[58] Maine's description of the development of ancient legal understanding indicates that the activity of law-making preceded theoretical speculation about the law. Law-making, from its very beginnings, was part of the activity of politics, that is, the activity "of attending to the general arrangements of a set of people whom chance or choice have brought together."[59] The development of theoretical or philosophic speculation on the subject of law did not obviate the need to understand law-making as an activity which takes place within the context of a particular set of people attending to its general arrangements. Maine taught that understanding ancient law in terms of its contribution to the present, or understanding a society's legal development in terms of abstract standards such as "progress" or "higher law" was significantly flawed, because "to understand an activity is to know it as a concrete whole; it is to recognize the activity as having the source of its movement within itself."[60] With this in mind, readers must beware the temptation to reduce the meaning of *Ancient Law* to its most famous tag line, "from status to contract," for this catch-phrase merely scratches the surface of what Maine understood to be a most complicated and fascinating matter: the development of legal codes, and the beguiling paradoxes and antinomies found within such histories.

Dante J. Scala
Saint Anselm College
Manchester, N. H.

Notes

1.   Shils, Edward, "Henry Sumner Maine in the Tradition of the Analysis of Society," in *The Victorian Achievement of Sir Henry Maine*, ed., Alan Diamond (Cambridge: Cambridge University Press, 1991).
2.   Ibid., p. 176-177.
3.   Maine, Henry Sumner. *Ancient Law* (London: John Murray, 1866), p. 305-306. Third Edition.
4.   Krishan Kumar, in a provocative essay on Maine and the history of the idea of progress, raises this question as follows: "But what should a theory of progress contain? There has always been some ambiguity about this—or rather, practically every major theorist of progress seems to have found it difficult to deal adequately with what are analytically two quite separate

things. Should an account of progress principally explain how or why societies evolve from one state or another, or should it rather tell us about the substance or content of progress? Ideally both, of course, but it is surprising how rare this has been in the history of the idea of progress." K. Kumar, "Maine and the Theory of Progress," p. 81-82, in *The Victorian Achievement of Sir Henry Maine.*

5. *Ancient Law*, p. 103.
6. Ibid., p. 289.
7. Ibid., p. 17.
8. Ibid., p. 135.
9. Ibid., p. 310-311.
10. Ibid., p. 189.
11. Ibid., p. 233.
12. Ibid., p. 171.
13. Ibid., p. 171.
14. The political philosopher Michael Oakeshott argued that "the activity of 'the historian' may be said (in virtue of its emancipation from a practical interest in the past) to represent an interest in past events for their own sake, or in respect of their independence of subsequent or present events... 'The historian' is disposed to decline the search for 'origins,' not because the expression 'origin' is ambiguous (opening the door to a confusion between a 'cause' and a 'beginning'), or because 'origins' are beyond the reach of discovery, or because they are of insignificant interest, but because to inquire into 'origins' is to read the past backwards and thus assimilate it to subsequent or present events... and imposes upon past events an arbitrary teleological structure." Oakeshott, Michael. "The Activity of Being an Historian," p. 170, 175-176, in *Rationalism in Politics and Other Essays* (Indianapolis: LibertyPress, 1991).
15. *Ancient Law*, p. 23.
16. Ibid., p. 24.
17. Ibid., p. 341-342.
18. Ibid., p. 340.
19. Ibid., p. 340.
20. Ibid., p. 341.
21. Ibid., p. 341.
22. Ibid., p. 364.

23. Ibid., p. 363-364.
24. Ibid., p. 361.
25. Ibid., p. 4-5.
26. Ibid., p. 11-13.
27. Ibid., p. 14-15.
28. Ibid., p. 15.
29. Ibid., p. 21-22.
30. Ibid., p. 360-361.
31. Ibid., p. 360-361.
32. Ibid., p. 361.
33. Ibid., p. 75.
34. Ibid., p. 28.
35. Ibid., p. 28.
36. Ibid., p. 67-68.
37. For more details on the role of the Praetor in Roman law, see p. 61-68.
38. Ibid., p. 68-69.
39. Ibid., p. 19.
40. Ibid., p. 19.
41. Ibid., p. 20.
42. Ibid., p. 70-71.
43. Ibid., p. 71.
44. Ibid., p. 45-46.
45. Ibid., p. 49.
46. Ibid., p. 52.
47. Ibid., p. 51-52.
48. Ibid., p. 53.
49. Ibid., p. 54.
50. Ibid., p. 54.
51. Ibid., p. 55.
52. Ibid., p. 56.
53. Ibid., p. 56-57.
54. Ibid., p. 57.
55. Ibid., p. 73-74.
56. Ibid., p. 77.   On this point, and on Maine's perceived need for a balance of continuity and innovation in order to achieve progress, see John W. Burrow, "Henry Maine and Mid-Victorian Ideas of Progress," p. 64-65, in *The Victorian Achievement of Sir Henry Maine.* Kumar defines Maine's definition of progress "in Darwinian terms as the achievement of order without the sacrifice of the potential for change," p. 86.

57. Ibid., p. 77.
58. Oakeshott, "The Activity of Being an Historian," p. 151, *Rationalism in Politics and Other Essays.*
59. Oakeshott, "Political Education," p. 44, *Rationalism in Politics and Other Essays.*
60. Oakeshott, "Political Education," p. 46; also see p. 67-68.

PREFACE

THE FIRST EDITION.

THE chief object of the following pages is to indicate
some of the earliest ideas of mankind, as they are
reflected in Ancient Law, and to point out the relation of those ideas to modern thought. Much of the
inquiry attempted could not have been prosecuted
with the slightest hope of a useful result if there had
not existed a body of law, like that of the Romans,
bearing in its earliest portions the traces of the most
remote antiquity and supplying from its later rules
the staple of the civil institutions by which modern
society is even now controlled. The necessity of
taking the Roman law as a typical system, has compelled the Author to draw from it what may appear
a disproportionate number of his illustrations ; but
it has not been his intention to write a treatise on

Roman jurisprudence, and he has as much as possible avoided all discussions which might give that appearance to his work. The space allotted in the Third and Fourth Chapters to certain philosophical theories of the Roman Jurisconsults, has been appropriated to them for two reasons. In the first place, those theories appear to the Author to have had a much wider and more permanent influence on the thought and action of the world than is usually supposed. Secondly, they are believed to be the ultimate source of most of the views which have been prevalent, till quite recently, on the subjects treated of in this volume. It was impossible for the Author to proceed far with his undertaking, without stating his opinion on the origin, meaning, and value of those speculations.

H. S. M.

LONDON : *January* 1861.

PREFACE

TO

THE THIRD EDITION.

THE Second and Third Editions of this work have been substantially reprints of the First. Some few errors have, however, been corrected.

It is necessary to remind the reader that the First Edition was published in 1861. The course of events since that period in Russia and in Northern America has taken away much of its application to existing facts from the language employed by the writer on the subject of serfage in Russia, of the Russian village-communities, and of negro-slavery in the United States. It may perhaps be interesting to the reader to observe the bearing of the changes which have taken place on the argument of that part of the work.

H. S. M.

CALCUTTA : *November* 1865.

ANCIENT LAW.

CHAPTER I.

ANCIENT CODES.

THE most celebrated system of jurisprudence known to the world begins, as it ends, with a Code. From the commencement to the close of its history, the expositors of Roman Law consistently employed language which implied that the body of their system rested on the Twelve Decemviral Tables, and therefore on a basis of written law. Except in one particular, no institutions anterior to the Twelve Tables were recognised at Rome. The theoretical descent of Roman jurisprudence from a code, the theoretical ascription of English law to immemorial unwritten tradition, were the chief reasons why the development of their system differed from the development of ours

Neither theory corresponded exactly with the facts, but each produced consequences of the utmost importance.

I need hardly say that the publication of the Twelve Tables is not the earliest point at which we can take up the history of law. The ancient Roman code belongs to a class of which almost every civilised nation in the world can show a sample, and which, so far as the Roman and Hellenic worlds were concerned, were largely diffused over them at epochs not widely distant from one another. They appeared under exceedingly similar circumstances, and were produced, to our knowledge, by very similar causes. Unquestionably, many jural phenomena lie behind these codes and preceded them in point of time. Not a few documentary records exist which profess to give us information concerning the early phenomena of law; but, until philology has effected a complete analysis of the Sanskrit literature, our best sources of knowledge are undoubtedly the Greek Homeric poems, considered of course not as a history of actual occurrences, but as a description, not wholly idealised, of a state of society known to the writer. However the fancy of the poet may have exaggerated certain features of the heroic age, the prowess of warriors and the potency of gods, there is no reason to believe that it has tampered with moral or metaphysical conceptions which were not yet the subjects of conscious observation; and in this respect the Homeric literature is far more trustworthy than those relatively later documents which pretend to give an account of times similarly early, but which were compiled under philosophical or theological influences.   If by any means we can determine the early forms of jural conceptions, they will be invaluable to us. These rudimentary ideas are to the jurist what the primary crusts of the earth are to the geologist. They contain, potentially, all the forms in which law has subsequently exhibited itself.   The haste or the prejudice which has generally refused them all but the most superficial examination, must bear the blame of the unsatisfactory condition in which we find the science of jurisprudence.   The inquiries of the jurist are in truth prosecuted much as inquiry in physics and physiology was prosecuted before observation had taken the place of assumption. Theories, plausible and comprehensive, but absolutely unverified, such as the Law of Nature or the Social Compact, enjoy a universal preference over sober research into the primitive history of society and law; and they obscure the truth not only by diverting attention from the only quarter in which it can be found, but by that most real and most important influence which, when once entertained and believed in, they are enabled to exercise on the later stages of jurisprudence.

The earliest notions connected with the conception, now so fully developed, of a law or rule of life, are those contained in the Homeric words " Themis " and " Themistes." " Themis," it is well known, appears in the later Greek pantheon as the Goddess of Justice, but this is a modern and much developed idea, and it is in a very different sense that Themis is described in the Iliad as the assessor of Zeus. It is now clearly seen by all trustworthy observers of the primitive condition of mankind that, in the infancy of the race, men could only account for sustained or periodically recurring action by supposing a personal agent. Thus, the wind blowing was a person and of course a divine person ; the sun rising, culminating, and setting was a person and a divine person ; the earth yielding her increase was a person and divine. As, then, in the physical world, so in the moral. When a king decided a dispute by a sentence, the judgment was assumed to be the result of direct inspiration. The divine agent, suggesting judicial awards to kings or to gods, the greatest of kings, was *Themis*. The peculiarity of the conception is brought out by the use of the plural. *Themistes*, Themises, the plural of Themis, are the awards themselves, divinely dictated to the judge. Kings are spoken of as if they had a store of " Themistes " ready to hand for use; but it must be distinctly understood that they are not laws, but judgments. " Zeus, or the human king on earth," says Mr. Grote, in his History of Greece, "is not a law-maker, but a judge." He is provided with Themistes, but, consistently with the belief in their emanation from above, they cannot be supposed to be connected by any thread of principle; they are separate, isolated judgments.

Even in the Homeric poems, we can see that these ideas are transient. Parities of circumstance were probably commoner in the simple mechanism of ancient society than they are now, and in the succession of similar cases awards are likely to follow and resemble each other. Here we have the germ or rudiment of a custom, a conception posterior to that of Themistes or judgments. However strongly we, with our modern associations, may be inclined to lay down à priori that the notion of a Custom must precede that of a judicial sentence, and that a judgment must affirm a Custom or punish its breach, it seems quite certain that the historical order of the ideas is that in which I have placed them. The Homeric word for a custom in the embryo is sometimes "Themis" in the singular—more often "Dike," the meaning of which visibly fluctuates between a "judgment" and a "custom" or "usage." Νόμος, a Law, so great and famous a term in the political vocabulary of the later Greek society, does not occur in Homer.

This notion of a divine agency, suggesting the

Themistes, and itself impersonated in Themis, must be kept apart from other primitive beliefs with which a superficial inquirer might confound it. The conception of the Deity dictating an entire code or body of law, as in the case of the Hindoo laws of Manu, seems to belong to a range of ideas more recent and more advanced. " Themis " and " Themistes " are much less remotely linked with that persuasion which clung so long and so tenaciously to the human mind, of a divine influence underlying and supporting every relation of life, every social institution. In early law, and amid the rudiments of political thought, symptoms of this belief meet us on all sides. A supernatural presidency is supposed to consecrate and keep together all the cardinal institutions of those times, the State, the Race, and the Family. Men, grouped together in the different relations which those institutions imply, are bound to celebrate periodically common rites and to offer common sacrifices; and every now and then the same duty is even more significantly recognised in the purifications and expiations which they perform, and which appear intended to deprecate punishment for involuntary or neglectful disrespect. Everybody acquainted with ordinary classical literature will remember the *sacra gentilicia*, which exercised so important an influence on the early Roman law of adoption and of wills. And to this hour the Hindoo

Customary Law, in which some of the most curious features of primitive society are stereotyped, makes almost all the rights of persons and all the rules of succession hinge on the due solemnisation of fixed ceremonies at the dead man's funeral, that is, at every point where a breach occurs in the continuity of the family.

Before we quit this stage of jurisprudence, a caution may be usefully given to the English student. Bentham, in his " Fragment on Government," and Austin, in his " Province of Jurisprudence Determined," resolve every law into a *command* of the lawgiver, an *obligation* imposed thereby on the citizen, and a *sanction* threatened in the event of disobedience ; and it is further predicated of the *command*, which is the first element in a law, that it must prescribe, not a single act, but a series or number of acts of the same class or kind. The results of this separation of ingredients tally exactly with the facts of mature jurisprudence ; and, by a little straining of language, they may be made to correspond in form with all law, of all kinds, at all epochs. It is not, however, asserted that the notion of law entertained by the generality is even now quite in conformity with this dissection ; and it is curious that, the farther we penetrate into the primitive history of thought, the farther we find ourselves from a conception of law which at all resembles a

compound of the elements which Bentham determined. It is certain that, in the infancy of mankind, no sort of legislature, not even a distinct
author of law, is contemplated or conceived of.
Law has scarcely reached the footing of custom;
it is rather a habit. It is, to use a French phrase,
"in the air." The only authoritative statement of
right and wrong is a judicial sentence after the
facts, not one presupposing a law which has been
violated, but one which is breathed for the first time
by a higher power into the judge's mind at the
moment of adjudication. It is of course extremely
difficult for us to realise a view so far removed
from us in point both of time and of association, but
it will become more credible when we dwell more
at length on the constitution of ancient society, in
which every man, living during the greater part of
his life under the patriarchal despotism, was practically
controlled in all his actions by a regimen not of law
but of caprice. I may add that an Englishman
should be better able than a foreigner to appreciate
the historical fact that the "Themistes" preceded
any conception of law, because, amid the many inconsistent theories which prevail concerning the character of English jurisprudence, the most popular, or
at all events the one which most affects practice, is
certainly a theory which assumes that adjudged
cases and precedents exist antecedently to rules,

principles, and distinctions. The " Themistes " have too, it should be remarked, the characteristic which, in the view of Bentham and Austin, distinguishes single or mere commands from laws. A true law enjoins on all the citizens indifferently a number of acts similar in class or kind; and this is exactly the feature of a law which has most deeply impressed itself on the popular mind, causing the term " law " to be applied to mere uniformities, successions, and similitudes. A *command* prescribes only a single act, and it is to commands, therefore, that " Themistes" are more akin than to laws. They are simply adjudications on insulated states of fact, and do not necessarily follow each other in any orderly sequence.

The literature of the heroic age discloses to us law in the germ under the " Themistes " and a little more developed in the conception of "Dike." The next stage which we reach in the history of jurisprudence is strongly marked and surrounded by the utmost interest. Mr. Grote, in the second part and second chapter of his History, has fully described the mode in which society gradually clothed itself with a different character from that delineated by Homer. Heroic kingship depended partly on divinely given prerogative, and partly on the possession of supereminent strength, courage, and wisdom. Gradually, as the impression of the monarch's sacredness became weakened, and feeble members occurred in

relative place in civilisation appears to have been the same, and they seem to have been exceedingly similar in general character. There is some evidence that the races which were subsequently united under the Persian monarchy, and those which peopled the peninsula of India, had all their heroic age and their era of aristocracies; but a military and a religious oligarchy appear to have grown up separately, nor was the authority of the king generally superseded. Contrary, too, to the course of events in the West, the religious element in the East tended to get the better of the military and political. Military and civil aristocracies disappear, annihilated or crushed into insignificance between the kings and the sacerdotal order ; and the ultimate result at which we arrive is, a monarch enjoying great power, but circumscribed by the privileges of a caste of priests. With these differences, however, that in the East aristocracies became religious, in the West civil or political, the proposition that a historical era of aristocracies succeeded a historical era of heroic kings may be considered as true, if not of all mankind, at all events of all branches of the Indo-European family of nations.

The important point for the jurist is that these aristocracies were universally the depositaries and administrators of law. They seem to have succeeded to the prerogatives of the king, with the important difference, however, that they do not appear to have pretended to direct inspiration for each sentence. The connection of ideas which caused the judgments of the patriarchal chieftain to be attributed to superhuman dictation still shows itself here and there in the claim of a divine origin for the entire body of rules, or for certain parts of it, but the progress of thought no longer permits the solution of particular disputes to be explained by supposing an extra-human interposition. What the juristical oligarchy now claims is to monopolise the *knowledge* of the laws, to have the exclusive possession of the principles by which quarrels are decided. We have in fact arrived at the epoch of Customary Law. Customs or Observances now exist as a substantive aggregate, and are assumed to be precisely known to the aristocratic order or caste. Our authorities leave us no doubt that the trust lodged with the oligarchy was sometimes abused, but it certainly ought not to be regarded as a mere usurpation or engine of tyranny. Before the invention of writing, and during the infancy of the art, an aristocracy invested with judicial privileges formed the only expedient by which accurate preservation of the customs of the race or tribe could be at all approximated to. Their genuineness was, so far as possible, insured by confiding them to the recollection of a limited portion of the community.

The epoch of Customary Law, and of its custody by a privileged order, is a very remarkable one. The condition of jurisprudence which it implies has left traces which may still be detected in legal and popular phraseology. The law, thus known exclusively to a privileged minority, whether a caste, an aristocracy, a priestly tribe, or a sacerdotal college, is true unwritten law. Except this, there is no such thing as unwritten law in the world. English case-law is sometimes spoken of as unwritten, and there are some English theorists who assure us that if a code of English jurisprudence were prepared we should be turning unwritten law into written—a conversion, as they insist, if not of doubtful policy, at all events of the greatest seriousness. Now, it is quite true that there was once a period at which the English common law might reasonably have been termed unwritten. The elder English judges did really pretend to knowledge of rules, principles, and distinctions which were not entirely revealed to the bar and to the lay-public. Whether all the law which they claimed to monopolise was really unwritten, is exceedingly questionable; but at all events, on the assumption that there was once a large mass of civil and criminal rules known exclusively to the judges, it presently ceased to be unwritten law. As soon as the Courts at Westminster Hall began to base their judgments on cases recorded, whether in the year books or elsewhere, the law which they administered became written law. At the present moment a rule of English law has first to be disentangled from the recorded facts of adjudged printed precedents, then thrown into a form of words varying with the taste, precision, and knowledge of the particular judge, and then applied to the circumstances of the case for adjudication. But at no stage of this process has it any characteristic which distinguishes it from written law. It is written case-law, and only different from code-law because it is written in a different way.

From the period of Customary Law we come to another sharply defined epoch in the history of jurisprudence. We arrive at the era of Codes, those ancient codes of which the Twelve Tables of Rome were the most famous specimen. In Greece, in Italy, on the Hellenised sea-board of Western Asia, these codes all made their appearance at periods much the same everywhere, not, I mean, at periods identical in point of time, but similar in point of the relative progress of each community. Everywhere, in the countries I have named, laws engraven on tablets and published to the people take the place of usages deposited with the recollection of a privileged oligarchy. It must not for a moment be supposed that the refined considerations now urged in favour of what is called codification had any part or place in the change I have described. The ancient codes were doubtless originally suggested by the discovery and diffusion of the art of writing. It is true that the aristocracies seem to have abused their monopoly of legal knowledge; and at all events their exclusive possession of the law was a formidable impediment to the success of those popular movements which began to be universal in the western world. But, though democratic sentiment may have added to their popularity, the codes were certainly in the main a direct result of the invention of writing. Inscribed tablets were seen to be a better depositary of law, and a better security for its accurate preservation, than the memory of a number of persons however strengthened by habitual exercise.

The Roman code belongs to the class of codes I have been describing. Their value did not consist in any approach to symmetrical classifications, or to terseness and clearness of expression, but in their publicity, and in the knowledge which they furnished to everybody, as to what he was to do, and what not to do. It is, indeed, true that the Twelve Tables of Rome do exhibit some traces of systematic arrangement, but this is probably explained by the tradition that the framers of that body of law called in the assistance of Greeks who enjoyed the later Greek experience in the art of law-making. The fragments of the Attic Code of Solon show, however, that it had but little order, and probably the laws of Draco had even less. Quite enough too remains of these collections, both in the East and in the West, to show that they mingled up religious, civil, and merely moral ordinances, without any regard to differences in their essential character; and this is consistent with all we know of early thought from other sources, the severance of law from morality, and of religion from law, belonging very distinctly to the *later* stages of mental progress.

But, whatever to a modern eye are the singularities of these Codes, their importance to ancient societies was unspeakable. The question—and it was one which affected the whole future of each community—was not so much whether there should be a code at all, for the majority of ancient societies seem to have obtained them sooner or later, and, but for the great interruption in the history of jurisprudence created by feudalism, it is likely that all modern law would be distinctly traceable to one or more of these fountain-heads. But the point on which turned the history of the race was, at what period, at what stage of their social progress, they should have their laws put into writing. In the western world the plebeian or popular element in each State successfully assailed the oligarchical monopoly, and a code was nearly universally obtained *early* in the history of the Commonwealth. But, in the East, as I

have before mentioned, the ruling aristocracies tended
to become religious rather than military or political,
and gained, therefore, rather than lost in power;
while in some instances the physical conformation
of Asiatic countries had the effect of making individual communities larger and more numerous
than in the West; and it is a known social law that
the larger the space over which a particular set of
institutions is diffused, the greater is its tenacity
and vitality.   From whatever cause, the codes
obtained by Eastern societies were obtained, relatively, much later than by Western, and wore
a very different character.   The religious oligarchies
of Asia, either for their own guidance, or for the
relief of their memory, or for the instruction of their
disciples, seem in all cases to have ultimately embodied
their legal learning in a code; but the opportunity of
increasing and consolidating their influence was probably too tempting to be resisted.   Their complete
monopoly of legal knowledge appears to have enabled
them to put off on the world collections, not so much
of the rules actually observed as of the rules which
the priestly order considered proper to be observed.
The Hindoo Code, called the Laws of Manu, which
is certainly a Brahmin compilation, undoubtedly enshrines many genuine observances of the Hindoo race,
but the opinion of the best contemporary orientalists
is, that it does not, as a whole, represent a set of rules

ever actually administered in Hindostan. It is, in great part, an ideal picture of that which, in the view of the Brahmins, *ought* to be the law. It is consistent with human nature and with the special motives of their authors, that codes like that of Manu should pretend to the highest antiquity and claim to have emanated in their complete form from the Deity. Manu, according to Hindoo mythology, is an emanation from the supreme God; but the compilation which bears his name, though its exact date is not easily discovered, is, in point of the relative progress of Hindoo jurisprudence, a recent production.

Among the chief advantages which the Twelve Tables and similar codes conferred on the societies which obtained them, was the protection which they afforded against the frauds of the privileged oligarchy and also against the spontaneous depravation and debasement of the national institutions. The Roman Code was merely an enunciation in words of the existing customs of the Roman people. Relatively to the progress of the Romans in civilisation, it was a remarkably early code, and it was published at a time when Roman society had barely emerged from that intellectual condition in which civil obligation and religious duty are inevitably confounded. Now a barbarous society practising a body of customs, is exposed to some especial dangers which may be absolutely fatal to its progress in civilisation. The usages which a particular community is found to

have adopted in its infancy and in its primitive seats
are generally those which are on the whole best
suited to promote its physical and moral well-being ;
and, if they are retained in their integrity until new
social wants have taught new practices, the upward
march of society is almost certain. But unhappily
there is a law of development which ever threatens
to operate upon unwritten usage. The customs are
of course obeyed by multitudes who are incapable of
understanding the true ground of their expediency,
and who are therefore left inevitably to invent superstitious reasons for their permanence. A process
then commences which may be shortly described
by saying that usage which is reasonable generates
usage which is unreasonable. Analogy, the most
valuable of instruments in the maturity of jurisprudence, is the most dangerous of snares in its infancy.
Prohibitions and ordinances, originally confined, for
good reasons, to a single description of acts, are made
to apply to all acts of the same class, because a man
menaced with the anger of the gods for doing one
thing, feels a natural terror in doing any other thing
which is remotely like it. After one kind of food
has been interdicted for sanitary reasons, the prohibition is extended to all food resembling it, though
the resemblance occasionally depends on analogies
the most fanciful. So, again, a wise provision for
insuring general cleanliness dictates in time long

routines of ceremonial ablution ; and that division into classes which at a particular crisis of social history is necessary for the maintenance of the national existence degenerates into the most disastrous and blighting of all human institutions—Caste. The fate of the Hindoo law is, in fact, the measure of the value of the Roman Code. Ethnology shows us that the Romans and the Hindoos sprang from the same original stock, and there is indeed a striking resemblance between what appear to have been their original customs. Even now, Hindoo jurisprudence has a substratum of forethought and sound judgment, but irrational imitation has engrafted in it an immense apparatus of cruel absurdities. From these corruptions the Romans were protected by their code. It was compiled while usage was still wholesome, and a hundred years afterwards it might have been too late. The Hindoo law has been to a great extent embodied in writing, but, ancient as in one sense are the compendia which still exist in Sanskrit, they contain ample evidence that they were drawn up after the mischief had been done. We are not of course entitled to say that if the Twelve Tables had not been published the Romans would have been condemned to a civilisation as feeble and perverted as that of the Hindoos, but thus much at least is certain, that *with* their code they were exempt from the very chance of so unhappy a destiny.

CHAPTER II.

LEGAL FICTIONS.

WHEN primitive law has once been embodied in a Code, there is an end to what may be called its spontaneous development. Henceforward the changes effected in it, if effected at all, are effected deliberately and from without. It is impossible to suppose that the customs of any race or tribe remained unaltered during the whole of the long—in some instances the immense—interval between their declaration by a patriarchal monarch and their publication in writing. It would be unsafe too to affirm that no part of the alteration was effected deliberately. But from the little we know of the progress of law during this period, we are justified in assuming that set purpose had the very smallest share in producing change. Such innovations on the earliest usages as disclose themselves appear to have been dictated by feelings and modes of thought which, under our present mental conditions, we are unable to comprehend. A new era begins, however, with the Codes. Wherever, after this epoch, we trace the course of legal modification, we are able to attribute it to the conscious desire of improvement, or at all events of compassing objects other than those which were aimed at in the primitive times.

It may seem at first sight that no general propositions worth trusting can be elicited from the history of legal systems subsequent to the codes. The field is too vast. We cannot be sure that we have included a sufficient number of phenomena in our observations, or that we accurately understand those which we have observed. But .the undertaking will be seen to be more feasible, if we consider that after the epoch of codes the distinction between stationary and progressive societies begins to make itself felt. It is only with the progressive societies that we are concerned, and nothing is more remarkable than their extreme fewness. In spite of overwhelming evidence, it is most difficult for a citizen of Western Europe to bring thoroughly home to himself the truth that the civilisation which surrounds him is a rare exception in the history of the world. The tone of thought common among us, all our hopes, fears, and speculations, would be materially affected, if we had vividly before us the relation of the progressive races to the totality of human life. It is indisputable that much the greatest part of mankind has never shown a particle of desire that its civil institutions should be improved since the moment when external completeness was first given to them by their embodiment in some permanent record. One set of usages has occasionally been violently overthrown and superseded by another ; here and there a primitive code, pretending to a supernatural origin, has been greatly extended, and distorted into the most surprising forms, by the perversity of sacerdotal commentators; but, except in a small section of the world, there has been nothing like the gradual amelioration of a legal system. There has been material civilisation, but, instead of the civilisation expanding the law, the law has limited the civilisation.   The study of races in their primitive condition affords us some clue to the point at which the development of certain societies has stopped.   We can see that Brahminical India has not passed beyond a stage which occurs in the history of all the families of mankind, the stage at which a rule of law is not yet discriminated from a rule of religion. The members of such a society consider that the transgression of a religious ordinance should be punished by civil penalties, and that the violation of a civil duty exposes the delinquent to divine correction. In China this point has been passed, but progress seems to have been there arrested, because the civil laws are coextensive with all the ideas of which the race is capable.   The difference between the stationary and progressive societies is, however, one of the great secrets which inquiry has yet to penetrate.   Among partial explanations of it I venture to place the considerations urged at the end of the last chapter.   It may further be remarked that no one is likely to succeed in the investigation who does not clearly realise that the stationary condition of the human race is the rule, the progressive the exception. And another indispensable condition of success is an accurate knowledge of Roman law in all its principal stages. The Roman jurisprudence has the longest known history of any set of human institutions. The character of all the changes which it underwent is tolerably well ascertained. From its commencement to its close, it was progressively modified for the better, or for what the authors of the modification conceived to be the better, and the course of improvement was continued through periods at which all the rest of human thought and action materially slackened its pace, and repeatedly threatened to settle down into stagnation.

I confine myself in what follows to the progressive societies. With respect to them it may be laid down that social necessities and social opinion are always more or less in advance of Law. We may come indefinitely near to the closing of the gap between them, but it has a perpetual tendency to reopen. Law is stable; the societies we are speaking of are progressive. The greater or less happiness of a people depends on the degree of promptitude with which the gulf is narrowed.

A general proposition of some value may be advanced with respect to the agencies by which Law is brought into harmony with society. These instrumentalities seem to me to be three in number, Legal Fictions, Equity, and Legislation. Their historical order is that in which I have placed them. Sometimes two of them will be seen operating together, and there are legal systems which have escaped the influence of one or other of them. But I know of no instance in which the order of their appearance has been changed or inverted. The early history of one of them, Equity, is universally obscure, and hence it may be thought by some that certain isolated statutes, reformatory of the civil law, are older than any equitable jurisdiction. My own belief is that remedial Equity is everywhere older than remedial Legislation; but, should this be not strictly true, it would only be necessary to limit the proposition respecting their order of sequence to the periods at which they exercise a sustained and substantial influence in transforming the original law.

I employ the word " fiction " in a sense considerably wider than that in which English lawyers are accustomed to use it, and with a meaning much more extensive than that which belonged to the Roman " fictiones." Fictio, in old Roman law, is properly a term of pleading, and signifies a false averment on the part of the plaintiff which the defendant was not allowed to traverse; such, for example, as an averment that the plaintiff was a Roman citizen, when in truth he was a foreigner. The object of these "fictiones" was, of course, to give jurisdiction, and they therefore strongly resembled the allegations in the writs of the English Queen's Bench and Exchequer, by which those Courts contrived to usurp the jurisdiction of the Common Pleas:—the allegation that the defendant was in custody of the king's marshal, or that the plaintiff was the king's debtor, and could not pay his debt by reason of the defendant's default. But I now employ the expression "Legal Fiction" to signify any assumption which conceals, or affects to conceal, the fact that a rule of law has undergone alteration, its letter remaining unchanged, its operation being modified. The words, therefore, include the instances of fictions which I have cited from the English and Roman law, but they embrace much more, for I should speak both of the English Case-law and of the Roman Responsa Prudentum as resting on fictions. Both these examples will be examined presently. The *fact* is in both cases that the law has been wholly changed; the *fiction* is that it remains what it always was. It is not difficult to understand why fictions in all their forms are particularly congenial to the infancy of society. They satisfy the desire for improvement, which is not quite wanting, at the same time that they do not offend the superstitious disrelish for change which is always present.

At a particular stage of social progress they are invaluable expedients for overcoming the rigidity of law, and, indeed, without one of them, the Fiction of Adoption which permits the family tie to be artificially created, it is difficult to understand how society would ever have escaped from its swaddling-clothes, and taken its first steps towards civilisation. We must, therefore, not suffer ourselves to be affected by the ridicule which Bentham pours on legal fictions wherever he meets them. To revile them as merely fraudulent is to betray ignorance of their peculiar office in the historical development of law. But at the same time it would be equally foolish to agree with those theorists who, discerning that fictions have had their uses, argue that they ought to be stereotyped in our system. There are several Fictions still exercising powerful influence on English jurisprudence which could not be discarded without a severe shock to the ideas, and considerable change in the language, of English practitioners; but there can be no doubt of the general truth that it is unworthy of us to effect an admittedly beneficial object by so rude a device as a legal fiction. I cannot admit any anomaly to be innocent, which makes the law either more difficult to understand or harder to arrange in harmonious order. Now, among other disadvantages, legal fictions are the greatest of obstacles to symmetrical classification. The rule of law remains sticking in the system, but it is a mere shell. It has been long ago undermined, and a new rule hides itself under its cover. Hence there is at once a difficulty in knowing whether the rule which is actually operative should be classed in its true or in its apparent place, and minds of different casts will differ as to the branch of the alternative which ought to be selected. If the English law is ever to assume an orderly distribution, it will be necessary to prune away the legal fictions which, in spite of some recent legislative improvements, are still abundant in it.

The next instrumentality by which the adaptation of law to social wants is carried on I call Equity, meaning by that word any body of rules existing by the side of the original civil law, founded on distinct principles and claiming incidentally to supersede the civil law in virtue of a superior sanctity inherent in those principles. The Equity whether of the Roman Prætors or of the English Chancellors, differs from the Fictions which in each case preceded it, in that the interference with law is open and avowed. On the other hand, it differs from Legislation, the agent of legal improvement which comes after it, in that its claim to authority is grounded, not on the prerogative of any external person or body, not even on that of the magistrate who enunciates it, but on the special nature of its principles, to which it is alleged that all law ought to conform. The very conception of a set of principles, invested with a higher sacredness than those of the original law and demanding application independently of the consent of any external body, belongs to a much more advanced stage of thought than that to which legal fictions originally suggested themselves.

Legislation, the enactments of a legislature which, whether it take the form of an autocratic prince or of a parliamentary assembly, is the assumed organ of the entire society, is the last of the ameliorating instrumentalities. It differs from Legal Fictions just as Equity differs from them, and it is also distinguished from Equity, as deriving its authority from an external body or person. Its obligatory force is independent of its principles. The legislature, whatever be the actual restraints imposed on it by public opinion, is in theory empowered to impose what obligations it pleases on the members of the community. There is nothing to prevent its legislating in the wantonness of caprice. Legislation may be dictated by equity, if that last word be used to indicate some standard of right and wrong to which its enactments happen to be adjusted; but then these enactments are indebted for their binding force to the authority of the legislature and not to that of the principles on which the legislature acted; and thus they differ from rules of Equity, in the technical sense of the word, which pretend to a paramount sacredness entitling them at

once to the recognition of the courts even without
the concurrence of prince or parliamentary assembly.
It is the more necessary to note these differences,
because a student of Bentham would be apt to confound Fictions, Equity, and Statute law under the
single head of legislation. They all, he would say,
involve *law-making*; they differ only in respect of
the machinery by which the new law is produced.
That is perfectly true, and we must never forget it;
but it furnishes no reason why we should deprive
ourselves of so convenient a term as Legislation in the
special sense. Legislation and Equity are disjoined
in the popular mind and in the minds of most lawyers; and it will never do to neglect the distinction
between them, however conventional, when important
practical consequences follow from it.

It would be easy to select from almost any regularly developed body of rules examples of *legal fictions*,
which at once betray their true character to the
modern observer. In the two instances which I
proceed to consider, the nature of the expedient employed is not so readily detected. The first authors
of these fictions did not perhaps intend to innovate,
certainly did not wish to be suspected of innovating.
There are, moreover, and always have been, persons
who refuse to see any fiction in the process, and
conventional language bears out their refusal. No
examples, therefore, can be better calculated to illus-

trate the wide diffusion of legal fictions, and the efficiency with which they perform their twofold office
of transforming a system of laws and of concealing
the transformation.

We in England are well accustomed to the extension, modification, and improvement of law by a
machinery which, in theory, is incapable of altering
one jot or one line of existing jurisprudence. The
process by which this virtual legislation is effected is
not so much insensible as unacknowledged. With
respect to that great portion of our legal system
which is enshrined in cases and recorded in law
reports, we habitually employ a double language, and
entertain, as it would appear, a double and inconsistent set of ideas. When a group of facts comes
before an English Court for adjudication, the whole
course of the discussion between the judge and the
advocates assumes that no question is, or can be,
raised which will call for the application of any
principles but old ones, or of any distinctions but
such as have long since been allowed. It is taken
absolutely for granted that there is somewhere a rule
of known law which will cover the facts of the
dispute now litigated, and that, if such a rule be not
discovered, it is only that the necessary patience,
knowledge, or acumen is not forthcoming to detect it.
Yet the moment the judgment has been rendered
and reported, we slide unconsciously or unavowedly

into a new language and a new train of thought.
We now admit that the new decision *has* modified
the law. The rules applicable have, to use the very
inaccurate expression sometimes employed, become
more elastic. In fact they have been changed. A
clear addition has been made to the precedents, and
the canon of law elicited by comparing the precedents is not the same with that which would have
been obtained if the series of cases had been curtailed
by a single example. The fact that the old rule has
been repealed, and that a new one has replaced it,
eludes us, because we are not in the habit of throwing
into precise language the legal formulas which we
derive from the precedents, so that a change in their
tenor is not easily detected unless it is violent and
glaring. I shall not now pause to consider at length
the causes which have led English lawyers to ac-
quiesce in these curious anomalies. Probably it will
be found that originally it was the received doctrine
that somewhere, *in nubibus* or *in gremio magistratuum*,
there existed a complete, coherent, symmetrical body
of English law, of an amplitude sufficient to furnish
principles which would apply to any conceivable
combination of circumstances. The theory was at
first much more thoroughly believed in than it is
now, and indeed it may have had a better foundation. The judges of the thirteenth century may
have really had at their command a mine of law

unrevealed to the bar and to the lay-public, for
there is some reason for suspecting that in secret
they borrowed freely, though not always wisely, from
current compendia of the Roman and Canon laws.
But that storehouse was closed as soon as the points
decided at Westminster Hall became numerous
enough to supply a basis for a substantive system of
jurisprudence; and now for centuries English practitioners have so expressed themselves as to convey
the paradoxical proposition that, except by Equity
and Statute law, nothing has been added to the basis
since it was first constituted.   We do not admit that
our tribunals legislate; we imply that they have
never legislated; and yet we maintain that the rules
of the English common law, with some assistance
from the Court of Chancery and from Parliament,
are coextensive with the complicated interests of
modern society.

A body of law bearing a very close and very instructive resemblance to our case-law in those particulars which I have noticed, was known to the
Romans under the name of the Responsa Prudentum,
the "answers of the learned in the law." The form
of these Responses varied a good deal at different periods of the Roman jurisprudence, but throughout its
whole course they consisted of explanatory glosses on
authoritative written documents, and at first they
were exclusively collections of opinions interpretative

of the Twelve Tables.   As with us, all legal language
adjusted itself to the assumption that the text of the
old Code remained unchanged.   There was the express rule.   It overrode all glosses and comments,
and no one openly admitted that any interpretation
of it, however eminent the interpreter, was safe from
revision on appeal to the venerable texts.   Yet in
point of fact, Books of Responses bearing the names of
leading jurisconsults obtained an authority at least
equal to that of our reported cases, and constantly
modified, extended, limited or practically overruled
the provisions of the Decemviral law.   The authors
of the new jurisprudence during the whole progress
of its formation professed the most sedulous respect
for the letter of the Code.   They were merely
explaining it, deciphering it, bringing out its full
meaning ; but then, in the result, by piecing texts
together, by adjusting the law to states of fact which
actually presented themselves and by speculating on
its possible application to others which might occur,
by introducing principles of interpretation derived
from the exegesis of other written documents which
fell under their observation, they educed a vast
variety of canons which had never been dreamed of by
the compilers of the Twelve Tables and which were
in truth rarely or never to be found there.   All
these treatises of the jurisconsults claimed respect on
the ground of their assumed conformity with the
Code, but their comparative authority depended on

the reputation of the particular jurisconsults who gave them to the world. Any name of universally acknowledged greatness clothed a Book of Responses with a binding force hardly less than that which belonged to enactments of the legislature ; and such a book in its turn constituted a new foundation on which a further body of jurisprudence might rest. The Responses of the early lawyers were not however published, in the modern sense, by their author. They were recorded and edited by his pupils, and were not therefore in all probability arranged according to any scheme of classification. The part of the students in these publications must be carefully noted, because the service they rendered to their teacher seems to have been generally repaid by his sedulous attention to the pupils' education. The educational treatises called Institutes or Commentaries, which are a later fruit of the duty then recognised, are among the most remarkable features of the Roman system. It was apparently in these Institutional works, and not in the books intended for trained lawyers, that the jurisconsults gave to the public their classifications and their proposals for modifying and improving the technical phraseology.

In comparing the Roman Responsa Prudentum with their nearest English counterpart, it must be carefully borne in mind that the authority by which this part of the Roman jurisprudence was expounded

was not the *bench*, but the *bar*. The decision of a
Roman tribunal, though conclusive in the particular
case, had no ulterior authority except such as was
given by the professional repute of the magistrate
who happened to be in office for the time. Properly
speaking, there was no institution at Rome during
the republic analogous to the English Bench, the
Chambers of Imperial Germany, or the Parliaments
of Monarchical France. There were magistrates
indeed, invested with momentous judicial functions
in their several departments, but the tenure of the
magistracies was but for a single year, so that they
are much less aptly compared to a permanent judicature than to a cycle of offices briskly circulating among
the leaders of the bar. Much might be said on the
origin of a condition of things which looks to us like
a startling anomaly, but which was in fact much more
congenial than our own system to the spirit of ancient societies, tending, as they always did, to split
into distinct orders which, however exclusive themselves, tolerated no professional hierarchy above them.

It is remarkable that this system did not produce
certain effects which might on the whole have been
expected from it. It did not, for example, *popularise*
the Roman law,—it did not, as in some of the Greek
republics, lessen the effort of intellect required for the
mastery of the science, although its diffusion and
authoritative exposition were opposed by no artificial

barriers.   On the contrary, if it had not been for the operation of a separate set of causes, there were strong probabilities that the Roman jurisprudence would have become as minute, technical, and difficult as any system which has since prevailed.   Again, a consequence which might still more naturally have been looked for, does not appear at any time to have exhibited itself.   The jurisconsults, until the liberties of Rome were overthrown, formed a class which was quite undefined and must have fluctuated greatly in numbers; nevertheless, there does not seem to have existed a doubt as to the particular individuals whose opinion, in their generation, was conclusive on the cases submitted to them.   The vivid pictures of a leading jurisconsult's daily practice which abound in Latin literature—the clients from the country flocking to his antechamber in the early morning, and the students standing round with their note-books to record the great lawyer's replies—are seldom or never identified at any given period with more than one or two conspicuous names.   Owing too to the direct contact of the client and the advocate, the Roman people itself seems to have been always alive to the rise and fall of professional reputation, and there is abundance of proof, more particularly in the well-known oration of Cicero, " Pro Muræna," that the reverence of the commons for forensic success was apt to be excessive rather than deficient.

We cannot doubt that the peculiarities which have been noted in the instrumentality by which the development of the Roman law was first effected, were the source of its characteristic excellence, its early wealth in principles. The growth and exuberance of principle was fostered, in part, by the competition among the expositors of the law, an influence wholly unknown where there exists a Bench, the depositaries intrusted by king or commonwealth with the prerogative of justice. But the chief agency, no doubt, was the uncontrolled multiplication of cases for legal decision. The state of facts which caused genuine perplexity to a country client was not a whit more entitled to form the basis of the jurisconsult's Response, or legal decision, than a set of hypothetical circumstances propounded by an ingenious pupil. All combinations of fact were on precisely the same footing, whether they were real or imaginary. It was nothing to the jurisconsult that his opinion was overruled for the moment by the magistrate who adjudicated on his client's case, unless that magistrate happened to rank above him in legal knowledge or the esteem of his profession. I do not, indeed, mean it to be inferred that he would wholly omit to consider his client's advantage, for the client was in earlier times the great lawyer's constituent and at a later period his paymaster, but the main road to the rewards of ambition lay through the good opinion of his order, and it is obvious that under such a system as I have been describing this was much more likely to be secured by viewing each case as an illustration of a great principle, or an exemplification of a broad rule, than by merely shaping it for an insulated forensic triumph. It is evident that powerful influence must have been exercised by the want of any distinct check on the suggestion or invention of possible questions. Where the data can be multiplied at pleasure, the facilities for evolving a general rule are immensely increased. As the law is administered among ourselves, the judge cannot travel out of the sets of facts exhibited before him or before his predecessors. Accordingly each group of circumstances which is adjudicated upon receives, to employ a Gallicism, a sort of consecration. It acquires certain qualities which distinguish it from every other case genuine or hypothetical. But at Rome, as I have attempted to explain, there was nothing resembling a Bench or Chamber of judges; and therefore no combination of facts possessed any particular value more than another. When a difficulty came for opinion before the jurisconsult, there was nothing to prevent a person endowed with a nice perception of analogy from at once proceeding to adduce and consider an entire class of supposed questions with which a particular feature connected it. Whatever were the practical advice given to the client, the

responsum treasured up in the note-books of listen-
ing pupils would doubtless contemplate the circumstances as governed by a great principle, or included
in a sweeping rule.   Nothing like this has ever been
possible among ourselves, and it should be acknowledged that in many criticisms passed on the English
law the manner in which it has been enunciated
seems to have been lost sight of.   The hesitation of
our courts in declaring principles may be much more
reasonably attributed to the comparative scantiness
of our precedents, voluminous as they appear to him
who is acquainted with no other system, than to the
temper of our judges.   It is true that in the wealth
of legal principle we are considerably poorer than
several modern European nations.   But they, it must
be remembered, took the Roman jurisprudence for
the foundation of their civil institutions.   They
built the *débris* of the Roman law into their walls ;
but in the materials and workmanship of the residue
there is not much which distinguishes it favourably
from the structure erected by the English judicature.

The period of Roman freedom was the period during
which the stamp of a distinctive character was impressed on the Roman jurisprudence; and through
all the earlier part of it, it was by the Responses of
the jurisconsults that the development of the law was
mainly carried on.   But as we approach the fall of
the republic there are signs that the Responses are

assuming a form which must have been fatal to their farther expansion. They are becoming systematised and reduced into compendia. Q. Mucius Scævola, the Pontifex, is said to have published a manual of the entire Civil Law, and there are traces in the writings of Cicero of growing disrelish for the old methods, as compared with the more active instruments of legal innovation. Other agencies had in fact by this time been brought to bear on the law. The Edict, or annual proclamation of the Prætor, had risen into credit as the principal engine of law reform, and L. Cornelius Sylla, by causing to be enacted the great group of statutes called the *Leges Corneliæ*, had shown what rapid and speedy improvements can be effected by direct legislation. The final blow to the Responses was dealt by Augustus, who limited to a few leading jurisconsults the right of giving binding opinions on cases submitted to them, a change which, though it brings us nearer the ideas of the modern world, must obviously have altered fundamentally the characteristics of the legal profession and the nature of its influence on Roman law. At a later period another school of jurisconsults arose, the great lights of jurisprudence for all time. But Ulpian and Paulus, Gaius and Papinian, were not authors of Responses. Their works were regular treatises on particular departments of the law, more especially on the Prætor's Edict.

The *Equity* of the Romans and the Prætorian Edict by which it was worked into their system, will be considered in the next chapter. Of the Statute Law it is only necessary to say that it was scanty during the republic, but became very voluminous under the empire. In the youth and infancy of a nation it is a rare thing for the legislature to be called into action for the general reform of private law. The cry of the people is not for change in the laws, which are usually valued above their real worth, but solely for their pure, complete and easy administration; and recourse to the legislative body is generally directed to the removal of some great abuse, or the decision of some incurable quarrel between classes or dynasties. There seems in the minds of the Romans to have been some association between the enactment of a large body of statutes and the settlement of society after a great civil commotion. Sylla signalised his reconstitution of the republic by the Leges Corneliæ; Julius Cæsar contemplated vast additions to the Statute Law; Augustus caused to be passed the all-important group of Leges Juliæ; and among later emperors the most active promulgators of constitutions are princes who, like Constantine, have the concerns of the world to readjust. The true period of Roman Statute Law does not begin till the establishment of the empire. The enactments of the emperors, clothed at first in the pretence of popular sanction, but afterwards emanating undisguisedly from the imperial prerogative, extend in increasing massiveness from the consolidation of Augustus's power to the publication of the Code of Justinian. It will be seen that even in the reign of the second emperor a considerable approximation is made to that condition of the law and that mode of administering it with which we are all familiar. A statute law and a limited board of expositors have arisen into being; a permanent court of appeal and a collection of approved commentaries will very shortly be added; and thus we are brought close on the ideas of our own day.

CHAPTER III.

LAW OF NATURE AND EQUITY.

THE theory of a set of legal principles entitled by their intrinsic superiority to supersede the older law, very early obtained currency both in the Roman State and in England. Such a body of principles, existing in any system, has in the foregoing chapters been denominated Equity, a term which, as will presently be seen, was one (though only one) of the designations by which this agent of legal change was known to the Roman jurisconsults. The jurisprudence of the Court of Chancery, which bears the name of Equity in England, could only be adequately discussed in a separate treatise. It is extremely complex in its texture, and derives its materials from several heterogeneous sources. The early ecclesiastical chancellors contributed to it, from the Canon Law, many of the principles which lie deepest in its structure. The Roman law, more fertile than the Canon Law in rules applicable to secular disputes, was not seldom resorted to by a later generation of Chancery judges, amid whose recorded dicta we often find entire texts from the *Corpus Juris Civilis* imbedded, with their terms unaltered, though their origin is never acknowledged. Still more recently, and particularly at the middle and during the latter half of the eighteenth century, the mixed systems of jurisprudence and morals constructed by the publicists of the Low Countries appear to have been much studied by English lawyers, and from the chancellorship of Lord Talbot to the commencement of Lord Eldon's chancellorship these works had considerable effect on the rulings of the Court of Chancery. The system, which obtained its ingredients from these various quarters, was greatly controlled in its growth by the necessity imposed on it of conforming itself to the analogies of the common law, but it has always answered the description of a body of comparatively novel legal principles claiming to override the older jurisprudence of the country on the strength of an intrinsic ethical superiority.

The Equity of Rome was a much simpler structure, and its development from its first appearance can be much more easily traced. Both its character and its history deserve attentive examination. It is the root of several conceptions which have exercised profound influence on human thought, and through human thought have seriously affected the destinies of mankind.

The Romans described their legal system as consisting of two ingredients. "All nations," says the

Institutional Treatise published under the authority of the Emperor Justinian, " who are ruled by laws and customs, are governed partly by their own particular laws, and partly by those laws which are common to all mankind. The law which a people enacts is called the Civil Law of that people, but that which natural reason appoints for all mankind is called the Law of Nations, because all nations use it." The part of the law " which natural reason appoints for all mankind " was the element which the Edict of the Prætor was supposed to have worked into Roman jurisprudence. Elsewhere it is styled more simply Jus Naturale, or the Law of Nature; and its ordinances are said to be dictated by Natural Equity (*naturalis æquitas*) as well as by natural reason. I shall attempt to discover the origin of these famous phrases, Law of Nations, Law of Nature, Equity, and to determine how the conceptions which they indicate are related to one another.

The most superficial student of Roman history must be struck by the extraordinary degree in which the fortunes of the republic were affected by the presence of foreigners, under different names, on her soil. The causes of this immigration are discernible enough at a later period, for we can readily understand why men of all races should flock to the mistress of the world; but the same phenomenon of a large population of foreigners and denizens meets us in the very earliest records of the Roman State. No doubt, the instability of society in ancient Italy, composed as it was in great measure of robber tribes, gave men considerable inducement to locate themselves in the territory of any community strong enough to protect itself and them from external attack, even though protection should be purchased at the cost of heavy taxation, political disfranchisement, and much social humiliation. It is probable, however, that this explanation is imperfect, and that it could only be completed by taking into account those active commercial relations which, though they are little reflected in the military traditions of the republic, Rome appears certainly to have had with Carthage and with the interior of Italy in pre-historic times. Whatever were the circumstances to which it was attributable, the foreign element in the commonwealth determined the whole course of its history, which, at all its stages, is little more than a narrative of conflicts between a stubborn nationality and an alien population. Nothing like this has been seen in modern times; on the one hand, because modern European communities have seldom or never received any accession of foreign immigrants which was large enough to make itself felt by the bulk of the native citizens, and on the other, because modern states, being held together by allegiance to a king or political superior, absorb considerable bodies of immigrant

assumed in disputes to which the parties were either foreigners or a native and a foreigner. The assumption of such a jurisdiction brought with it the immediate necessity of discovering some principles on which the questions to be adjudicated upon could be settled, and the principles applied to this object by the Roman lawyers were eminently characteristic of the time. They refused, as I have said before, to decide the new cases by pure Roman Civil Law. They refused, no doubt because it seemed to involve some kind of degradation, to apply the law of the particular State from which the foreign litigant came. The expedient to which they resorted was that of selecting the rules of law common to Rome and to the different Italian communities in which the immigrants were born. In other words, they set themselves to form a system answering to the primitive and literal meaning of Jus Gentium, that is, Law common to all Nations. Jus Gentium was, in fact, the sum of the common ingredients in the customs of the old Italian tribes, for they were *all the nations* whom the Romans had the means of observing, and who sent successive swarms of immigrants to Roman soil. Whenever a particular usage was seen to be practised by a large number of separate races in common, it was set down as part of the Law common to all Nations, or Jus Gentium. Thus, although the conveyance of property was certainly accompanied by very different forms in the different commonwealths surrounding Rome, the actual transfer, tradition, or delivery of the article intended to be conveyed was a part of the ceremonial in all of them. It was, for instance, a part, though a subordinate part, in the Mancipation or conveyance peculiar to Rome. Tradition, therefore, being in all probability the only common ingredient in the modes of conveyance which the jurisconsults had the means of observing, was set down as an institution Juris Gentium, or rule of the Law common to all Nations. A vast number of other observances were scrutinised with the same result. Some common characteristic was discovered in all of them, which had a common object, and this characteristic was classed in the Jus Gentium. The Jus Gentium was accordingly a collection of rules and principles, determined by observation to be common to the institutions which prevailed among the various Italian tribes.

The circumstances of the origin of the Jus Gentium are probably a sufficient safeguard against the mistake of supposing that the Roman lawyers had any special respect for it. It was the fruit in part of their disdain for all foreign law, and in part of their disinclination to give the foreigner the advantage of their own indigenous Jus Civile. It is true that we, at the present day, should probably take a very different view of the Jus Gentium, if we w ee performing the operation which was effected by the

Roman jurisconsults. We should attach some vague superiority or precedence to the element which we had thus discerned underlying and pervading so great a variety of usage. We should have a sort of respect for rules and principles so universal. Perhaps we should speak of the common ingredient as being of the essence of the transaction into which it entered, and should stigmatise the remaining apparatus of ceremony, which varied in different communities, as adventitious and accidental. Or it may be, we should infer that the races which we were comparing once obeyed a great system of common institutions of which the Jus Gentium was the reproduction, and that the complicated usages of separate commonwealths were only corruptions and depravations of the simpler ordinances which had once regulated their primitive state. But the results to which modern ideas conduct the observer are, as nearly as possible, the reverse of those which were instinctively brought home to the primitive Roman. What we respect or admire, he disliked or regarded with jealous dread. The parts of jurisprudence which he looked upon with affection were exactly those which a modern theorist leaves out of consideration as accidental and transitory; the solemn gestures of the mancipation; the nicely adjusted questions and answers of the verbal contract; the endless formalities of pleading and procedure. The Jus Gentium was merely a system forced on his attention by a political necessity. He loved it as little as he loved the foreigners from whose institutions it was derived and for whose benefit it was intended. A complete revolution in his ideas was required before it could challenge his respect, but so complete was it when it did occur, that the true reason why our modern estimate of the Jus Gentium differs from that which has just been described, is that both modern jurisprudence and modern philosophy have inherited the matured views of the later jurisconsults on this subject. There did come a time when, from an ignoble appendage of the Jus Civile, the Jus Gentium came to be considered a great though as yet imperfectly developed model to which all law ought as far as possible to conform. This crisis arrived when the Greek theory of a Law of Nature was applied to the practical Roman administration of the Law common to all Nations.

The Jus Naturale, or Law of Nature, is simply the Jus Gentium or Law of Nations seen in the light of a peculiar theory. An unfortunate attempt to discriminate them was made by the jurisconsult Ulpian, with the propensity to distinguish characteristic of a lawyer, but the language of Gaius, a much higher authority, and the passage quoted before from the Institutes, leave no room for doubt, that the expressions were practically convertible. The difference between them was entirely historical, and no distinction in essence could ever be established between them. It is almost unnecessary to add that the confusion between Jus Gentium, or Law common to all Nations, and *international law* is entirely modern. The classical expression for international law is Jus Feciale, or the law of negotiation and diplomacy. It is, however, unquestionable that indistinct impressions as to the meaning of Jus Gentium had considerable share in producing the modern theory that the relations of independent states are governed by the Law of Nature.

It becomes necessary to investigate the Greek conceptions of Nature and her law. The word φύσις which was rendered in the Latin *natura* and our *nature*, denoted beyond all doubt originally the material universe, but it was the material universe contemplated under an aspect which—such is our intellectual distance from those times—it is not very easy to delineate in modern language. Nature sig·· nified the physical world regarded as the result of some primordial element or law. The oldest Greek philosophers had been accustomed to explain the fabric of creation as the manifestation of some single principle which they variously asserted to be movement, fire, moisture, or generation. In its simplest and most ancient sense, Nature is precisely the physical universe looked upon in this way as the manifestation of a principle. Afterwards, the later Greek sects, returning to a path from which the greatest intellects of Greece had meanwhile strayed, added the *moral* to the *physical* world in the conception of Nature. They extended the term till it embraced not merely the visible creation, but the thoughts, observances, and aspirations of mankind. Still, as before, it was not solely the moral phenomena of human society which they understood by *Nature*, but these phenomena considered as resolvable into some general and simple laws.

Now, just as the oldest Greek theorists supposed that the sports of chance had changed the material universe from its simple primitive form into its present heterogeneous condition, so their intellectual descendants imagined that but for untoward accident the human race would have conformed itself to simpler rules of conduct and a less tempestuous life. To live according to *nature* came to be considered as the end for which man was created, and which the best men were bound to compass. To live according to *nature* was to rise above the disorderly habits and gross indulgences of the vulgar to higher laws of action which nothing but self-denial and self-command would enable the aspirant to observe. It is notorious that this proposition— live according to nature—was the sum of the tenets of the famous Stoic philosophy. Now on the subjugation of Greece that philosophy made instantaneous progress in Roman society. It possessed natural fascinations for the powerful class who, in theory at least, adhered to the simple habits of the ancient Italian race, and disdained to surrender themselves to the innovations of foreign fashion. Such persons began immediately to affect the Stoic precepts of life according to nature—an affectation all the more grateful, and, I may add, all the more noble, from its contrast with the unbounded profligacy which was being diffused through the imperial city by the pillage of the world and by the example of its most luxurious races. In the front of the disciples of the new Greek school, we might be sure, even if we did not know it historically, that the Roman lawyers figured. We have abundant proof that, there being substantially but two professions in the Roman republic, the military men were generally identified with the party of movement, but the lawyers were universally at the head of the party of resistance.

The alliance of the lawyers with the Stoic philosophers lasted through many centuries. Some of the earliest names in the series of renowned jurisconsults are associated with Stoicism, and ultimately we have the golden age of Roman jurisprudence fixed by general consent at the era of the Antonine Cæsars, the most famous disciples to whom that philosophy has given a rule of life. The long diffusion of these doctrines among the members of a particular profession was sure to affect the art which they practised and influenced. Several positions which we find in the remains of the Roman jurisconsults are scarcely intelligible, unless we use the Stoic tenets as our key; but at the same time it is a serious, though a very common, error to measure the influence of Stoicism on Roman law by counting up the number of legal rules which can be confidently affiliated on Stoical dogmas. It has often been observed that the strength of Stoicism resided not in its canons of conduct, which were often repulsive or ridiculous, but in the great though vague principle which it inculcated of resistance to passion. Just in the same way the influence on jurisprudence of the Greek theories, which had their most distinct expression in Stoicism, consisted not in the number of specific positions which they contributed to Roman law, but in the single fundamental assumption which they lent to it. After Nature had become a household word in the mouths of the Romans, the belief gradually prevailed among the Roman lawyers that the old Jus Gentium was in fact the lost code of Nature, and that the Prætor in framing an Edictal jurisprudence on the principles of the Jus Gentium was gradually restoring a type from which law had only departed to deteriorate. The inference from this belief was immediate that it

was the Prætor's duty to supersede the Civil Law as
much as possible by the Edict, to revive as far as
might be the institutions by which Nature had governed man in the primitive state. Of course there
were many impediments to the amelioration of law by
this agency. There may have been prejudices to overcome even in the legal profession itself, and Roman
habits were far too tenacious to give way at once
to mere philosophical theory. The indirect methods
by which the Edict combated certain technical anomalies, show the caution which its authors were compelled
to observe, and down to the very days of Justinian
there was some part of the old law which had obstinately resisted its influence. But on the whole,
the progress of the Romans in legal improvement
was astonishingly rapid as soon as stimulus was
applied to it by the theory of Natural Law. The
ideas of simplification and generalisation had always
been associated with the conception of Nature; simplicity, symmetry, and intelligibility came therefore
to be regarded as the characteristics of a good legal
system, and the taste for involved language, multiplied ceremonials, and useless difficulties disappeared altogether. The strong will and unusual
opportunities of Justinian were needed to bring the
Roman law to its existing shape, but the groundplan of the system had been sketched long before
the imperial reforms were effected.

What was the exact point of contact between the old Jus Gentium and the Law of Nature? I think that they touch and blend through Æquitas, or Equity in its original sense; and here we seem to come to the first appearance in jurisprudence of this famous term Equity. In examining an expression which has so remote an origin and so long a history as this, it is always safest to penetrate, if possible, to the simple metaphor or figure which at first shadowed forth the conception. It has generally been supposed that Æquitas is the equivalent of the Greek ἰσότης, i. e. the principle of equal or proportionate distribution. The equal division of numbers or physical magnitudes is doubtless closely entwined with our perceptions of justice; there are few associations which keep their ground in the mind so stubbornly or are dismissed from it with such diffi-culty by the deepest thinkers. Yet in tracing the history of this association, it certainly does not seem to have suggested itself to very early thought, but is rather the offspring of a comparatively late philosophy. It is remarkable too that the " equality" of laws on which the Greek democracies prided themselves—that equality which, in the beautiful drinking song of Callistratus, Harmodius and Ari-stogiton are said to have given to Athens—had little in common with the " equity " of the Romans. The first was an equal administration of civil laws

among the citizens, however limited the class of
citizens might be; the last implied the applicability
of a law, which was not civil law, to a class which
did not necessarily consist of citizens. The first
excluded a despot; the last included foreigners, and
for some purposes slaves. On the whole, I should
be disposed to look in another direction for the germ
of the Roman "Equity." The Latin word " æquus "
carries with it more distinctly than the Greek " ἴσος "
the sense of *levelling*. Now its levelling tendency
was exactly the characteristic of the Jus Gentium,
which would be most striking to a primitive Roman.
The pure Quiritarian law recognised a multitude of
arbitrary distinctions between classes of men and
kinds of property; the Jus Gentium, generalised from
a comparison of various customs, neglected the
Quiritarian divisions. The old Roman law established, for example, a fundamental difference between " Agnatic " and " Cognatic " relationship,
that is, between the Family considered as based
upon common subjection to patriarchal authority
and the Family considered (in conformity with modern ideas) as united through the mere fact of a
common descent. This distinction disappears in the
" law common to all nations," as also does the
difference between the archaic forms of property,
Things " Mancipi " and Things " nec Mancipi." The
neglect of demarcations and boundaries seems to

me, therefore, the feature of the Jus Gentium which was depicted in Æquitas. I imagine that the word was at first a mere description of that constant *levelling* or removal of irregularities which went on wherever the prætorian system was applied to the cases of foreign litigants. Probably no colour of ethical meaning belonged at first to the expression; nor is there any reason to believe that the process which it indicated was otherwise than extremely distasteful to the primitive Roman mind.

On the other hand, the feature of the Jus Gentium which was presented to the apprehension of a Roman by the word Equity, was exactly the first and most vividly realised characteristic of the hypothetical state of nature. Nature implied symmetrical order, first in the physical world, and next in the moral, and the earliest notion of order doubtless involved straight lines, even surfaces, and measured distances. The same sort of picture or figure would be unconsciously before the mind's eye, whether it strove to form the outlines of the supposed natural state, or whether it took in at a glance the actual administration of the " law common to all nations ; " and all we know of primitive thought would lead us to conclude that this ideal similarity would do much to encourage the belief in an identity of the two conceptions. But then, while the Jus Gentium had little or no antecedent credit at Rome, the theory of a Law of Nature came

states, but which had little in common with those
passages of political affairs which we now term revolutions. It may best be described by saying that
the monarchy was put into commission. The powers
heretofore accumulated in the hands of a single person were parcelled out among a number of elective
functionaries, the very name of the kingly office
being retained and imposed on a personage known
subsequently as the Rex Sacrorum or Rex Sacrificulus. As part of the change, the settled duties of
the supreme judicial office devolved on the Prætor,
at the time the first functionary in the commonwealth,
and together with these duties was transferred the
undefined supremacy over law and legislation which
always attached to ancient sovereigns, and which is
not obscurely related to the patriarchal and heroic
authority they had once enjoyed. The circumstances
of Rome gave great importance to the more indefinite
portion of the functions thus transferred, as with the
establishment of the republic began that series of
recurrent trials which overtook the state, in the difficulty of dealing with a multitude of persons who,
not coming within the technical description of indigenous Romans, were nevertheless permanently located
within Roman jurisdiction. Controversies between
such persons, or between such persons and native-born
citizens, would have remained without the pale of the
remedies provided by Roman law, if the Prætor had

not undertaken to decide them, and he must soon have addressed himself to the more critical disputes which in the extension of commerce arose between Roman subjects and avowed foreigners. The great increase of such cases in the Roman Courts about the period of the first Punic War is marked by the appointment of a special Prætor, known subsequently as the Prætor Peregrinus, who gave them his undivided attention. Meantime, one precaution of the Roman people against the revival of oppression, had consisted in obliging every magistrate whose duties had any tendency to expand their sphere, to publish, on commencing his year of office, an Edict or proclamation in which he declared the manner in which he intended to administer his department. The Prætor fell under the rule with other magistrates; but as it was necessarily impossible to construct each year a separate system of principles, he seems to have regularly republished his predecessor's Edict with such additions and changes as the exigency of the moment or his own views of the law compelled him to introduce. The Prætor's proclamation, thus lengthened by a new portion every year, obtained the name of the Edictum Perpetuum, that is, the *continuous* or *unbroken* edict. The immense length to which it extended, together perhaps with some distaste for its necessarily disorderly texture, caused the practice of increasing it to be stopped in the year of Salvius Julianus, who occupied the magistracy in the reign of the Emperor Hadrian. The edict of that Prætor embraced therefore the whole body of equity jurisprudence, which it probably disposed in new and symmetrical order, and the perpetual edict is therefore often cited in Roman law merely as the Edict of Julianus.

Perhaps the first inquiry which occurs to an Englishman who considers the peculiar mechanism of the Edict is, what were the limitations by which these extensive powers of the Prætor were restrained? How was authority so little definite to be reconciled with a settled condition of society and of law? The answer can only be supplied by careful observation of the conditions under which our own English law is administered. The Prætor, it should be recollected, was a jurisconsult himself, or a person entirely in the hands of advisers who were jurisconsults, and it is probable that every Roman lawyer waited impatiently for the time when he should fill or control the great judicial magistracy. In the interval, his tastes, feelings, prejudices, and degree of enlightenment were inevitably those of his own order, and the qualifications which he ultimately brought to office were those which he had acquired in the practice and study of his profession. An English Chancellor goes through precisely the same training, and carries to the woolsack the same qualifications. It is certain when he

assumes office that he will have, to some extent, modified the law before he leaves it; but until he has
quitted his seat, and the series of his decisions in the
Law Reports has been completed, we cannot discover
how far he has elucidated or added to the principles
which his predecessors bequeathed to him.   The influence of the Prætor on Roman jurisprudence differed
only in respect of the period at which its amount was
ascertained.   As was before stated, he was in office
but for a year, and his decisions rendered during his
year, though of course irreversible as regarded the
litigants, were of no ulterior value.   The most natural moment for declaring the changes he proposed to
effect, occurred therefore at his entrance on the præ-
torship; and hence, when commencing his duties, he
did openly and avowedly that which in the end his
English representative does insensibly and sometimes
unconsciously.   The checks on his apparent liberty
are precisely those imposed on an English judge.
Theoretically there seems to be hardly any limit to
the powers of either of them, but practically the
Roman Prætor, no less than the English Chancellor,
was kept within the narrowest bounds by the prepossessions imbibed from early training, and by the
strong restraints of professional opinion, restraints
of which the stringency can only be appreciated by
those who have personally experienced them.   It may
be added that the lines within which movement is

permitted, and beyond which there is to be no travelling, were chalked with as much distinctness in the one case as in the other. In England the judge follows the analogies of reported decisions on insulated groups of facts. At Rome, as the intervention of the Prætor was at first dictated by simple concern for the safety of the state, it is likely that in the earliest times it was proportioned to the difficulty which it attempted to get rid of. Afterwards, when the taste for principle had been diffused by the Responses, he no doubt used the Edict as the means of giving a wider application to those fundamental principles which he and the other practising jurisconsults, his contemporaries, believed themselves to have detected underlying the law. Latterly he acted wholly under the influence of Greek philosophical theories, which at once tempted him to advance and confined him to a particular course of progress.

The nature of the measures attributed to Salvius Julianus has been much disputed. Whatever they were, their effects on the Edict are sufficiently plain. It ceased to be extended by annual additions, and henceforward the equity jurisprudence of Rome was developed by the labours of a succession of great jurisconsults who fill with their writings the interval between the reign of Hadrian and the reign of Alexander Severus. A fragment of the wonderful system which they built up survives in the

Pandects of Justinian, and supplies evidence that their works took the form of treatises on all parts of Roman law, but chiefly that of commentaries on the Edict. Indeed, whatever be the immediate subject of a jurisconsult of this epoch, he may always be called an expositor of Equity. The principles of the Edict had, before the epoch of its cessation, made their way into every part of Roman jurisprudence. The Equity of Rome, it should be understood, even when most distinct from the Civil Law, was always administered by the same tribunals. The Prætor was the chief equity judge as well as the great common law magistrate, and as soon as the Edict had evolved an equitable rule the Prætor's court began to apply it in place of or by the side of the old rule of the Civil Law, which was thus directly or indirectly repealed without any express enactment of the legislature. The result, of course, fell considerably short of a complete fusion of law and equity, which was not carried out till the reforms of Justinian. The technical severance of the two elements of jurisprudence entailed some confusion and some inconvenience, and there were certain of the stubborner doctrines of the Civil Law with which neither the authors nor the expositors of the Edict had ventured to interfere. But at the same time there was no corner of the field of jurisprudence which was not more or less swept over by the influence of Equity. It sup-

plied the jurist with all his materials for generalisation, with all his methods of interpretation, with
his elucidations of first principles, and with that
great mass of limiting rules which are rarely interfered with by the legislator, but which seriously
control the application of every legislative act.

The period of jurists ends with Alexander Severus.
From Hadrian to that emperor the improvement of
law was carried on, as it is at the present moment in
most continental countries, partly by approved commentaries and partly by direct legislation. But in
the reign of Alexander Severus the power of growth
in Roman Equity seems to be exhausted, and the succession of jurisconsults comes to a close. The remaining history of the Roman law is the history of the
imperial constitutions, and, at the last, of attempts to
codify what had now become the unwieldy body of
Roman jurisprudence. We have the latest and most
celebrated experiment of this kind in the *Corpus Juris*
of Justinian.

It would be wearisome to enter on a detailed comparison or contrast of English and Roman Equity;
but it may be worth while to mention two features
which they have in common. The first may be
stated as follows. Each of them tended, and all
such systems tend, to exactly the same state in
which the old common law was when Equity first
interfered with it. A time always comes at which

the moral principles originally adopted have been
carried out to all their legitimate consequences, and
then the system founded on them becomes as rigid,
as unexpansive, and as liable to fall behind moral
progress as the sternest code of rules avowedly legal.
Such an epoch was reached at Rome in the reign
of Alexander Severus; after which, though the
whole Roman world was undergoing a moral revolution, the Equity of Rome ceased to expand. The
same point of legal history was attained in England under the chancellorship of Lord Eldon, the
first of our equity judges who, instead of enlarging the jurisprudence of his court by indirect
legislation, devoted himself through life to explaining and harmonising it. If the philosophy of legal
history were better understood in England, Lord
Eldon's services would be less exaggerated on the
one hand and better appreciated on the other than
they appear to be among contemporary lawyers.
Other misapprehensions too, which bear some practical fruit, would perhaps be avoided. It is easily
seen by English lawyers that English Equity is a
system founded on moral rules; but it is forgotten
that these rules are the morality of past centuries—
not of the present—that they have received nearly
as much application as they are capable of, and that,
though of course they do not differ largely from the
ethical creed of our own day, they are not necessarily

on a level with it. The imperfect theories of the subject which are commonly adopted have generated errors of opposite sorts. Many writers of treatises on Equity, struck with the completeness of the system in its present state, commit themselves expressly or implicitly to the paradoxical assertion that the founders of the chancery jurisprudence contemplated its present fixity of form when they were settling its first bases. Others, again, complain— and this is a grievance frequently observed upon in forensic arguments—that the moral rules enforced by the Court of Chancery fall short of the ethical standard of the present day. They would have each Lord Chancellor perform precisely the same office for the jurisprudence which he finds ready to his hand, which was performed for the old common law by the fathers of English equity. But this is to invert the order of the agencies by which the improvement of the law is carried on. Equity has its place and its time; but I have pointed out that another instrumentality is ready to succeed it when its energies are spent.

Another remarkable characteristic of both English and Roman Equity is the falsehood of the assumptions upon which the claim of the equitable to superiority over the legal rule is originally defended. Nothing is more distasteful to men, either as individuals or as masses, than the admission of their moral progress as a substantive reality. This unwillingness shows itself, as regards individuals, in the exaggerated respect which is ordinarily paid to the doubtful virtue of consistency. The movement of the collective opinion of a whole society is too palpable to be ignored, and is generally too visibly for the better to be decried; but there is the greatest disinclination to accept it as a primary phenomenon, and it is commonly explained as the recovery of a lost perfection—the gradual return to a state from which the race has lapsed. This tendency to look backward instead of forward for the goal of moral progress produced anciently, as we have seen, on Roman jurisprudence effects the most serious and permanent. The Roman jurisconsults, in order to account for the improvement of their jurisprudence by the Prætor, borrowed from Greece the doctrine of a Natural state of man—a Natural society—anterior to the organisation of commonwealths governed by positive laws. In England, on the other hand, a range of ideas especially congenial to Englishmen of that day, explained the claim of Equity to override the common law by supposing a general right to superintend the administration of justice which was assumed to be vested in the king as a natural result of his paternal authority. The same view appears in a different and a quainter form in the old doctrine that Equity flowed from the king's conscience—the improvement which had in fact taken place in the moral standard of the community being thus referred to an inherent elevation in the moral sense of the sovereign. The growth of the English constitution rendered such a theory unpalatable after a time; but, as the jurisdiction of the Chancery was then firmly established, it was not worth while to devise any formal substitute for it. The theories found in modern manuals of Equity are very various, but all are alike in their untenability. Most of them are modifications of the Roman doctrine of a natural law, which is indeed adopted in terms by those writers who begin a discussion of the jurisdiction of the Court of Chancery by laying down a distinction between natural justice and civil.

CHAPTER IV.

THE MODERN HISTORY OF THE LAW OF NATURE.

IT will be inferred from what has been said that
the theory which transformed the Roman jurisprudence had no claim to philosophical precision.   It
involved, in fact, one of those "mixed modes of
thought" which are now acknowledged to have
characterised all but the highest minds during the
infancy of speculation, and which are far from undiscoverable even in the mental efforts of our own
day.   The Law of Nature confused the Past and the
Present.   Logically, it implied a state of Nature
which had once been regulated by natural law; yet
the jurisconsults do not speak clearly or confidently
of the existence of such a state, which indeed is little
noticed by the ancients except where it finds a
poetical expression in the fancy of a golden age.
Natural law, for all practical purposes, was something belonging to the present, something entwined
with existing institutions, something which could be
distinguished from them by a competent observer.
The test which separated the ordinances of Nature

from the gross ingredients with which they were mingled was a sense of simplicity and harmony; yet it
was not on account of their simplicity and harmony
that these finer elements were primarily respected, but
on the score of their descent from the aboriginal reign
of Nature. This confusion has not been successfully
explained away by the modern disciples of the jurisconsults, and in truth modern speculations on the
Law of Nature betray much more indistinctness of
perception and are vitiated by much more hopeless
ambiguity of language than the Roman lawyers can
be justly charged with. There are some writers on
the subject who attempt to evade the fundamental
difficulty by contending that the code of Nature
exists in the future and is the goal to which all civil
laws are moving, but this is to reverse the assumptions on which the old theory rested, or rather
perhaps to mix together two inconsistent theories.
The tendency to look not to the past but to the future
for types of perfection was brought into the world
by Christianity. Ancient literature gives few or
no hints of a belief that the progress of society is
necessarily from worse to better.

But the importance of this theory to mankind has
been very much greater than its philosophical de-
ficiencies would lead us to expect. Indeed, it is not
easy to say what turn the history of thought, and
therefore of the human race, would have taken, if the

belief in a law natural had not become universal in the ancient world.

There are two special dangers to which law, and society which is held together by law, appear to be liable in their infancy. One of them is that law may be too rapidly developed. This occurred with the codes of the more progressive Greek communities, which disembarrassed themselves with astonishing facility from cumbrous forms of procedure and needless terms of art, and soon ceased to attach any superstitious value to rigid rules and prescriptions. It was not for the ultimate advantage of mankind that they did so, though the immediate benefit conferred on their citizens may have been considerable. One of the rarest qualities of national character is the capacity for applying and working out the law, as such, at the cost of constant miscarriages of abstract justice, without at the same time losing the hope or the wish that law may be conformed to a higher ideal. The Greek intellect, with all its mobility and elasticity, was quite unable to confine itself within the strait waistcoat of a legal formula; and, if we may judge them by the popular courts of Athens, of whose working we possess accurate knowledge, the Greek tribunals exhibited the strongest tendency to confound law and fact. The remains of the Orators and the forensic commonplaces preserved by Aristotle in his Treatise on Rhetoric, show

that questions of pure law were constantly argued
on every consideration which could possibly influence
the mind of the judges. No durable system of
jurisprudence could be produced in this way. A
community which never hesitated to relax rules of
written law whenever they stood in the way of an
ideally perfect decision on the facts of particular
cases, would only, if it bequeathed any body of
judicial principles to posterity, bequeath one consisting of the ideas of right and wrong which happened to be prevalent at the time. Such a jurisprudence would contain no framework to which the
more advanced conceptions of subsequent ages could
be fitted. It would amount at best to a philosophy,
marked with the imperfections of the civilisation
under which it grew up.

Few national societies have had their jurisprudence menaced by this peculiar danger of precocious
maturity and untimely disintegration. It is certainly doubtful whether the Romans were ever
seriously threatened by it, but at any rate they had
adequate protection in their theory of Natural Law.
For the Natural Law of the jurisconsults was distinctly conceived by them as a system which ought
gradually to absorb civil laws, without superseding
them so long as they remained unrepealed. There
was no such impression of its sanctity abroad, that
an appeal to it would be likely to overpower the

mind of a judge who was charged with the superintendence of a particular litigation. The value and
serviceableness of the conception arose from its
keeping before the mental vision a type of perfect
law, and from its inspiring the hope of an indefinite
approximation to it, at the same time that it never
tempted the practitioner or the citizen to deny the
obligation of existing laws which had not yet been
adjusted to the theory. It is important too to observe
that this model system, unlike many of those which
have mocked men's hopes in later days, was not
entirely the product of imagination. It was never
thought of as founded on quite untested principles.
The notion was that it underlay existing law and
must be looked for through it. Its functions were
in short remedial, not revolutionary or anarchical.
And this, unfortunately, is the exact point at which
the modern view of a Law of Nature has often ceased
to resemble the ancient.

The other liability to which the infancy of society
is exposed has prevented or arrested the progress of
far the greater part of mankind. The rigidity of
primitive law, arising chiefly from its early association and identification with religion, has chained
down the mass of the human race to those views
of life and conduct which they entertained at the
time when their usages were first consolidated into
a systematic form. There were one or two races

exempted by a marvellous fate from this calamity,
and grafts from these stocks have fertilised a few
modern societies; but it is still true that, over the
larger part of the world, the perfection of law has
always been considered as consisting in adherence to
the groundplan supposed to have been marked out
by the original legislator.   If intellect has in such
cases been exercised on jurisprudence, it has uniformly
prided itself on the subtle perversity of the conclusions it could build on ancient texts, without discoverable departure from their literal tenour.   I know
no reason why the law of the Romans should be superior to the laws of the Hindoos, unless the theory
of Natural Law had given it a type of excellence
different from the usual one.   In this one exceptional
instance, simplicity and symmetry were kept before
the eyes of a society whose influence on mankind was
destined to be prodigious from other causes, as the
characteristics of an ideal and absolutely perfect law.
It is impossible to overrate the importance to a nation
or profession of having a distinct object to aim at
in the pursuit of improvement.   The secret of
Bentham's immense influence in England during the
past thirty years is his success in placing such an
object before the country.   He gave us a clear rule
of reform.   English lawyers of the last century were
probably too acute to be blinded by the paradoxical
commonplace that English law was the perfection of

human reason, but they acted as if they believed it for want of any other principle to proceed upon. Bentham made the good of the community take precedence of every other object, and thus gave escape to a current which had long been trying to find its way outwards.

It is not an altogether fanciful comparison if we call the assumptions we have been describing the ancient counterpart of Benthamism. The Roman theory guided men's efforts in the same direction as the theory put into shape by the Englishman ; its practical results were not widely different from those which would have been attained by a sect of law-reformers who maintained a steady pursuit of the general good of the community. It would be a mistake, however, to suppose it a conscious antici-pation of Bentham's principles. The happiness of mankind is, no doubt, sometimes assigned, both in the popular and in the legal literature of the Romans, as the proper object of remedial legislation, but it is very remarkable how few and faint are the testimonies to this principle compared with the tributes which are constantly offered to the overshadowing claims of the Law of Nature. It was not to anything resembling philanthropy, but to their sense of simplicity and harmony—of what they significantly termed " ele-gance "—that the Roman jurisconsults freely surren-dered themselves. The coincidence of their labours with those which a more precise philosophy would have counselled has been part of the good fortune of mankind.

Turning to the modern history of the law of nature, we find it easier to convince ourselves of the vastness of its influence than to pronounce confidently whether that influence has been exerted for good or for evil. The doctrines and institutions which may be attributed to it are the material of some of the most violent controversies debated in our time, as will be seen when it is stated that the theory of Natural Law is the source of almost all the special ideas as to law, politics, and society which France during the last hundred years has been the instrument of diffusing over the western world. The part played by jurists in French history, and the sphere of jural conceptions in French thought, have always been remarkably large. It was not indeed in France, but in Italy, that the juridical science of modern Europe took its rise, but of the schools founded by emissaries of the Italian universities in all parts of the continent, and attempted (though vainly) to be set up in our island, that established in France produced the greatest effect on the fortunes of the country. The lawyers of France immediately formed a strict alliance with the kings of the houses of Capet and Valois, and it was as much through their assertions of royal prerogative, and through their interpretations of the rules of feudal succession, as by the power of the

sword, that the French monarchy at last grew together out of the agglomeration of provinces and
dependencies. The enormous advantage which their
understanding with the lawyers conferred on the
French kings in the prosecution of their struggle
with the great feudatories, the aristocracy, and the
church, can only be appreciated if we take into
account the ideas which prevailed in Europe far down
into the middle ages. There was, in the first place,
a great enthusiasm for generalisation and a curious
admiration for all general propositions, and consequently, in the field of law, an involuntary reverence
for every general formula which seemed to embrace
and sum up a number of the insulated rules which
were practised as usages in various localities. Such
general formulas it was, of course, not difficult for
practitioners familiar with the Corpus Juris or the
Glosses to supply in almost any quantity. There was,
however, another cause which added yet more considerably to the lawyers' power. At the period of
which we are speaking, there was universal vagueness
of ideas as to the degree and nature of the authority
residing in written texts of law. For the most part,
the peremptory preface, *Ita scriptum est*, seems to
have been sufficient to silence all objections. Where
a mind of our own day would jealously scrutinise the
formula which had been quoted, would inquire its
source, and would (if necessary) deny that the body

of law to which it belonged had any authority to
supersede local customs, the elder jurist would not
probably have ventured to do more than question the
applicability of the rule, or at best cite some counter-
proposition from the Pandects or the Canon Law. It
is extremely necessary to bear in mind the uncertainty of men's notions on this most important side
of juridical controversies, not only because it helps to
explain the weight which the lawyers threw into the
monarchical scale, but on account of the light which
it sheds on several curious historical problems. The
motives of the author of the Forged Decretals and
his extraordinary success are rendered more intelligible by it. And, to take a phenomenon of smaller
interest, it assists us, though only partially, to understand the plagiarisms of Bracton. That an English
writer of the time of Henry III. should have been
able to put off on his countrymen as a compendium
of pure English law a treatise of which the entire
form and a third of the contents were directly borrowed from the Corpus Juris, and that he should have
ventured on this experiment in a country where the
systematic study of the Roman law was formally
proscribed, will always be among the most hopeless
enigmas in the history of jurisprudence; but still it
is something to lessen our surprise when we comprehend the state of opinion at the period as to the
obligatory force of written texts, apart from all consideration of the source whence they were derived.

When the kings of France had brought their long struggle for supremacy to a successful close, an epoch which may be placed roughly at the accession of the branch of Valois-Angoulême to the throne, the situation of the French jurists was peculiar, and continued to be so down to the outbreak of the revolution. On the one hand, they formed the best instructed and nearly the most powerful class in the nation. They had made good their footing as a privileged order by the side of the feudal aristocracy, and they had assured their influence by an organisation which distributed their profession over France in great chartered corporations possessing large defined powers and still larger indefinite claims. In all the qualities of the advocate, the judge, and the legislator, they far excelled their compeers throughout Europe. Their juridical tact, their ease of expression, their fine sense of analogy and harmony, and (if they may be judged by the highest names among them) their passionate devotion to their conceptions of justice, were as remarkable as the singular variety of talent which they included, a variety covering the whole ground between the opposite poles of Cujas and Montesquieu, of D'Aguesseau and Dumoulin. But, on the other hand, the system of laws which they had to administer stood in striking contrast with the habits of mind which they had cultivated. The France which had been in great part constituted by their efforts was smitten with the

curse of an anomalous and dissonant jurisprudence
beyond every other country in Europe. One great
division ran through the country and separated it
into *Pays de Droit Écrit* and *Pays de Droit Coutumier*, the first acknowledging the written Roman law
as the basis of their jurisprudence, the last admitting
it only so far as it supplied general forms of expression, and courses of juridical reasoning, which were
reconcileable with the local usages. The sections
thus formed were again variously subdivided. In
the *Pays de Droit Coutumier* province differed from
province, county from county, municipality from
municipality, in the nature of its customs. In the
Pays de Droit Écrit the stratum of feudal rules
which overlay the Roman law was of the most miscellaneous composition. No such confusion as this ever
existed in England. In Germany it did exist, but
was too much in harmony with the deep political and
religious divisions of the country to be lamented or
even felt. It was the special peculiarity of France
that an extraordinary diversity of laws continued
without sensible alteration while the central authority
of the monarchy was constantly strengthening itself,
while rapid approaches were being made to complete
administrative unity, and while a fervid national
spirit had been developed among the people. The
contrast was one which fructified in many serious
results, and among them we must rank the effect

which it produced on the minds of the French lawyers. Their speculative opinions and their intellectual bias were in the strongest opposition to their interests and professional habits. With the keenest sense and the fullest recognition of those perfections of jurisprudence which consist in simplicity and uniformity, they believed, or seemed to believe, that the vices which actually invested French law were ineradicable; and in practice they often resisted the reformation of abuses with an obstinacy which was not shown by many among their less enlightened countrymen. But there was a way to reconcile these contradictions. They became passionate enthusiasts for Natural Law. The Law of Nature overleapt all provincial and municipal boundaries; it disregarded all distinctions between noble and burgess, between burgess and peasant; it gave the most exalted place to lucidity, simplicity, and system; but it committed its devotees to no specific improvement, and did not directly threaten any venerable or lucrative technicality. Natural law may be said to have become the common law of France, or, at all events, the admission of its dignity and claims was the one tenet which all French practitioners alike subscribed to. The language of the præ-revolutionary jurists in its eulogy is singularly unqualified, and it is remarkable that the writers on the Customs, who often made it their duty to speak disparagingly of the pure Roman law,

speak even more fervidly of Nature and her rules
than the civilians who professed an exclusive respect
for the Digest and the Code. Dumoulin, the highest
of all authorities on old French Customary Law, has
some extravagant passages on the Law of Nature;
and his panegyrics have a peculiar rhetorical turn
which indicates a considerable departure from the
caution of the Roman jurisconsults. The hypothesis
of a Natural Law had become not so much a theory
guiding practice as an article of speculative faith,
and accordingly we shall find that, in the transformation which it more recently underwent, its weakest
parts rose to the level of its strongest in the esteem
of its supporters.

The eighteenth century was half over when the
most critical period in the history of Natural Law
was reached. Had the discussion of the theory and
of its consequences continued to be exclusively the
employment of the legal profession, there would possibly have been an abatement of the respect which it
commanded; for by this time the *Esprit des Lois* had
appeared. Bearing in some exaggerations the marks
of the excessive violence with which its author's
mind had recoiled from assumptions usually suffered
to pass without scrutiny, yet showing in some ambiguities the traces of a desire to compromise with
existing prejudice, the book of Montesquieu, with all
its defects, still proceeded on that Historical Method

before which the Law of Nature has never maintained its footing for an instant. Its influence on thought ought to have been as great as its general popularity; but, in fact, it was never allowed time to put it forth, for the counter-hypothesis which it seemed destined to destroy passed suddenly from the forum to the street, and became the key-note of controversies far more exciting than are ever agitated in the courts or the schools. The person who launched it on its new career was that remarkable man who, without learning, with few virtues, and with no strength of character, has nevertheless stamped himself ineffaceably on history by the force of a vivid imagination, and by the help of a genuine and burning love for his fellow-men, for which much will always have to be forgiven him. We have never seen in our own generation—indeed the world has not seen more than once or twice in all the course of history—a literature which has exercised such prodigious influence over the minds of men, over every cast and shade of intellect, as that which emanated from Rousseau between 1749 and 1762. It was the first attempt to re-erect the edifice of human belief after the purely iconoclastic efforts commenced by Bayle, and in part by our own Locke, and consummated by Voltaire ; and besides the superiority which every constructive effort will always enjoy over one that is merely destructive, it possessed the immense advantage of appearing amid an all but universal scepticism as to the soundness of all foregone knowledge in matters speculative. Now, in all the speculations of Rousseau, the central figure, whether arrayed in an English dress as the signatary of a social compact, or simply stripped naked of all historical qualities, is uniformly Man, in a supposed state of nature. Every law or institution which would misbeseem this imaginary being under these ideal circumstances is to be condemned as having lapsed from an original perfection; every transformation of society which would give it a closer resemblance to the world over which the creature of Nature reigned, is admirable and worthy to be effected at any apparent cost. The theory is still that of the Roman lawyers, for in the phantasmagoria with which the Natural Condition is peopled, every feature and characteristic eludes the mind except the simplicity and harmony which possessed such charms for the jurisconsult; but the theory is, as it were, turned upside down. It is not the Law of Nature, but the State of Nature, which is now the primary subject of contemplation. The Roman had conceived that by careful observation of existing institutions parts of them could be singled out which either exhibited already, or could by judicious purification be made to exhibit, the vestiges of that reign of nature whose reality he faintly affirmed. Rousseau's belief was that a perfect social order could be evolved from the unassisted consideration of the natural state, a social order wholly irrespective of the actual condition of the world and wholly unlike it. The great difference between the views is that one bitterly and broadly condemns the present for its unlikeness to the ideal past ; while the other, assuming the present to be as necessary as the past, does not affect to disregard or censure it. It is not worth our while to analyse with any particularity that philosophy of politics, art, education, ethics, and social relation which was constructed on the basis of a state of nature. It still possesses singular fascination for the looser thinkers of every country, and is no doubt the parent, more or less remote, of almost all the prepossessions which impede the employment of the Historical Method of inquiry, but its discredit with the higher minds of our day is deep enough to astonish those who are familiar with the extraordinary vitality of speculative error. Perhaps the question most frequently asked nowadays is not what is the value of these opinions, but what were the causes which gave them such overshadowing prominence a hundred years ago. The answer is, I conceive, a simple one. The study which in the last century would best have corrected the misapprehensions into which an exclusive attention to legal antiquities is apt to betray was the

study of religion. But Greek religion, as then understood, was dissipated in imaginative myths. The
Oriental religions, if noticed at all, appeared to be
lost in vain cosmogonies. There was but one body
of primitive records which was worth studying—the
early history of the Jews. But resort to this was
prevented by the prejudices of the time. One of the
few characteristics which the school of Rousseau had
in common with the school of Voltaire was an utter
disdain of all religious antiquities; 'and, more than
all, of those of the Hebrew race. It is well known
that it was a point of honour with the reasoners of
that day to assume not merely that the institutions
called after Moses were not divinely dictated, nor
even that they were codified at a later date than that
attributed to them, but that they and the entire
Pentateuch were a gratuitous forgery, executed after
the return from the Captivity. Debarred, therefore,
from one chief security against speculative delusion,
the philosophers of France, in their eagerness to
escape from what they deemed a superstition of the
priests, flung themselves headlong into a superstition
of the lawyers.

But though the philosophy founded on the hypothesis of a state of nature has fallen low in general
esteem, in so far as it is looked upon under its coarser
and more palpable aspect, it does not follow that in
its subtler disguises it has lost plausibility, popu-

larity, or power.   I believe, as I have said, that it is
still the great antagonist of the Historical Method;
and whenever (religious objections apart) any mind
is seen to resist or contemn that mode of investigation, it will generally be found under the influence
of a prejudice or vicious bias traceable to a conscious
or unconscious reliance on a non-historic, natural,
condition of society or the individual.   It is chiefly,
however, by allying themselves with political and
social tendencies that the doctrines of Nature and
her law have preserved their energy.   Some of these
tendencies they have stimulated, others they have
actually created, to a great number they have given
expression and form.   They visibly enter largely
into the ideas which constantly radiate from France
over the civilised world, and thus become part of the
general body of thought by which its civilisation is
modified.   The value of the influence which they
thus exercise over the fortunes of the race is of course
one of the points which our age debates most warmly,
and it is beside the purpose of this treatise to discuss
it.   Looking back, however, to the period at which
the theory of the state of nature acquired the maxi-
mum of political importance, there are few who will
deny that it helped most powerfully to bring about
the grosser disappointments of which the first
French Revolution was fertile.   It gave birth, or
intense stimulus, to the vices of mental habit all but

universal at the time, disdain of positive law, impatience of experience, and the preference of *à priori* to all other reasoning. In proportion too as this philosophy fixes its grasp on minds which have thought less than others and fortified themselves with smaller observation, its tendency is to become distinctly anarchical. It is surprising to note how many of the *Sophismes Anarchiques* which Dumont published for Bentham, and which embody Bentham's exposure of errors distinctively French, are derived from the Roman hypothesis in its French transformation, and are unintelligible unless referred to it. On this point too it is a curious exercise to consult the *Moniteur* during the principal eras of the Revolution. The appeals to the Law and State of Nature become thicker as the times grow darker.

There is a single example which very strikingly illustrates the effects of the theory of natural law on modern society, and indicates how very far are those effects from being exhausted. There cannot, I conceive, be any question that to the assumption of a Law Natural we owe the doctrine of the fundamental equality of human beings. That "all men are equal" is one of a large number of legal propositions which in progress of time, have become political. The Roman jurisconsults of the Antonine era lay down that " omnes homines naturâ æquales sunt," but in their eyes this is a strictly juridical axiom. They intend to affirm that, under the hypothetical Law of Nature, and in so far as positive law approximates to it, the arbitrary distinctions which the Roman Civil Law maintained between classes of persons cease to have a legal existence. The rule was one of considerable importance to the Roman practitioner, who required to be reminded that, wherever Roman jurisprudence was assumed to conform itself exactly to the code of Nature, there was no difference in the contemplation of the Roman tribunals between citizen and foreigner, between freeman and slave, between Agnate and Cognate. The jurisconsults who thus expressed themselves most certainly never intended to censure the social arrangements under which civil law fell somewhat short of its speculative type; nor did they apparently believe that the world would ever see human society completely assimilated to the economy of nature. But when the doctrine of human equality makes its appearance in a modern dress it has evidently clothed itself with a new shade of meaning. Where the Roman jurisconsult had written " æquales sunt," meaning exactly what he said, the modern civilian wrote " all men are equal " in the sense of " all men ought to be equal." The peculiar Roman idea that natural law coexisted with civil law and gradually absorbed it, had evidently been lost sight of, or had become unintelligible, and the words which had at most conveyed a theory concerning the origin, composition, and development of human institutions, were beginning to express the sense of a great standing wrong suffered by mankind. As early as the beginning of the fourteenth century, the current language concerning the birth-state of men, though visibly intended to be identical with that of Ulpian and his contemporaries, has assumed an altogether different form and meaning. The preamble to the celebrated ordinance of King Louis Hutin, enfranchising the serfs of the royal domains, would have sounded strangely to Roman ears. "Whereas, according to natural law, everybody ought to be born free; and by some usages and customs which, from long antiquity, have been introduced and kept until now in our realm, and peradventure by reason of the misdeeds of their predecessors, many persons of our common people have fallen into servitude, therefore, We," &c. This is the enunciation not of a legal rule but of a political dogma; and from this time the equality of men is spoken of by the French lawyers just as if it were a political truth which happened to have been preserved among the archives of their science. Like all other deductions from the hypothesis of a Law Natural, and like the belief itself in a Law of Nature, it was languidly assented to and suffered to have little influence on opinion and practice until it passed out of the possession of the lawyers into that of the literary men of the eighteenth century and of the public which sat at their feet. With them it became the most distinct tenet of their creed, and was even regarded as a summary of all the others. It is probable, however, that the power which it ultimately acquired over the events of 1789 was not entirely owing to its popularity in France, for in the middle of the century it passed over to America. The American lawyers of the time, and particularly those of Virginia, appear to have possessed a stock of knowledge which differed chiefly from that of their English contemporaries in including much which could only have been derived from the legal literature of continental Europe. A very few glances at the writings of Jefferson will show how strongly his mind was affected by the semi-juridical, semi-popular opinions which were fashionable in France, and we cannot doubt that it was sympathy with the peculiar ideas of the French jurists which led him and the other colonial lawyers who guided the course of events in America to join the specially French assumption that "all men are born equal" with the assumption, more familiar to Englishmen, that all men are born free, in the very first lines of their Declaration of Independence. The passage was one of great importance to the history of the doctrine before us. The American lawyers, in thus prominently and emphatically affirming the fundamental equality of human beings, gave an impulse to political movements in their own country, and in a less degree. in Great Britain, which is far from having yet spent itself; but besides this they returned the dogma they had adopted to its home in France, endowed with vastly greater energy and enjoying much greater claims on general reception and respect. Even the more cautious politicians of the first Constituent Assembly repeated Ulpian's proposition as if it at once commended itself to the instincts and intuitions of mankind; and of all the " principles of 1789 " it is the one which has been least strenuously assailed, which has most thoroughly leavened modern opinion, and which promises to modify most deeply the constitution of societies and the politics of states.

The grandest function of the Law of Nature was discharged in giving birth to modern International Law and to the modern Law of War, but this part of its effects must here be dismissed with consideration very unequal to its importance.

Among the postulates which form the foundation of International Law, or of so much of it as retains the figure which it received from its original architects, there are two or three of preeminent importance. The first of all is expressed in the position that there is a determinable Law of Nature. Grotius and his successors took the assumption directly from the Romans, but they differed widely from the Roman jurisconsults and from each other in their ideas as to the mode of determination. The

ambition of almost every Publicist who has flourished
since the revival of letters has been to provide new
and more manageable definitions of Nature and of her
law, and it is indisputable that the conception in
passing through the long series of writers on Public
Law has gathered round it a large accretion, consisting of fragments of ideas derived from nearly
every theory of ethics which has in its turn taken
possession of the schools.   Yet it is a remarkable
proof of the essentially historical character of the
conception that, after all the efforts which have been
made to evolve the code of nature from the necessary
characteristics of the natural state, so much of the
result is just what it would have been if men had
been satisfied to adopt the dicta of the Roman
lawyers without questioning or reviewing them.
Setting aside the Conventional or Treaty Law of
Nations, it is surprising how large a part of the
system is made up of pure Roman law.   Wherever
there is a doctrine of the jurisconsults affirmed by
them to be in harmony with the Jus Gentium, the
Publicists have found a reason for borrowing it,
however plainly it may bear the marks of a distinctively Roman origin.   We may observe too that the
derivative theories are afflicted with the weakness
of the primary notion.   In the majority of the
Publicists, the mode of thought is still " mixed."
In studying these writers, the great difficulty is

always to discover whether they are discussing law or morality—whether the state of international relations they describe is actual or ideal—whether they lay down that which is, or that which, in their opinion, ought to be.

The assumption that Natural Law is binding on states *inter se* is the next in rank of those which underlie International Law. A series of assertions or admissions of this principle may be traced up to the very infancy of modern juridical science, and at first sight it seems a direct inference from the teaching of the Romans. The civil condition of society being distinguished from the natural by the fact that in the first there is a distinct author of law, while in the last there is none, it appears as if the moment a number of *units* were acknowledged to obey no common sovereign or political superior they were thrown back on the ulterior behests of the Law Natural. States are such units; the hypothesis of their independence excludes the notion of a common lawgiver, and draws with it, therefore, according to a certain range of ideas, the notion of subjection to the primeval order of nature. The alternative is to consider independent communities as not related to each other by any law, but this condition of lawlessness is exactly the vacuum which the Nature of the jurisconsults abhorred. There is certainly apparent reason for thinking that if the mind of a Roman lawyer rested on any sphere from which civil law was banished, it would instantly fill the void with the ordinances of Nature. It is never safe, however, to assume that conclusions, however certain and immediate in our own eyes, were actually drawn at any period of history. No passage has ever been adduced from the remains of Roman law which, in my judgment, proves the jurisconsults to have believed natural law to have obligatory force between independent commonwealths; and we cannot but see that to citizens of the Roman empire, who regarded their sovereign's dominions as conterminous with civilisation, the equal subjection of states to the Law of Nature, if contemplated at all, must have seemed at most an extreme result of curious speculation. The truth appears to be that modern International Law, undoubted as is its descent from Roman law, is only connected with it by an irregular filiation. The early modern interpreters of the jurisprudence of Rome, misconceiving the meaning of Jus Gentium, assumed without hesitation that the Romans had bequeathed to them a system of rules for the adjustment of international transactions. This "Law of Nations" was at first an authority which had formidable competitors to strive with, and the condition of Europe was long such as to preclude its universal reception. Gradually, however, the western world arranged itself in a form more favourable to the theory of the civilians; circumstances destroyed the credit of rival

doctrines; and at last, at a peculiarly felicitous con-
juncture, Ayala and Grotius were able to obtain for it
the enthusiastic assent of Europe, an assent which has
been over and over again renewed in every variety of
solemn engagement.   The great men to whom its
triumph is chiefly owing attempted, it need scarcely be
said, to place it on an entirely new basis, and it is unquestionable that in the course of this displacement
they altered much of its structure, though far less
of it than is commonly supposed.   Having adopted
from the Antonine jurisconsults the position that the
Jus Gentium and the Jus Naturæ were identical,
Grotius, with his immediate predecessors and his immediate successors, attributed to the Law of Nature
an authority which would never perhaps have been
claimed for it, if " Law of Nations " had not in that
age been an ambiguous expression.   They laid down
unreservedly that Natural Law is the code of states,
and thus put in operation a process which has continued almost down to our own day, the process of
engrafting on the international system rules which
are supposed to have been evolved from the unassisted contemplation of the conception of Nature.
There is too one consequence of immense practical
importance to mankind which, though not unknown
during the early modern history of Europe, was
never clearly or universally acknowledged till the
doctrines of the Grotian school had prevailed.   If

the society of nations is governed by Natural Law, the atoms which compose it must be absolutely equal. Men under the sceptre of Nature are all equal, and accordingly commonwealths are equal if the international state be one of nature. The proposition that independent communities, however different in size and power, are all equal in the view of the law of nations, has largely contributed to the happiness of mankind, though it is constantly threatened by the political tendencies of each successive age. It is a doctrine which probably would never have obtained a secure footing at all if International Law had not been entirely derived from the majestic claims of Nature by the Publicists who wrote after the revival of letters.

On the whole, however, it is astonishing, as I have observed before, how small a proportion the additions made to International Law since Grotius's day bear to the ingredients which have been simply taken from the most ancient stratum of the Roman Jus Gentium. Acquisition of territory has always been the great spur of national ambition, and the rules which govern this acquisition, together with the rules which moderate the wars in which it too frequently results, are merely transcribed from the part of the Roman law which treats of the modes of acquiring property *jure gentium*. These modes of acquisition were obtained by the elder jurisconsults, as I have attempted to

explain, by abstracting a common ingredient from
the usages observed to prevail among the various
tribes surrounding Rome; and, having been classed
on account of their origin in the "law common to
all nations," they were thought by the later lawyers
to fit in, on the score of their simplicity, with the
more recent conception of a Law Natural.   They thus
made their way into the modern Law of Nations, and
the result is that those parts of the international
system which refer to *dominion*, its nature, its limitations, the modes of acquiring and securing it, are
pure Roman Property Law—so much, that is to say,
of the Roman Law of Property as the Antonine jurisconsults imagined to exhibit a certain congruity with
the natural state.   In order that these chapters of
International Law may be capable of application, it is
necessary that sovereigns should be related to each
other like the members of a group of Roman proprietors.   This is another of the postulates which lie
at the threshold of the International Code, and it is
also one which could not possibly have been subscribed to during the first centuries of modern
European history.   It is resolvable into the double
proposition that "sovereignty is territorial," *i. e.* that
it is always associated with the proprietorship of a
limited portion of the earth's surface, and that " sovereigns *inter se* are to be deemed not *paramount*, but
absolute, owners of the state's territory."

Many contemporary writers on International Law tacitly assume that the doctrines of their system, founded on principles of equity and common sense, were capable of being readily reasoned out in every stage of modern civilisation. But this assumption, while it conceals some real defects of the international theory, is altogether untenable so far as regards a large part of modern history. It is not true that the authority of the Jus Gentium in the concerns of nations was always uncontradicted; on the contrary, it had to struggle long against the claims of several competing systems. It is again not true that the territorial character of sovereignty was always recognised, for long after the dissolution of the Roman dominion the minds of men were under the empire of ideas irreconcileable with such a conception. An old order of things, and of views founded on it, had to decay—a new Europe, and an apparatus of new notions congenial to it, had to spring up—before two of the chiefest postulates of International Law could be universally conceded.

It is a consideration well worthy to be kept in view, that during a large part of what we usually term modern history no such conception was entertained as that of "*territorial sovereignty.*" Sovereignty was not associated with dominion over a portion or subdivision of the earth. The world had

lain for so many centuries under the shadow of
Imperial Rome as to have forgotten that distribution of the vast spaces comprised in the empire
which had once parcelled them out into a number of
independent commonwealths, claiming immunity from
extrinsic interference, and pretending to equality of
national rights.   After the subsidence of the barbarian irruptions, the notion of sovereignty that
prevailed seems to have been twofold.   On the one
hand it assumed the form of what may be called
" *tribe*-sovereignty."   The Franks, the Burgundians,
the Vandals, the Lombards, and Visigoths were
masters, of course, of the territories which they
occupied, and to which some of them have given a
geographical appellation; but they based no claim
of right upon the fact of territorial possession, and
indeed attached no importance to it whatever.   They
appear to have retained the traditions which they
brought with them from the forest and the steppe,
and to have still been in their own view a patriarchal
society, a nomad horde, merely encamped for the time
upon the soil which afforded them sustenance.   Part
of Transalpine Gaul, with part of Germany, had now
become the country *de facto* occupied by the Franks
—it was France; but the Merovingian line of chieftains, the descendants of Clovis, were not Kings of
France, they were Kings of the Franks.   Territorial
titles were not unknown, but they seem at first to

have come into use only as a convenient mode of
designating the ruler of a *portion* of the tribe's
possessions; the king of a *whole* tribe was king of
his people, not of his people's lands. The alternative to this peculiar notion of sovereignty appears
to have been—and this is the important point—the
idea of universal dominion. When a monarch departed from the special relation of chief to clansmen, and became solicitous, for purposes of his own,
to invest himself with a novel form of sovereignty,
the precedent which suggested itself for his adoption
was the domination of the Emperors of Rome. To
parody a common quotation, he became " *aut Cæsar
aut nullus.*" Either he pretended to the full prerogative of the Byzantine Emperor, or he had no
political status. In our own age, when a new dynasty
is desirous of obliterating the prescriptive title of a
deposed line of sovereigns, it takes its designation
from the *people*, instead of the *territory*. Thus we
have Emperors and Kings of the French, and a King
of the Belgians. At the period of which we have
been speaking, under similar circumstances, a different alternative presented itself. The Chieftain who
would no longer call himself King of the tribe
must claim to be Emperor of the world. Thus,
when the hereditary Mayors of the Palace had
ceased to compromise with the monarchs they had
long since virtually dethroned, they soon became

unwilling to call themselves Kings of the Franks, a title which belonged to the displaced Merovings; but they could not style themselves Kings of France, for such a designation, though apparently not unknown, was not a title of dignity. Accordingly they came forward as aspirants to universal empire. Their motive has been greatly misapprehended. It has been taken for granted by recent French writers that Charlemagne was far before his age, quite as much in the character of his designs as in the energy with which he prosecuted them. Whether it be true or not that anybody is at any time before his age, it is certainly true that Charlemagne, in aiming at an unlimited dominion, was emphatically taking the only course which the characteristic ideas of his age permitted him to follow. Of his intellectual eminence there cannot be a question, but it is proved by his acts and not by his theory.

These singularities of view were not altered on the partition of the inheritance of Charlemagne among his three grandsons. Charles the Bald, Lewis, and Lothair were still theoretically—if it be proper to use the word—Emperors of Rome. Just as the Cæsars of the Eastern and Western Empires had each been *de jure* emperor of the whole world, with *de facto* control over half of it, so the three Carlovingians appear to have considered their power as limited, but their title as unqualified. The same speculative universality of sovereignty continued to be associated

with the Imperial throne after the second division on
the death of Charles the Fat, and, indeed, was never
thoroughly dissociated from it so long as the empire
of Germany lasted.   Territorial sovereignty—the
view which connects sovereignty with the possession
of a limited portion of the earth's surface—was distinctly an offshoot, though a tardy one, of *feudalism*.
This might have been expected *à priori*, for it was
feudalism which for the first time linked personal
duties, and by consequence personal rights, to the
ownership of land.   Whatever be the proper view of
its origin and legal nature, the best mode of vividly
picturing to ourselves the feudal organisation is to
begin with the basis; to consider the relation of the
tenant to the patch of soil which created and limited
his services—and then to mount up, through narrow-
ing circles of super-feudation, till we approximate to
the apex of the system.   Where that summit exactly
was during the later portion of the dark ages it is not
easy to decide.   Probably, wherever the conception
of tribe sovereignty had really decayed, the topmost
point was always assigned to the supposed successor
of the Cæsars of the West. But before long, when the
actual sphere of Imperial authority had immensely
contracted, and when the emperors had concentrated
the scanty remains of their power upon Germany and
North Italy, the highest feudal superiors in all the
outlying portions of the former Carlovingian empire
found themselves practically without a supreme head.

Gradually they habituated themselves to the new situation, and the fact of immunity put at last out of sight the theory of dependence; but there are many symptoms that this change was not quite easily accomplished; and, indeed, to the impression that in the nature of things there must necessarily be a culminating domination somewhere, we may, no doubt, refer the increasing tendency to attribute secular superiority to the See of Rome. The completion of the first stage in the revolution of opinion is marked, of course, by the accession of the Capetian dynasty in France. Before that epoch arrived, several of the holders of the great territorial fiefs into which the Carlovingian empire was now split up, had begun to call themselves Kings, instead of Dukes or Counts; but the important change occurred when the feudal prince of a limited territory surrounding Paris began, from the accident of his uniting an unusual number of suzerainties in his own person, to call himself *King of France*, at the same time that he usurped from the earlier house their dynastic title of *Kings of the French*. Hugues Capet and his descendants were kings in quite a new sense, sovereigns standing in the same relation to the soil of France as the baron to his estate, the tenant to his freehold. The form of the monarchy in France had visible effects in hastening changes which were elsewhere proceeding in the same direction. The kingship of our Anglo-Saxon regal houses was midway between the chieftainship of a tribe and a territorial supremacy; but the superiority of the Norman monarchs, imitated from that of the King of France, was distinctly a territorial sovereignty. Every subsequent dominion which was established or consolidated was formed on the latter model. Spain, Naples, and the principalities founded on the ruins of municipal freedom in Italy, were all under rulers whose sovereignty was territorial. Few things, I may add, are more curious than the gradual lapse of the *Venetians* from one view to the other. At the commencement of its foreign conquests, the republic regarded itself as an antitype of the Roman commonwealth, governing a number of subject provinces. Move a century onwards, and you find that it wishes to be looked upon as a corporate sovereign, claiming the rights of a feudal suzerain over its possessions in Italy and the Ægean.

During the period through which the popular ideas on the subject of sovereignty were undergoing this remarkable change, the system which stood in the place of what we now call International Law was heterogeneous in form and inconsistent in the principles to which it appealed. Over so much of Europe as was comprised in the Romano-German empire, the connexion of the confederate states was regulated by the complex and as yet incomplete mechanism of the Imperial constitution; and, surprising as it may seem to us, it was a favourite notion of German lawyers that the relations of commonwealths, whether inside

or outside the empire, ought to be regulated not by
the *Jus Gentium*, but by the pure Roman jurisprudence, of which Cæsar was still the centre. This
doctrine was less confidently repudiated in the outlying countries than we might have supposed antecedently ; but substantially, through the rest of Europe
feudal subordinations furnished a substitute for a
public law ; and when those were undetermined or
ambiguous, there lay behind, in theory at least, a
supreme regulating force in the authority of the head
of the Church.   It is certain, however, that both
feudal and ecclesiastical influences were rapidly decaying during the fifteenth, and even the fourteenth
century ; and if we closely examine the current pre-
texts of wars, and the avowed motives of alliances,
it will be seen that, step by step with the displacement of the old principles, the views afterwards har-
monised and consolidated by Ayala and Grotius were
making considerable progress, though it was silent
and but slow.   Whether the fusion of all the sources
of authority would ultimately have evolved a system
of international relations, and whether that system
would have exhibited material differences from the
fabric of Grotius, is not now possible to decide, for
as a matter of fact the Reformation annihilated all
its potential elements except one.   Beginning in
Germany, it divided the princes of the empire by a
gulf too broad to be bridged over by the Imperial
supremacy, even if the Imperial superior had stood

neutral. He, however, was forced to take colour with the church against the reformers ; the Pope was, as a matter of course, in the same predicament; and thus the two authorities to whom belonged the office of mediation between combatants became themselves the chiefs of one great faction in the schism of the nations. Feudalism, already enfeebled and discredited as a principle of public relations, furnished no bond whatever which was stable enough to countervail the alliances of religion. In a condition, therefore, of public law which was little less than chaotic, those views of a state system to which the Roman jurisconsults were supposed to have given their sanction alone remained standing. The shape, the symmetry, and the prominence which they assumed in the hands of Grotius are known to every educated man ; but the great marvel of the Treatise "De Jure Belli et Pacis," was its rapid, complete, and universal success. The horrors of the Thirty Years' War, the boundless terror and pity which the unbridled license of the soldiery was exciting, must, no doubt, be taken to explain that success in some measure, but they do not wholly account for it. Very little penetration into the ideas of that age is required to convince one that, if the ground plan of the international edifice which was sketched in the great book of Grotius had not appeared to be theoretically perfect, it would have been discarded by jurists and neglected by statesmen and soldiers.

It is obvious that the speculative perfection of the Grotian system is intimately connected with that conception of territorial sovereignty which we have been discussing. The theory of International Law assumes that commonwealths are, relatively to each other, in a state of nature ; but the component atoms of a natural society must, by the fundamental assumption, be insulated and independent of each other. If there be a higher power connecting them, however slightly and occasionally, by the claim of common supremacy, the very conception of a common superior introduces the notion of positive law, and excludes the idea of a law natural. It follows, therefore, that if the universal suzerainty of an Imperial head had been admitted even in bare theory, the labours of Grotius would have been idle. Nor is this the only point of junction between modern public law and those views of sovereignty of which I have endeavoured to describe the development. I have said that there are entire departments of international jurisprudence which consist of the Roman Law of Property. What then is the inference ? It is, that if there had been no such change as I have described in the estimate of sovereignty—if sovereignty had not been associated with the proprietorship of a limited portion of the earth, had not, in other words, become territorial—three parts of the Grotian theory would have been incapable of application.

CHAPTER V.

PRIMITIVE SOCIETY AND ANCIENT LAW.

THE necessity of submitting the subject of jurisprudence to scientific treatment has never been entirely
lost sight of in modern times, and the essays which
the consciousness of this necessity has produced
have proceeded from minds of very various calibre,
but there is not much presumption, I think, in asserting that what has hitherto stood in the place of
a science has for the most part been a set of guesses,
those very guesses of the Roman lawyers which were
examined in the two preceding chapters.   A series
of explicit statements, recognising and adopting
these conjectural theories of a natural state, and of a
system of principles congenial to it, has been continued with but brief interruption from the days of
their inventors to our own.   They appear in the
annotations of the Glossators who founded modern
jurisprudence, and in the writings of the scholastic
jurists who succeeded them.   They are visible in
the dogmas of the canonists.   They are thrust into
prominence by those civilians of marvellous erudi-
tion, who flourished at the revival of ancient letters.

Grotius and his successors invested them not more with brilliancy and plausibility than with practical importance. They may be read in the introductory chapters of our own Blackstone, who has transcribed them textually from Burlamaqui, and wherever the manuals published in the present day for the guidance of the student or the practitioner begin with any discussion of the first principles of law, it always resolves itself into a restatement of the Roman hypothesis. It is however from the disguises with which these conjectures sometimes clothe themselves, quite as much as from their native form, that we gain an adequate idea of the subtlety with which they mix themselves in human thought. The Lockeian theory of the origin of Law in a Social Compact scarcely conceals its Roman derivation, and indeed is only the dress by which the ancient views were rendered more attractive to a particular generation of the moderns ; but on the other hand the theory of Hobbes on the same subject was purposely devised to repudiate the reality of a law of nature as conceived by the Romans and their disciples. Yet these two theories, which long divided the reflecting politicians of England into hostile camps, resemble each other strictly in their fundamental assumption of a non-historic, unverifiable, condition of the race. Their authors differed as to the characteristics of the præ-social state, and as to the nature of the abnormal action by which men lifted themselves out of it into that social organisation with which alone we are acquainted, but they agreed in thinking that a great chasm separated man in his primitive condition from man in society, and this notion we cannot doubt that they borrowed, consciously or unconsciously, from the Romans. If indeed the phenomena of law be regarded in the way in which these theorists regarded them—that is, as one vast complex whole—it is not surprising that the mind should often evade the task it has set to itself by falling back on some ingenious conjecture which (plausibly interpreted) will seem to reconcile everything, or else that it should sometimes abjure in despair the labour of systematization.

From the theories of jurisprudence which have the same speculative basis as the Roman doctrine two of much celebrity must be excepted. The first of them is that associated with the great name of Montesquieu. Though there are some ambiguous expressions in the early part of the *Esprit des Lois*, which seem to show its writer's unwillingness to break quite openly with the views hitherto popular, the general drift of the book is certainly to indicate a very different conception of its subject from any which had been entertained before. It has often been noticed that, amidst the vast variety of examples which, in its immense width of survey, it sweeps together from supposed systems of jurisprudence, there is an evident anxiety to thrust into especial prominence those manners and institutions which astonish the civilised reader by their uncouthness, strangeness, or indecency. The inference constantly suggested is, that laws are the creatures of climate, local situation, accident, or imposture—the fruit of any causes except those which appear to operate with tolerable constancy. Montesquieu seems, in fact, to have looked on the nature of man as entirely plastic, as passively reproducing the impressions, and submitting implicitly to the impulses, which it receives from without. And here no doubt lies the error which vitiates his system as a system. He greatly underrates the stability of human nature. He pays little or no regard to the inherited qualities of the race, those qualities which each generation receives from its predecessors, and transmits but slightly altered to the generation which follows it. It is quite true, indeed, that no complete account can be given of social phenomena, and consequently of laws, till due allowance has been made for those modifying causes which are noticed in the *Esprit des Lois*; but their number and their force appear to have been overestimated by Montesquieu. Many of the anomalies which he parades have since been shown to rest on false report or erroneous construction, and of those which remain not a few prove the permanence rather than the variableness of man's nature, since they are relics of older stages of the race which have obstinately defied the influences that have elsewhere had effect. The truth is that the stable part of our mental, moral, and physical constitution is the largest part of it, and the resistance it opposes to change is such that, though the variations of human society in a portion of the world are plain enough, they are neither so rapid nor so extensive that their amount, character, and general direction cannot be ascertained. An approximation to truth may be all that is attainable with our present knowledge, but there is no reason for thinking that it is so remote, or (what is the same thing) that it requires so much future correction, as to be entirely useless and uninstructive.

The other theory which has been adverted to is, the historical theory of Bentham. This theory which is obscurely (and, it might even be said, timidly) propounded in several parts of Bentham's works is quite distinct from that analysis of the conception of law which he commenced in the " Fragment on Government," and which was more recently completed by Mr. John Austin. The resolution of a law into a command of a particular nature, imposed under special conditions, does not affect to do more than protect us against a difficulty—a most formidable one certainly—of language. The whole question remains open as to the motives of societies in imposing these commands on themselves, as to the connexion of these commands with each other, and the nature of their dependence on those which preceded them, and which they have superseded. Bentham suggests the answer that societies modify, and have always modified, their laws according to modifications of their views of general expediency. It is difficult to say that this proposition is false, but it certainly appears to be unfruitful. For that which seems expedient to a society, or rather to the governing part of it, when it alters a rule of law is surely the same thing as the object, whatever it may be, which it has in view when it makes the change. Expediency and the greatest good are nothing more than different names for the impulse which prompts the modification; and when we lay down expediency as the rule of change in law or opinion, all we get by the proposition is the substitution of an express term for a term which is necessarily implied when we say that a change takes place.

There is such wide-spread dissatisfaction with existing theories of jurisprudence, and so general a conviction that they do not really solve the questions they pretend to dispose of, as to justify the suspicion that some line of inquiry, necessary to a perfect result, has been incompletely followed or altogether omitted by their authors. And indeed there is one remarkable omission with which all these speculations are chargeable, except perhaps those of Montesquieu. They take no account of what law has actually been at epochs remote from the particular period at which they made their appearance. Their originators carefully observed the institutions of their own age and civilisation, and those of other ages and civilisations with which they had some degree of intellectual sympathy, but, when they turned their attention to archaic states of society which exhibited much superficial difference from their own, they uniformly ceased to observe and began guessing. The mistake which they committed is therefore analogous to the error of one who, in investigating the laws of the material universe, should commence by contemplating the existing physical world as a whole, instead of beginning with the particles which are its simplest ingredients. One does not certainly see why such a scientific solecism should be more defensible in jurisprudence than in any other region of thought. It would seem antecedently that we ought to commence with the simplest social forms in a state as near as possible to their rudimentary condition. In other words, if we followed the course usual in such inquiries, we should penetrate as far up as we could in the history of primitive societies. The phenomena which early societies present us with are not easy at first to understand, but the difficulty of grappling with them bears no proportion to the perplexities which beset us in considering the baffling entanglement of modern social organisation. It is a difficulty arising from their strangeness and uncouthness, not from their number and complexity. One does not readily get over the surprise which they occasion when looked at from a modern point of view; but when that is surmounted they are few enough and simple enough. But, even if they gave more trouble than they do, no pains would be wasted in ascertaining the germs out of which has assuredly been unfolded every form of moral restraint which controls our actions and shapes our conduct at the present moment.

The rudiments of the social state, so far as they are known to us at all, are known through testimony of three sorts—accounts by contemporary observers of civilisations less advanced than their own, the records which particular races have preserved concerning their primitive history, and ancient law. The first kind of evidence is the best we could have expected. As societies do not advance concurrently, but at different rates of progress, there have been epochs at which men trained to habits of methodical observation have really been in a position to watch and describe the infancy of mankind. Tacitus made the most of such an opportunity; but the *Germany*, unlike most celebrated classical books, has not induced others to follow the excellent example set by its author, and the amount of this sort of testimony which we possess is exceedingly small. The lofty contempt which a civilised people entertains for barbarous neighbours has caused a remarkable negligence in observing them, and this carelessness has been aggravated at times by fear, by religious prejudice, and even by the use of these very terms—civilisation and barbarism—which convey to most persons the impression of a difference not merely in degree but in kind. Even the *Germany* has been suspected by some critics of sacrificing fidelity to poignancy of contrast and picturesqueness of narrative. Other histories too, which have been handed down to us among the archives of the people to whose infancy they relate, have been thought distorted by the pride of race or by the religious sentiment of a newer age. It is important then to observe that these suspicions, whether groundless or rational, do not attach to a great deal of archaic law. Much of the old law which has descended to us was preserved merely because it was old. Those who practised and obeyed it did not pretend to understand it; and in some cases they even ridiculed and despised it. They offered no account of it except that it had come down to them from their ancestors. If we confine our attention, then, to those fragments of ancient institutions which cannot reasonably be supposed to have been tampered with, we are able to gain a clear conception of certain great characteristics of the society to which they originally belonged. Advancing a step further, we can apply our knowledge to systems of law which, like the Code of Manu, are as a whole of suspicious authenticity; and, using the key we have obtained, we are in a position to discriminate those portions of them which are truly archaic from those which have been affected by the prejudices, interests, or ignorance of the compiler. It will at least be acknowledged that, if the materials for this process are sufficient, and if the comparisons be accurately executed, the methods followed are as little objectionable as those which have led to such surprising results in comparative philology.

The effect of the evidence derived from comparative jurisprudence is to establish that view of the primeval condition of the human race which is known as the Patriarchal Theory. There is no doubt, of course, that this theory was originally based on the Scriptural history of the Hebrew patriarchs in Lower Asia; but, as has been explained already, its connexion with Scripture rather militated than otherwise against its reception as a complete theory, since the majority of the inquirers who till recently addressed themselves with most earnestness to the colligation of social phenomena, were either influenced by the strongest prejudice against Hebrew antiquities or by the strongest desire to construct their system without the assistance of religious records. Even now there is perhaps a disposition to undervalue these accounts, or rather to decline generalising from them, as forming part of the traditions of a Semitic people. It is to be noted, however, that the legal testimony comes nearly exclusively from the institutions of societies belonging to the Indo-European stock, the Romans, Hindoos, and Sclavonians supplying the greater part of it; and indeed the difficulty, at the present stage of the inquiry, is to know where to stop, to say of what races of men it is *not* allowable to lay down that the society in which they are united was originally organised on the patriarchal model. The chief lineaments of such a society, as collected from the early chapters in Genesis, I need not attempt to depict with any minuteness, both because they are familiar to most of us from our earliest childhood, and because, from the interest once attaching to the controversy which takes its name from the debate between Locke and Filmer, they fill a whole chapter, though not a very profitable one, in English litera-ture. The points which lie on the surface of the history are these:—The eldest male parent—the eldest ascendant—is absolutely supreme in his house-hold. His dominion extends to life and death, and is as unqualified over his children and their houses as over his slaves; indeed the relations of sonship and serfdom appear to differ in little beyond the higher capacity which the child in blood possesses of becoming one day the head of a family himself. The flocks and herds of the children are the flocks and herds of the father, and the possessions of the parent, which he holds in a representative rather than in a proprietary character, are equally divided at his death among his descendants in the first degree, the eldest son sometimes receiving a double share under the name of birthright, but more generally endowed with no hereditary advantage beyond an honorary precedence. A less obvious inference from the Scriptural accounts is that they seem to plant us on the traces of the breach which is first effected in the empire of the parent. The families of Jacob and Esau separate and form two nations; but the families of Jacob's children hold together and become a people. This looks like the immature germ of a state or commonwealth, and of an order of rights superior to the claims of family relation.

If I were attempting, for the more special purposes of the jurist, to express compendiously the characteristics of the situation in which mankind disclose themselves at the dawn of their history, I should be satisfied to quote a few verses from the *Odyssee* of Homer:

> τοῖσιν δ' οὔτ' ἀγοραὶ βουληφόροι οὔτε θέμιστες.
> .   .   .   θεμιστεύει δὲ ἕκαστος
> παίδων ἠδ' ἀλόχων οὐδ' ἀλλήλων ἀλέγουσιν.

" They have neither assemblies for consultation nor *themistes*, but every one exercises jurisdiction over his wives and his children, and they pay no regard to one another." These lines are applied to the Cyclops, and it may not perhaps be an altogether fanciful idea when I suggest that the Cyclops is Homer's type of an alien and less advanced civilisation ; for the almost physical loathing which a primitive community feels for men of widely different manners from its own usually expresses itself by describing them as monsters, such as giants, or even (which is almost always the case in Oriental mythology) as demons. However that may be, the verses condense in themselves the sum of the hints which are given us by legal antiquities. Men are first seen distributed in perfectly insulated groups, held together by obe· dience to the parent. Law is the parent's word, but it is not yet in the condition of those *themistes* which were analysed in the first chapter of this work. When we go forward to the state of society in which these early legal conceptions show themselves as formed, we find that they still partake of the mystery and spontaneity which must have seemed to characterise a despotic father's commands, but that at the same time, inasmuch as they proceed from a sovereign, they presuppose a union of family groups in some wider organisation. The next question is, what is the nature of this union and the degree of intimacy which it involves? It is just here that archaic law renders us one of the greatest of its services and fills up a gap which otherwise could only have been bridged by conjecture. It is full, in all its provinces, of the clearest indications that society in primitive times was not what it is assumed to be at present, a collection of *individuals*. In fact, and in the view of the men who composed it, it was *an aggregation of families*. The contrast may be most forcibly expressed by saying that the *unit* of an ancient society was the Family, of a modern society the Individual. We must be prepared to find in ancient law all the consequences of this difference. It is so framed as to be adjusted to a system of small independent corporations. It is therefore scanty, because it is supplemented by the despotic commands of the heads of households. It is ceremonious, because the transactions to which it pays regard resemble international concerns much more than the quick play of intercourse between individuals. Above all it has a peculiarity of which the full importance cannot be shown at present. It takes a view of *life* wholly unlike any which appears in developed jurisprudence. Corporations *never die*, and accordingly primitive law considers the entities with which it deals, *i. e.* the patriarchal or family groups, as perpetual and inextinguishable. This view is closely allied to the peculiar aspect under which, in very ancient times, moral attributes present themselves. The moral elevation and moral debasement of the individual appear to be confounded with, or postponed to, the merits and offences of the group to which the individual belongs. If the community sins, its guilt is much more than the sum of the offences committed by its members; the crime is a corporate act, and extends in its consequences to many more persons than have shared in its actual perpetration. If, on the other hand, the individual is conspicuously guilty, it is his children, his kinsfolk, his tribesmen, or his fellow-citizens, who suffer with him, and sometimes for him. It thus happens that the ideas of moral responsibility and retribution often seem to be more clearly realised at very ancient than at more advanced periods, for, as the family group is immortal, and its liability to punishment indefinite, the primitive mind is not perplexed by the questions which become troublesome as soon as the individual is conceived as altogether separate from the group. One step in the transition from the ancient and simple view of the matter to the theological or metaphysical explanations of later days is marked by the early Greek notion of an inherited curse. The bequest received by his posterity from the original criminal was not a liability to punishment, but a liability to the commission of fresh offences which drew with them a condign retribution; and thus the responsibility of the family was reconciled with the newer phase of thought which limited the consequences of crime to the person of the actual delinquent.

It would be a very simple explanation of the origin of society if we could base a general conclusion on the hint furnished us by the Scriptural example already adverted to, and could suppose that communities began to exist wherever a family held together instead of separating at the death of its patriarchal chieftain. In most of the Greek states and in Rome there long remained the vestiges of an ascending series of groups out of which the State was at first constituted. The Family, House, and Tribe of the Romans may be taken as the type of them, and they are so described to us that we can scarcely help conceiving them as a system of concentric circles which have gradually expanded from the same point. The elementary group is the Family, connected by common subjection to the highest male ascendant. The aggregation of Families forms the Gens or House. The aggregation of Houses makes the Tribe. The aggregation of Tribes constitutes the Commonwealth. Are we at liberty to follow these indications, and to lay down that the commonwealth is a collection of persons united by common descent from the progenitor of an original family ? Of this we may at least be certain, that all ancient societies regarded themselves as having proceeded from one original stock, and even laboured under an incapacity for comprehending any reason except this for their holding together in political union. The history of political ideas begins, in fact, with the assumption that kinship in blood is the sole possible ground of community in political functions; nor is there any of those subversions of feeling, which we term emphatically revolutions, so startling and so complete as the change which is accomplished when some other principle—such as that, for instance, of *local contiguity*—establishes itself for the first time as the basis of common political action. It may be affirmed then of early commonwealths that their citizens considered all the groups in which they claimed membership to be founded on common lineage. What was obviously true of the Family was believed to be true first of the House, next of the Tribe, lastly of the State. And yet we find that along with this belief, or, if we may use the word, this theory, each community preserved records or traditions which distinctly showed that the fundamental assumption was false. Whether we look to the Greek states, or to Rome, or to the Teutonic aristocracies in Ditmarsh which furnished Niebuhr with so many valuable illustrations, or to the Celtic clan associations, or to that strange social organisation of the Sclavonic Russians and Poles which has only lately attracted notice, everywhere we discover traces of passages in their history when men of alien descent were admitted to, and amalgamated with, the original brotherhood. Adverting to Rome singly, we perceive that the primary group, the Family, was being constantly adulterated by the practice of adoption, while stories seem to have been always current respecting the exotic extraction of one of the original Tribes and concerning a large addition to the Houses made by one of the early kings. The composition of the state uniformly assumed to be natural, was nevertheless known to be in great measure artificial. This conflict between belief or theory and notorious fact is at first sight extremely perplexing; but what it really illustrates is the efficiency with which Legal Fictions do their work in the infancy of society. The earliest and most extensively employed of legal fictions was that which permitted family relations to be created artificially, and there is none to which I conceive mankind to be more deeply indebted. If it had never existed, I do not see how any one of the primitive groups, whatever were their nature, could have absorbed another, or on what terms any two of them could have combined, except those of absolute superiority on one side and absolute subjection on the other. No doubt, when with our modern ideas we contemplate the union of independent communities, we can suggest a hundred modes of carrying it out, the simplest of all being that the individuals comprised in the coalescing groups shall vote or act together

according to local propinquity; but the idea that a
number of persons should exercise political rights in
common simply because they happened to live within
the same topographical limits was utterly strange and
monstrous to primitive antiquity. The expedient
which in those times commanded favour was that the
incoming population should *feign themselves* to be
descended from the same stock as the people on
whom they were engrafted ; and it is precisely the
good faith of this fiction, and the closeness with
which it seemed to imitate reality, that we cannot
now hope to understand. One circumstance, however, which it is important to recollect, is that the
men who formed the various political groups were
certainly in the habit of meeting together periodically,
for the purpose of acknowledging and consecrating
their association by common sacrifices. Strangers
amalgamated with the brotherhood were doubtless
admitted to these sacrifices ; and when that was once
done, we can believe that it seemed equally easy, or
not more difficult, to conceive them as sharing in the
common lineage. The conclusion then which is suggested by the evidence is, not that all early societies
were formed by descent from the same ancestor, but
that all of them which had any permanence and
solidity either were so descended or assumed that they
were. An indefinite number of causes may have
shattered the primitive groups, but wherever their

ingredients recombined, it was on the model or principle of an association of kindred. Whatever were the
fact, all thought, language, and law adjusted themselves to the assumption. But though all this seems
to me to be established with reference to the communities with whose records we are acquainted, the
remainder of their history sustains the position before
laid down as to the essentially transient and termi-
nable influence of the most powerful Legal Fictions.
At some point of time—probably as soon as they felt
themselves strong enough to resist extrinsic pressure—all these states ceased to recruit themselves
by factitious extensions of consanguinity. They necessarily, therefore, became Aristocracies, in all cases
where a fresh population from any cause collected
around them which could put in no claim to community of origin. Their sternness in maintaining the
central principle of a system under which political
rights were attainable on no terms whatever except
connexion in blood, real or artificial, taught their
inferiors another principle, which proved to be endowed with a far higher measure of vitality. This
was the principle of *local contiguity*, now recognised
everywhere as the condition of community in political functions. A new set of political ideas came at
once into existence, which, being those of ourselves,
our contemporaries, and in great measure of our
ancestors, rather obscure our perception of the older
theory which they vanquished and dethroned.

The Family then is the type of an archaic society in all the modifications which it was capable of assuming ; but the family here spoken of is not exactly the family as understood by a modern. In order to reach the ancient conception we must give to our modern ideas an important extension and an important limitation. We must look on the family as constantly enlarged by the absorption of strangers within its circle, and we must try to regard the fiction of adoption as so closely simulating the reality of kinship that neither law nor opinion makes the slightest difference between a real and an adoptive connexion. On the other hand, the persons theoretically amalgamated into a family by their common descent are practically held together by common obedience to their highest living ascendant, the father, grandfather, or great-grandfather. The patriarchal authority of a chieftain is as necessary an ingredient in the notion of the family group as the fact (or assumed fact) of its having sprung from his loins; and hence we must understand that if there be any persons who, however truly included in the brotherhood by virtue of their blood-relationship, have nevertheless *de facto* withdrawn themselves from the empire of its ruler, they are always, in the beginnings of law, considered as lost to the family. It is this patriarchal aggregate—the modern family thus cut down on one side and extended on the other—which meets us on the threshold of primitive jurisprudence. Older probably than the State, the Tribe, and the House, it left traces of itself on private law long after the House and the Tribe had been forgotten, and long after consanguinity had ceased to be associated with the composition of States. It will be found to have stamped itself on all the great departments of jurisprudence, and may be detected, I think, as the true source of many of their most important and most durable characteristics. At the outset, the peculiarities of law in its most ancient state lead us irresistibly to the conclusion that it took precisely the same view of the family group which is taken of individual men by the systems of rights and duties now prevalent throughout Europe. There are societies open to our observation at this very moment whose laws and usages can scarcely be explained unless they are supposed never to have emerged from this primitive condition; but in communities more fortunately circumstanced the fabric of jurisprudence fell gradually to pieces, and if we carefully observe the disintegration we shall perceive that it took place principally in those portions of each system which were most deeply affected by the primitive conception of the family. In one all-important instance, that of the Roman law, the change was effected so slowly, that from epoch to epoch we can observe the line and direction which it followed, and can even give some idea of the ultimate result to which it was tending. And, in pursuing this last inquiry, we need not suffer ourselves to be stopped by the imaginary barrier which separates the modern from the ancient world. For one effect of that mixture of refined Roman law with primitive barbaric usage, which is known to us by the deceptive name of feudalism, was to revive many features of archaic jurisprudence which had died out of the Roman world, so that the decomposition which had seemed to be over commenced again, and to some extent is still proceeding.

On a few systems of law the family organisation of the earliest society has left a plain and broad mark in the life-long authority of the Father or other ancestor over the person and property of his descendants, an authority which we may conveniently call by its later Roman name of Patria Potestas. No feature of the rudimentary associations of mankind is deposed to by a greater amount of evidence than this, and yet none seems to have disappeared so generally and so rapidly from the usages of advancing communities. Gaius, writing under the Antonines, describes the institution as distinctively Roman. It is true that, had he glanced across the Rhine or the Danube to those tribes of barbarians which were exciting the curiosity of some among his contemporaries, he would have seen examples of patriarchal power in its crudest form; and in the far East a branch of the same ethnical

stock from which the Romans sprang was repeating
their Patria Potestas in some of its most technical
incidents. But among the races understood to be
comprised within the Roman empire, Gaius could
find none which exhibited an institution resembling
the Roman "Power of the Father," except only the
Asiatic Galatæ. There are reasons, indeed, as it seems
to me, why the direct authority of the ancestor should,
in the greater number of progressive societies, very
shortly assume humbler proportions than belonged to
it in their earliest state. The implicit obedience of
rude men to their parent is doubtless a primary fact,
which it would be absurd to explain away altogether by
attributing to them any calculation of its advantages;
but, at the same time, if it is natural in the sons to
obey the father, it is equally natural that they should
look to him for superior strength or superior wisdom.
Hence, when societies are placed under circumstances
which cause an especial value to be attached to
bodily and mental vigour, there is an influence at
work which tends to confine the Patria Potestas to
the cases where its possessor is actually skilful and
strong. When we obtain our first glimpse of organised Hellenic society, it seems as if supereminent
wisdom would keep alive the father's power in persons whose bodily strength had decayed; but the
relations of Ulysses and Laertes in the *Odyssee* appear
to show that, where extraordinary valour and sagacity

were united in the son, the father in the decrepitude
of age was deposed from the headship of the family.
In the mature Greek jurisprudence, the rule advances
a few steps on the practice hinted at in the Homeric
literature; and though very many traces of stringent
family obligation remain, the direct authority of the
parent is limited, as in European codes, to the non-
age or minority of the children, or, in other words,
to the period during which their mental and physical
inferiority may always be presumed. The Roman
law, however, with its remarkable tendency to innovate on ancient usage only just so far as the exigency
of the commonwealth may require, preserves both
the primeval institution and the natural limitation to
which I conceive it to have been subject. In every
relation of life in which the collective community
might have occasion to avail itself of his wisdom and
strength, for all purposes of counsel or of war, the
filius familias, or Son under Power, was as free as his
father. It was a maxim of Roman jurisprudence
that the Patria Potestas did not extend to the Jus
Publicum. Father and son voted together in the
city, and fought side by side in the field; indeed, the
son, as general, might happen to command the father,
or, as magistrate, decide on his contracts and punish
his delinquencies. But in all the relations created by
Private Law, the son lived under a domestic despotism
which, considering the severity it retained to the

last, and the number of centuries through which it endured, constitutes one of the strangest problems in legal history.

The Patria Potestas of the Romans, which is necessarily our type of the primeval paternal authority, is equally difficult to understand as an institution of civilised life, whether we consider its incidence on the person or its effects on property. It is to be regretted that a chasm which exists in its history cannot be more completely filled. So far as regards the person, the parent, when our information commences, has over his children the *jus vitæ necisque*, the power of life and death, and *à fortiori* of uncontrolled corporal chastisement; he can modify their personal condition at pleasure; he can give a wife to his son; he can give his daughter in marriage; he can divorce his children of either sex; he can transfer them to another family by adoption; and he can sell them. Late in the Imperial period we find vestiges of all these powers, but they are reduced within very narrow limits. The unqualified right of domestic chastisement has become a right of bringing domestic offences under the cognisance of the civil magistrate; the privilege of dictating marriage has declined into a conditional veto; the liberty of selling has been virtually abolished, and adoption itself, destined to lose almost all its ancient importance in the reformed system of Justinian, can no longer be effected without the assent of the child transferred to the adoptive parentage. In short, we are brought very close to the verge of the ideas which have at length prevailed in the modern world. But between these widely distant epochs there is an interval of obscurity, and we can only guess at the causes which permitted the Patria Potestas to last as long as it did by rendering it more tolerable than it appears. The active discharge of the most important among the duties which the son owed to the state must have tempered the authority of his parent if they did not annul it. We can readily persuade ourselves that the paternal despotism could not be brought into play without great scandal against a man of full age occupying a high civil office. During the earlier history, however, such cases of practical emancipation would be rare compared with those which must have been created by the constant wars of the Roman republic. The military tribune and the private soldier who were in the field three quarters of a year during the earlier contests, at a later period the proconsul in charge of a province, and the legionaries who occupied it, cannot have had practical reason to regard themselves as the slaves of a despotic master; and all these avenues of escape tended constantly to multiply themselves. Victories led to conquests, conquests to occupations; the mode of occupation by colonies was exchanged for the system of occupying provinces by standing armies. Each step in advance was a call for the expatriation of more Roman citizens and a fresh draft on the blood of the failing Latin race. We may infer, I think, that a strong sentiment in favour of the relaxation of the Patria Potestas had become fixed by the time that the pacification of the world commenced on the establishment of the Empire. The first serious blows at the ancient institution are attributed to the earlier Cæsars, and some isolated interferences of Trajan and Hadrian seem to have prepared the ground for a series of express enactments which, though we cannot always determine their dates, we know to have limited the father's powers on the one hand, and on the other to have multiplied facilities for their voluntary surrender. The older mode of getting rid of the Potestas, by effecting a triple sale of the son's person, is evidence, I may remark, of a very early feeling against the unnecessary prolongation of the powers. The rule which declared that the son should be free after having been three times sold by his father seems to have been originally meant to entail penal consequences on a practice which revolted even the imperfect morality of the primitive Roman. But even before the publication of the Twelve Tables, it had been turned, by the ingenuity of the jurisconsults, into an expedient for destroying the parental authority wherever the father desired that it should cease.

Many of the causes which helped to mitigate the stringency of the father's power over the persons of his children are doubtless among those which do not lie upon the face of history. We cannot tell how far public opinion may have paralysed an authority which the law conferred, or how far natural affection may have rendered it endurable. But though the powers over the *person* may have been latterly nominal, the whole tenour of the extant Roman jurisprudence suggests that the father's rights over the son's *property* were always exercised without scruple to the full extent to which they were sanctioned by law. There is nothing to astonish us in the latitude of these rights when they first show themselves. The ancient law of Rome forbade the Children under Power to hold property apart from their parent, or (we should rather say) never contemplated the possibility of their claiming a separate ownership. The father was entitled to take the whole of the son's acquisitions, and to enjoy the benefit of his contracts without being entangled in any compensating liability. So much as this we should expect from the constitution of the earliest Roman society, for we can hardly form a notion of the primitive family group unless we suppose that its members brought their earnings of all kinds into the common stock while they were unable to bind it by improvident individual engagements. The true enigma of the

Patria Potestas does not reside here, but in the slow-
ness with which these proprietary privileges of the
parent were curtailed, and in the circumstance that,
before they were seriously diminished, the whole
civilised world was brought within their sphere. No
innovation of any kind was attempted till the first
years of the Empire, when the acquisitions of soldiers
on service were withdrawn from the operation of the
Patria Potestas, doubtless as part of the reward of
the armies which had overthrown the free commonwealth. Three centuries afterwards the same immunity was extended to the earnings of persons who
were in the civil employment of the state. Both
changes were obviously limited in their application,
and they were so contrived in technical form as
to interfere as little as possible with the principle
of Patria Potestas. A certain qualified and dependent
ownership had always been recognised by the Roman
law in the perquisites and savings which slaves and
sons under power were not compelled to include in
the household accounts, and the special name of this
permissive property, Peculium, was applied to the acquisitions newly relieved from Patria Potestas, which
were called in the case of soldiers Castrense Peculium,
and Quasi-castrense Peculium in the case of civil servants. Other modifications of the parental privileges
followed, which showed a less studious outward
respect for the ancient principle. Shortly after the

introduction of the Quasi-castrense Peculium, Constantine the Great took away the father's absolute control over property which his children had inherited from their mother, and reduced it to a *usufruct*, or life-interest. A few more changes of slight importance followed in the Western Empire, but the furthest point reached was in the East, under Justinian, who enacted that unless the acquisitions of the child were derived from the parent's own property, the parent's right over them should not extend beyond enjoying their produce for the period of his life. Even this, the utmost relaxation of the Roman Patria Potestas, left it far ampler and severer than any analogous institution of the modern world. The earliest modern writers on jurisprudence remark that it was only the fiercer and ruder of the conquerors of the empire, and notably the nations of Sclavonic origin, which exhibited a Patria Potestas at all resembling that which was described in the Pandects and the Code. All the Germanic immigrants seem to have recognised a corporate union of the family under the *mund*, or authority of a patriarchal chief; but his powers are obviously only the relics of a decayed Patria Potestas, and fell far short of those enjoyed by the Roman father. The Franks are particularly mentioned as not having the Roman Institution, and accordingly the old French lawyers, even when most busily engaged in filling the interstices of barbarous customs with rules of Roman law, were obliged to protect themselves against the intrusion of the Potestas by the express maxim, *Puyssance de père en France n'a lieu*. The tenacity of the Romans in maintaining this relic of their most ancient condition is in itself remarkable, but it is less remarkable than the diffusion of the Potestas over the whole of a civilisation from which it had once disappeared. While the Castrense Peculium constituted as yet the sole exception to the father's power over property, and while his power over his children's persons was still extensive, the Roman citizenship, and with it the Patria Potestas, were spreading into every corner of the Empire. Every African or Spaniard, every Gaul, Briton, or Jew, who received this honour by gift, purchase, or inheritance, placed himself under the Roman Law of Persons, and, though our authorities intimate that children born before the acquisition of citizenship could not be brought under Power against their will, children born after it and all ulterior descendants were on the ordinary footing of a Roman *filius familias*. It does not fall within the province of this treatise to examine the mechanism of the later Roman society, but I may be permitted to remark that there is little foundation for the opinion which represents the constitution of Antoninus Caracalla conferring Roman citizenship on the whole of his subjects as a measure of small importance. However we may interpret it, it must have enormously enlarged the sphere of the Patria Potestas, and it seems to me that the tightening of family relations which it effected is an agency which ought to be kept in view more than it has been, in accounting for the great moral revolution which was transforming the world.

Before this branch of our subject is dismissed, it should be observed that the Paterfamilias was answerable for the delicts (or *torts*) of his Sons under Power. He was similarly liable for the torts of his slaves ; but in both cases he originally possessed the singular privilege of tendering the delinquent's person in full satisfaction of the damage. The responsibility thus incurred on behalf of sons, coupled with the mutual incapacity of Parent and Child under Power to sue one another, has seemed to some jurists to be best explained by the assumption of a "unity of person" between the Paterfamilias and the Filius-familias. In the Chapter on Successions I shall attempt to show in what sense, and to what extent, this " unity" can be accepted as a reality. I can only say at present that these responsibilities of the Paterfamilias, and other legal phenomena which will be discussed hereafter, appear to me to point at certain *duties* of the primitive Patriarchal chieftain which balanced his *rights*. I conceive that, if he disposed absolutely of the persons and fortune of his clansmen, this representative ownership was coextensive with a liability to provide for all members of the brotherhood out of the common fund. The difficulty is to throw ourselves out of our habitual associations sufficiently for conceiving the nature of his obligation. It was not a legal duty, for law had not yet penetrated into the precinct of the Family. To call it *moral* is perhaps to anticipate the ideas belonging to a later stage of mental development; but the expression "moral obligation" is significant enough for our purpose, if we understand by it a duty semi-consciously followed and enforced rather by instinct and habit than by definite sanctions.

The Patria Potestas, in its normal shape, has not been, and, as it seems to me, could not have been, a generally durable institution. The proof of its former universality is therefore incomplete so long as we consider it by itself; but the demonstration may be carried much further by examining other departments of ancient law which depend on it ultimately, but not by a thread of connexion visible in all its parts or to all eyes. Let us turn for example to Kinship, or in other words, to the scale on which the proximity of relatives to each other is calculated in archaic jurisprudence. Here again it will be convenient to employ the Roman terms, Agnatic and Cognatic relationship. *Cognatic* relationship is simply the conception of kinship familiar to modern ideas: it is the relationship arising through common descent from the same pair of married persons, whether the descent be traced through males or females. *Agnatic* relationship is something very different : it excludes a number of persons whom we in our day should certainly consider of kin to ourselves, and it includes many more whom we should never reckon among our kindred. It is in truth the connexion existing between the members of the Family, conceived as it was in the most ancient times. The limits of this connexion are far from conterminous with those of modern relationship.

Cognates then are all those persons who can trace their blood to a single ancestor and ancestress; or, if we take the strict technical meaning of the word in Roman law, they are all who trace their blood to the legitimate marriage of a common pair. " Cognation " is therefore a relative term, and the degree of connexion in blood which it indicates depends on the particular marriage which is selected as the commencement of the calculation. If we begin with the marriage of father and mother, Cognation will only express the relationship of brothers and sisters; if we take that of the grandfather and grandmother, then uncles, aunts, and their descendants will also be included in the notion of Cognation, and following the same process a larger number of Cognates may be continually obtained by choosing the starting point

higher and higher up in the line of ascent.   All this
is easily understood by a modern; but who are the
Agnates? In the first place, they are all the Cognates
who trace their connexion exclusively through males.
A table of Cognates is, of course, formed by taking
each lineal ancestor in turn and including all his
descendants of both sexes in the tabular view; if
then, in tracing the various branches of such a ge-
nealogical table or tree, we stop whenever we come
to the name of a female and pursue that particular
branch or ramification no further, all who remain
after the descendants of women have been excluded
are Agnates, and their connexion together is Agnatic
Relationship.   I dwell a little on the process which
is practically followed in separating them from the
Cognates, because it explains a memorable legal
maxim, " Mulier est finis familiæ "—a woman is the
terminus of the family.   A female name closes the
branch or twig of the genealogy in which it occurs.
None of the descendants of a female are included in
the primitive notion of family relationship.

If the system of archaic law at which we are looking be one which admits Adoption, we must add to
the Agnates thus obtained all persons, male or female,
who have been brought into the Family by the artificial extension of its boundaries.   But the descendants
of such persons will only be Agnates, if they satisfy
the conditions which have just been described.

What then is the reason of this arbitrary inclusion
and exclusion? Why should a conception of Kinship,
so elastic as to include strangers brought into the
family by adoption, be nevertheless so narrow as to
shut out the descendants of a female member? To
solve these questions, we must recur to the Patria
Potestas. The foundation of Agnation is not the
marriage of Father and Mother, but the authority of
the Father. All persons are Agnatically connected
together who are under the same Paternal Power, or
who have been under it, or who might have been under it if their lineal ancestor had lived long enough
to exercise his empire. In truth, in the primitive
view, Relationship is exactly limited by Patria Potestas. Where the Potestas begins, Kinship begins;
and therefore adoptive relatives are among the kindred. Where the Potestas ends, Kinship ends; so
that a son emancipated by his father loses all rights
of Agnation. And here we have the reason why the
descendants of females are outside the limits of archaic kinship. If a woman died unmarried, she could
have no legitimate descendants. If she married, her
children fell under the Patria Potestas, not of her
Father, but of her Husband, and thus were lost to her
own family. It is obvious that the organisation of
primitive societies would have been confounded, if men
had called themselves relatives of their mother's relatives. The inference would have been that a person

might be subject to two distinct Patriæ Potestates; but distinct Patriæ Potestates implied distinct jurisdictions, so that anybody amenable to two of them at the same time would have lived under two different dispensations. As long as the Family was an imperium in imperio, a community within the commonwealth, governed by its own institutions of which the parent was the source, the limitation of relationship to the Agnates was a necessary security against a conflict of laws in the domestic forum.

The Paternal Powers proper are extinguished by the death of the Parent, but Agnation is as it were a mould which retains their imprint after they have ceased to exist. Hence comes the interest of Agnation for the inquirer into the history of jurisprudence. The powers themselves are discernible in comparatively few monuments of ancient law, but Agnatic Relationship, which implies their former existence, is discoverable almost everywhere. There are few indigenous bodies of law belonging to communities of the Indo-European stock, which do not exhibit peculiarities in the most ancient part of their structure which are clearly referable to Agnation. In Hindoo law, for example, which is saturated with the primitive notions of family dependency, kinship is entirely Agnatic, and I am informed that in Hindoo genealogies the names of women are generally omitted altogether. The same view of relationship pervades

so much of the laws of the races who overran the
Roman Empire as appears to have really formed part
of their primitive usage, and we may suspect that
it would have perpetuated itself even more than it
has in modern European jurisprudence, if it had not
been for the vast influence of the later Roman law
on modern thought.   The Prætors early laid hold on
Cognation as the *natural* form of kinship, and spared
no pains in purifying their system from the older
conception.   Their ideas have descended to us, but
still traces of Agnation are to be seen in many of the
modern rules of succession after death. The exclusion
of females and their children from governmental
functions, commonly attributed to the usage of the
Salian Franks, has certainly an agnatic origin, being
descended from the ancient German rule of succession
to allodial property.   In Agnation too is to be sought
the explanation of that extraordinary rule of English
Law, only recently repealed, which prohibited brothers
of the half-blood from succeeding to one another's
lands.   In the Customs of Normandy, the rule applies
to *uterine* brothers only, that is, to brothers by the
same mother but not by the same father; and,
limited in this way, it is a strict deduction from
the system of Agnation, under which uterine brothers
are no relations at all to one another.   When it
was transplanted to England, the English judges,
who had no clue to its principle, interpreted it as

a general prohibition against the succession of the half-blood, and extended it to *consanguineous* brothers, that is to sons of the same father by different wives. In all the literature which enshrines the pretended philosophy of law, there is nothing more curious than the pages of elaborate sophistry in which Blackstone attempts to explain and justify the exclusion of the half-blood.

It may be shown, I think, that the Family, as held together by the Patria Potestas, is the nidus out of which the entire Law of Persons has germinated. Of all the chapters of that Law the most important is that which is concerned with the status of Females. It has just been stated that Primitive Jurisprudence, though it does not allow a Woman to communicate any rights of Agnation to her descendants, includes herself nevertheless in the Agnatic bond. Indeed, the relation of a female to the family in which she was born is much stricter, closer, and more durable than that which unites her male kinsmen. We have several times laid down that early law takes notice of Families only; this is the same thing as saying that it only takes notice of persons exercising Patria Potestas, and accordingly the only principle on which it enfranchises a son or grandson at the death of his Parent, is a consideration of the capacity inherent in such son or grandson to become himself the head of a new family and the root of a new set of Parental

Powers. But a woman, of course, has no capacity of the kind, and no title accordingly to the liberation which it confers. There is therefore a peculiar contrivance of archaic jurisprudence for retaining her in the bondage of the Family for life. This is the institution known to the oldest Roman law as the Perpetual Tutelage of Women, under which a Female, though relieved from her Parent's authority by his decease, continues subject through life to her nearest male relations, or to her Father's nominees, as her Guardians. Perpetual Guardianship is obviously neither more nor less than an artificial prolongation of the Patria Potestas, when for other purposes it has been dissolved. In India, the system survives in absolute completeness, and its operation is so strict that a Hindoo Mother frequently becomes the ward of her own sons. Even in Europe, the laws of the Scandinavian nations respecting women preserved it until quite recently. The invaders of the Western Empire had it universally among their indigenous usages, and indeed their ideas on the subject of Guardianship, in all its forms, were among the most retrogressive of those which they introduced into the Western world. But from the mature Roman jurisprudence it had entirely disappeared. We should know almost nothing about it, if we had only the compilations of Justinian to consult; but the discovery of the manuscript of Gaius discloses it to us at a most interesting epoch, just when it had fallen into complete discredit and was verging on extinction.   The great jurisconsult himself scouts the popular apology offered for it in the mental inferiority of the female sex, and a considerable part of his volume is taken up with descriptions of the numerous expedients, some of them displaying extraordinary ingenuity, which the Roman lawyers had devised for enabling Women to defeat the ancient rules.   Led by their theory of Natural Law, the jurisconsults had evidently at this time assumed the equality of the sexes as a principle of their code of equity.   The restrictions which they attacked were, it is to be observed, restrictions on the disposition of property, for which the assent of the woman's guardians was still formally required.   Control of her person was apparently quite obsolete.

Ancient law subordinates the woman to her blood-relations, while a prime phenomenon of modern jurisprudence has been her subordination to her husband. The history of the change is remarkable.   It begins far back in the annals of Rome.   Anciently, there were three modes in which marriage might be contracted according to Roman usage, one involving a religious solemnity, the other two the observance of certain secular formalities.   By the religious marriage or *Confarreation*; by the higher form of civil marriage, which was called *Coemption* ;   and by the lower form, which was termed *Usus*, the Husband acquired a

number of rights over the person and property of his
wife, which were on the whole in excess of such as are
conferred on him in any system of modern jurisprudence. But in what capacity did he acquire them?
Not as *Husband*, but as *Father*. By the Confarreation,
Coemption, and Usus, the woman passed *in manum
viri*, that is, in law she became the *Daughter* of
her husband. She was included in his Patria
Potestas. She incurred all the liabilities springing
out of it while it subsisted, and surviving it when it
had expired. All her property became absolutely
his, and she was retained in tutelage after his death
to the guardian whom he had appointed by will.
These three ancient forms of marriage fell, however,
gradually into disuse, so that, at the most splendid
period of Roman greatness, they had almost entirely
given place to a fashion of wedlock—old apparently,
but not hitherto considered reputable—which was
founded on a modification of the lower form of civil
marriage. Without explaining the technical mechanism of the institution now generally popular, I may
describe it as amounting in law to little more than a
temporary deposit of the woman by her family. The
rights of the family remained unimpaired, and the
lady continued in the tutelage of guardians whom her
parents had appointed and whose privileges of control overrode, in many material respects, the inferior
authority of her husband. The consequence was

that the situation of the Roman female, whether married or unmarried, became one of great personal and proprietary independence, for the tendency of the later law, as I have already hinted, was to reduce the power of the guardian to a nullity, while the form of marriage in fashion conferred on the husband no compensating superiority. But Christianity tended somewhat from the very first to narrow this remarkable liberty. Led at first by justifiable disrelish for the loose practices of the decaying heathen world, but afterwards hurried on by a passion of asceticism, the professors of the new faith looked with disfavour on a marital tie which was in fact the laxest the Western world has seen. The latest Roman law, so far as it is touched by the Constitutions of the Christian Emperors, bears some marks of a reaction against the liberal doctrines of the great Antonine jurisconsults. And the prevalent state of religious sentiment may explain why it is that modern jurisprudence, forged in the furnace of barbarian conquest, and formed by the fusion of Roman jurisprudence with patriarchal usage, has absorbed, among its rudiments, much more than usual of those rules concerning the position of women which belong peculiarly to an imperfect civilisation. During the troubled era which begins modern history, and while the laws of the Germanic and Sclavonic immigrants remained superposed like a separate layer above the Roman jurisprudence of their provincial subjects, the women of the dominant races are seen everywhere under various forms of archaic guardianship, and the husband who takes a wife from any family except his own pays a money-price to her relations for the tutelage which they surrender to him. When we move onwards, and the code of the middle ages has been formed by the amalgamation of the two systems, the law relating to women carries the stamp of its double origin. The principle of the Roman jurisprudence is so far triumphant that unmarried females are generally (though there are local exceptions to the rule) relieved from the bondage of the family ; but the archaic principle of the barbarians has fixed the position of married women, and the husband has drawn to himself in his marital character the powers which had once belonged to his wife's male kindred, the only difference being that he no longer purchases his privileges. At this point therefore the modern law of Western and Southern Europe begins to be distinguished by one of its chief characteristics, the comparative freedom it allows to unmarried women and widows, the heavy disabilities it imposes on wives. It was very long before the subordination entailed on the other sex by marriage was sensibly diminished. The principal and most powerful solvent of the revived barbarism of Europe was always the codified jurisprudence of Justinian, wherever it was studied with that passionate enthusiasm which it seldom failed to awaken. It covertly but most efficaciously undermined the customs which it pretended merely to interpret. But the Chapter of law relating to married women was for the most part read by the light, not of Roman, but of Canon Law, which in no one particular departs so widely from the spirit of the secular jurisprudence as in the view it takes of the relations created by marriage. This was in part inevitable, since no society which preserves any tincture of Christian institution is likely to restore to married women the personal liberty conferred on them by the middle Roman law, but the proprietary disabilities of married females stand on quite a different basis from their personal incapacities, and it is by the tendency of their doctrines to keep alive and consolidate the former, that the expositors of the Canon Law have deeply injured civilisation. There are many vestiges of a struggle between the secular and ecclesiastical principles, but the Canon Law nearly everywhere prevailed. In some of the French provinces, married women, of a rank below nobility, obtained all the powers of dealing with property which Roman jurisprudence had allowed, and this local law has been largely followed by the Code Napoleon ; but the state of the Scottish law shows that scrupulous deference to the doctrines of the Roman jurisconsults did not always extend to mitigating the disabilities of wives.

The systems however which are least indulgent to married women are invariably those which have followed the Canon Law exclusively, or those which, from the lateness of their contact with European civilisation, have never had their archaisms weeded out. The Danish and Swedish laws, harsh for many centuries to all females, are still much less favourable to wives than the generality of Continental codes. And yet more stringent in the proprietary incapacities it imposes is the English Common Law, which borrows far the greatest number of its fundamental principles from the jurisprudence of the Canonists. Indeed, the part of the Common Law which prescribes the legal situation of married women may serve to give an Englishman clear notions of the great institution which has been the principal subject of this chapter. I do not know how the operation and nature of the ancient Patria Potestas can be brought so vividly before the mind as by reflecting on the prerogatives attached to the husband by the pure English Common Law, and by recalling the rigorous consistency with which the view of a complete legal subjection on the part of the wife is carried by it, where it is untouched by equity or statutes, through every department of rights, duties and remedies. The distance between the eldest and latest Roman law on the subject of Children under Power may be considered as equivalent to the difference between

the Common Law and the jurisprudence of the Court
of Chancery in the rules which they respectively
apply to wives.

If we were to lose sight of the true origin of
Guardianship in both its forms, and were to employ
the common language on these topics, we should find
ourselves remarking that, while the Tutelage of
Women is an instance in which systems of archaic
law push to an extravagant length the fiction of
suspended rights, the rules which they lay down for
the Guardianship of Male Orphans are an example of
a fault in precisely the opposite direction. Such
systems terminate the Tutelage of Males at an extraordinary early period. Under the ancient Roman
law, which may be taken as their type, the son who
was delivered from Patria Potestas by the death of
his Father or Grandfather remained under guardianship till an epoch which for general purposes may be
described as arriving with his fifteenth year; but the
arrival of that epoch placed him at once in the full
enjoyment of personal and proprietary independence.
The period of minority appears therefore to have
peen as unreasonably short as the duration of the
disabilities of women was preposterously long. But,
in point of fact, there was no element either of
excess or of shortcoming in the circumstances which
gave their original form to the two kinds of guardianship. Neither the one nor the other of them was
based on the slightest consideration of public or

private convenience. The guardianship of male orphans was no more designed originally to shield them till the arrival of years of discretion than the tutelage of women was intended to protect the other sex against its own feebleness. The reason why the death of the father delivered the son from the bondage of the family was the son's capacity for becoming himself the head of a new family and the founder of a new Patria Potestas: no such capacity was possessed by the woman, and therefore she was *never* enfranchised. Accordingly the Guardianship of Male Orphans was a contrivance for keeping alive the semblance of subordination to the family of the Parent, up to the time when the child was supposed capable of becoming a parent himself. It was a prolongation of the Patria Potestas up to the period of bare physical manhood. It ended with puberty, for the rigour of the theory demanded that it should do so. Inasmuch, however, as it did not profess to conduct the orphan ward to the age of intellectual maturity or fitness for affairs, it was quite unequal to the purposes of general convenience; and this the Romans seem to have discovered at a very early stage of their social progress. One of the very oldest monuments of Roman legislation is the *Lex Lætoria* or *Plætoria*, which placed all free males who were of full years and rights under the temporary control of a new class of guardians, called *Curatores*, whose sanction was required to validate their acts or contracts. The twenty-sixth year of the young man's age was the limit of this statutory supervision ; and it is exclusively with reference to the age of twenty-five that the terms " majority " and " minority " are employed in Roman law. *Pupilage* or *wardship* in modern jurisprudence has adjusted itself with tolerable regularity to the simple principle of protection to the immaturity of youth both bodily and mental. It has its natural termination with years of discretion. But for protection against physical weakness and for protection against intellectual incapacity, the Romans looked to two different institutions, distinct both in theory and design. The ideas attendant on both are combined in the modern idea of guardianship.

The Law of Persons contains but one other chapter which can be usefully cited for our present purpose. The legal rules by which systems of mature jurisprudence regulate the connexion of *Master* and *Slave*, present no very distinct traces of the original condition common to ancient societies. But there are reasons for this exception. There seems to be something in the institution of Slavery which has at all times either shocked or perplexed mankind, however little habituated to reflection, and however slightly advanced in the cultivation of its moral instincts. The compunction which ancient communities almost unconsciously experienced appears to have always resulted in the adoption of some imaginary principle upon which a defence, or at least a rationale, of slavery could be plausibly founded. Very early in their history the Greeks explained the institution as grounded on the intellectual inferiority of certain races and their consequent natural aptitude for the servile condition. The Romans, in a spirit equally characteristic, derived it from a supposed agreement between the victor and the vanquished, in which the first stipulated for the perpetual services of his foe ; and the other gained in consideration the life which he had legitimately forfeited. Such theories were not only unsound but plainly unequal to the case for which they affected to account. Still they exercised powerful influence in many ways. They satisfied the conscience of the Master. They perpetuated and probably increased the debasement of the Slave. And they naturally tended to put out of sight the relation in which servitude had originally stood to the rest of the domestic system. This relation, though not clearly exhibited, is casually indicated in many parts of primitive law, and more particularly in the typical system—that of ancient Rome.

Much industry and some learning have been bestowed in the United States of America on the question whether the Slave was in the early stages of society a recognised member of the Family. There is a sense in which an affirmative answer must certainly be given. It is clear, from the testimony both of ancient law and of many primeval histories, that the Slave might under certain conditions be made the Heir, or Universal Successor, of the Master, and this significant faculty, as I shall explain in the Chapter on Succession, implies that the government and representation of the Family might, in a particular state of circumstances, devolve on the bondman. It seems, however, to be assumed in the American arguments on the subject that, if we allow Slavery to have been a primitive Family institution, the acknowledgment is pregnant with an admission of the moral defensibility of Negro-servitude at the present moment. What then is meant by saying that the Slave was originally included in the Family ? Not that his situation may not have been the fruit of the coarsest motives which can actuate man. The simple wish to use the bodily powers of another person as a means of ministering to one's own ease or pleasure is doubtless the foundation of Slavery, and as old as human nature. When we speak of the Slave as anciently included in the Family, we intend to assert nothing as to the motives of those who brought him into it or kept him there; we merely imply that the tie which bound him to his master was regarded as one of the same general character with that which united every other member of the group to its chieftain. This consequence is, in fact, carried in the general assertion already made that the primitive ideas of mankind

were unequal to comprehending any basis of the connexion *inter se* of individuals, apart from the relations of family. The Family consisted primarily of
those who belonged to it by consanguinity, and next
of those who had been engrafted on it by adoption;
but there was still a third class of persons who were
only joined to it by common subjection to its head,
and these were the Slaves. The born and the adopted
subjects of the chief were raised above the Slave by
the certainty that in the ordinary course of events
they would be relieved from bondage and entitled to
exercise powers of their own; but that the inferiority
of the Slave was not such as to place him outside the
pale of the Family, or such as to degrade him to the
footing of inanimate property, is clearly proved, I
think, by the many traces which remain of his ancient
capacity for inheritance in the last resort. It would,
of course, be unsafe in the highest degree to hazard
conjectures how far the lot of the Slave was mitigated,
in the beginnings of society, by having a definite
place reserved to him in the empire of the Father. It
is, perhaps, more probable that the son was practically assimilated to the Slave, than that the Slave
shared any of the tenderness which in later times was
shown to the son. But it may be asserted with some
confidence of advanced and matured codes that,
wherever servitude is sanctioned, the Slave has uniformly greater advantages under systems which preserve some memento of his earlier condition than

under those which have adopted some other theory of
his civil degradation.   The point of view from which
jurisprudence regards the Slave is always of great
importance to him.   The Roman law was arrested
in its growing tendency to look upon him more and
more as an article of property by the theory of the
Law of Nature; and hence it is that, wherever servitude is sanctioned by institutions which have been
deeply affected by Roman jurisprudence, the servile
condition is never intolerably wretched.   There is a
great deal of evidence that in those American States
which have taken the highly Romanised code of
Louisiana as the basis of their jurisprudence, the lot
and prospects of the Negro-population were better in
many material respects, until the letter of the fundamental law was overlaid by recent statutory enactments passed under the influence of panic, than
under institutions founded on the English Common
Law, which, as recently interpreted, has no true place
for the Slave, and can only therefore regard him as a
chattel.

We have now examined all parts of the ancient
Law of Persons which fall within the scope of this
treatise, and the result of the inquiry is, I trust, to
give additional definiteness and precision to our view
of the infancy of jurisprudence.   The Civil laws of
States first make their appearance as the Themistes
of a patriarchal sovereign, and we can now see that
these Themistes are probably only a developed form

of the irresponsible commands which, in a still earlier
condition of the race, the head of each isolated household may have addressed to his wives, his children,
and his slaves. But, even after the State has been
organised, the laws have still an extremely limited
application. Whether they retain their primitive
character as Themistes, or whether they advance to
the condition of Customs or Codified Texts, they are
binding not on individuals, but on Families. Ancient
jurisprudence, if a perhaps deceptive comparison may
be employed, may be likened to International Law,
filling nothing, as it were, excepting the interstices
between the great groups which are the atoms of society. In a community so situated, the legislation
of assemblies and the jurisdiction of Courts reach
only to the heads of families, and to every other
individual the rule of conduct is the law of his home,
of which his Parent is the legislator. But the sphere
of civil law, small at first, tends steadily to enlarge
itself. The agents of legal change, Fictions, Equity,
and Legislation, are brought in turn to bear, on the
primeval institutions, and at every point of the progress, a greater number of personal rights and a
larger amount of property are removed from the domestic forum to the cognizance of the public tribunals. The ordinances of the government obtain
gradually the same efficacy in private concerns as
in matters of state, and are no longer liable to be
overridden by the behests of a despot enthroned by

each hearthstone. We have in the annals of Roman law a nearly complete history of the crumbling away of an archaic system, and of the formation of new institutions from the re-combined materials, institutions some of which descended unimpaired to the modern world, while others, destroyed or corrupted by contact with barbarism in the dark ages, had again to be recovered by mankind. When we leave this jurisprudence at the epoch of its final reconstruction by Justinian, few traces of archaism can be discovered in any part of it except in the single article of the extensive powers still reserved to the living Parent. Everywhere else principles of convenience, or of symmetry, or of simplification—new principles at any rate—have usurped the authority of the jejune considerations which satisfied the conscience of ancient times. Everywhere a new morality has displaced the canons of conduct and the reasons of acquiescence which were in unison with the ancient usages, because in fact they were born of them.

The movement of the progressive societies has been uniform in one respect. Through all its course it has been distinguished by the gradual dissolution of family dependency and the growth of individual obligation in its place. The Individual is steadily substituted for the Family, as the unit of which civil laws take account. The advance has been accomplished at varying rates of celerity, and there are societies not absolutely stationary in which the collapse of the ancient organisation can only be perceived by careful study of the phenomena they present. But, whatever its pace, the change has not been subject to reaction or recoil, and apparent retardations will be found to have been occasioned through the absorption of archaic ideas and customs from some entirely foreign source. Nor is it difficult to see what is the tie between man and man which replaces by degrees those forms of reciprocity in rights and duties which have their origin in the Family. It is Contract. Starting, as from one terminus of history, from a condition of society in which all the relations of Persons are summed up in the relations of Family, we seem to have steadily moved towards a phase of social order in which all these relations arise from the free agreement of Individuals. In Western Europe the progress achieved in this direction has been considerable. Thus the status of the Slave has disappeared—it has been superseded by the contractual relation of the servant to his master. The status of the Female under Tutelage, if the tutelage be understood of persons other than her husband, has also ceased to exist; from her coming of age to her marriage all the relations she may form are relations of contract. So too the status of the Son under Power has no true place in the law of modern European societies. If any civil obligation binds together the Parent and the child of full age, it is one to which only contract gives its legal validity. The apparent exceptions are exceptions of that stamp which illustrate the rule. The child before years of discretion, the orphan under guardianship, the adjudged lunatic, have all their capacities and incapacities regulated by the Law of Persons. But why? The reason is differently expressed in the conventional language of different systems, but in substance it is stated to the same effect by all. The great majority of Jurists are constant to the principle that the classes of persons just mentioned are subject to extrinsic control on the single ground that they do not possess the faculty of forming a judgment on their own interests ; in other words, that they are wanting in the first essential of an engagement by Contract.

The word Status may be usefully employed to construct a formula expressing the law of progress thus indicated, which, whatever be its value, seems to me to be sufficiently ascertained. All the forms of Status taken notice of in the Law of Persons were derived from, and to some extent are still coloured by, the powers and privileges anciently residing in the Family. If then we employ Status, agreeably with the usage of the best writers, to signify these personal conditions only, and avoid applying the term to such conditions as are the immediate or remote result of agreement, we may say that the movement of the progressive societies has hitherto been a movement *from Status to Contract.*

CHAPTER VI.

THE EARLY HISTORY OF TESTAMENTARY SUCCESSION.

IF an attempt were made to demonstrate in England the superiority of the historical method of investigation to the modes of inquiry concerning Jurisprudence which are in fashion among us, no department of Law would better serve as an example than Testaments or Wills. Its capabilities it owes to its great length and great continuity. At the beginning of its history we find ourselves in the very infancy of the social state, surrounded by conceptions which it requires some effort of mind to realise in their ancient form; while here, at the other extremity of its line of progress, we are in the midst of legal notions which are nothing more than those same conceptions disguised by the phraseology and by the habits of thought which belong to modern times, and exhibiting therefore a difficulty of another kind, the difficulty of believing that ideas which form part of our every-day mental stock can really stand in need of analysis and examination. The growth of the Law of

Wills between these extreme points can be traced
with remarkable distinctness.   It was much less interrupted at the epoch of the birth of feudalism, than
the history of most other branches of law.   It is, indeed, true that as regards all provinces of jurisprudence, the break caused by the division between
ancient and modern history, or in other words by the
dissolution of the Roman Empire, has been very
greatly exaggerated.   Indolence has disinclined many
writers to be at the pains of looking for threads of
connexion entangled and obscured by the confusions
of six troubled centuries, while other inquirers, not
naturally deficient in patience and industry, have
been misled by idle pride in the legal system of their
country, and by consequent unwillingness to confess
its obligations to the jurisprudence of Rome.   But
these unfavourable influences have had comparatively
little effect on the province of Testamentary Law.
The barbarians were confessedly strangers to any
such conception as that of a Will.   The best
authorities agree that there is no trace of it in
those parts of their written codes which comprise
the customs practised by them in their original seats,
and in their subsequent settlements on the edge
of the Roman Empire.   But soon after they became
mixed with the population of the Roman provinces
they appropriated from the Imperial jurisprudence
the conception of a Will, at first in part, and after-

wards in all its integrity. The influence of the
Church had much to do with this rapid assimilation.
The ecclesiastical power had very early succeeded to
those privileges of custody and registration of Testaments which several of the heathen temples had enjoyed; and even thus early it was almost exclusively
to private bequests that the religious foundations
owed their temporal possessions. Hence it is that
the degrees of the earliest Provincial Councils perpetually contain anathemas against those who deny
the sanctity of Wills. Here, in England, Church influence was certainly chief among the causes which
by universal acknowledgment have prevented that
discontinuity in the history of Testamentary Law
which is sometimes believed to exist in the history of
other provinces of Jurisprudence. The jurisdiction
over one class of Wills was delegated to the Ecclesiastical Courts, which applied to them, though not
always intelligently, the principles of Roman jurisprudence; and, though neither the courts of Common
Law nor the Court of Chancery owned any positive
obligation to follow the Ecclesiastical tribunals, they
could not escape the potent influence of a system of
settled rules in course of application by their side.
The English law of testamentary succession to personalty has become a modified form of the dispen-
sation under which the inheritances of Roman citizens
were administered.

It is not difficult to point out the extreme difference of the conclusions forced on us by the historical treatment of the subject, from those to which we are conducted when, without the help of history, we merely strive to analyse our *primâ facie* impressions. I suppose there is nobody who, starting from the popular or even the legal conception of a Will, would not imagine that certain qualities are necessarily attached to it. He would say, for example, that a Will necessarily takes effect *at death only*,—that it is *secret*, not known as a matter of course to persons taking interests under its provisions,—that it is *revocable*, i.e. always capable of being superseded by a new act of testation. Yet I shall be able to show that there was a time when none of these characteristics belonged to a Will. The Testaments from which our Wills are directly descended at first took effect immediately on their execution; they were not secret; they were not revocable. Few legal agencies are, in fact, the fruit of more complex historical agencies than that by which a man's written intentions control the posthumous disposition of his goods. Testaments very slowly and gradually gathered round them the qualities I have mentioned; and they did this from causes and under pressure of events which may be called casual, or which at any rate have no interest for us at present, except so far as they have affected the history of law.

At a time when legal theories were more abundant than at present,—theories which, it is true, were for the most part gratuitous and premature enough, but which nevertheless rescued jurisprudence from that worse and more ignoble condition, not unknown to ourselves, in which nothing like a generalisation is aspired to, and law is regarded as a mere empirical pursuit—it was the fashion to explain the ready and apparently intuitive perception which we have of certain qualities in a Will, by saying that they were natural to it, or, as the phrase would run in full, attached to it by the Law of Nature. Nobody, I imagine, would affect to maintain such a doctrine, when once it was ascertained that all these characteristics had their origin within historical memory; at the same time, vestiges of the theory of which the doctrine is an offshoot, linger in forms of expression which we all of us use and perhaps scarcely know how to dispense with. I may illustrate this by mentioning a position common in the legal literature of the seventeenth century. The jurists of that period very commonly assert that the power of Testation itself is of Natural Law, that it is a right conferred by the Law of Nature. Their teaching, though all persons may not at once see the connexion, is in substance followed by those who affirm that the right of dictating or controlling the posthumous disposal of property is a necessary or natural consequence of the proprietary

second assertion we must object that it is contrary to the best-ascertained facts in the early history of law, and I venture to affirm generally that, in all indigenous societies, a condition of jurisprudence in which Testamentary privileges are *not* allowed, or rather not contemplated, has preceded that later stage of legal development in which the mere will of the proprietor is permitted under more or less of restriction to override the claims of his kindred in blood.

The conception of a Will or Testament cannot be considered by itself. It is a member, and not the first, of a series of conceptions. In itself a Will is simply the instrument by which the intention of the testator is declared. It must be clear, I think, that before such an instrument takes its turn for discussion, there are several preliminary points to be examined—as for example, what is it, what sort of right or interest, which passes from a dead man on his decease? to whom and in what form does it pass? and how came it that the dead were allowed to control the posthumous disposition of their property? Thrown into technical language, the dependence of the various conceptions which contribute to the notion of a Will is thus expressed. A Will or Testament is an instrument by which the devolution of an inheritance is prescribed. Inheritance is a form of universal succession. A universal succession is a succession to a *universitas juris*, or university of rights and duties. Inverting this order we have therefore to inquire what is a *universitas juris*; what is a universal succession; what is the form of universal succession which is called an inheritance? And there are also two further questions, independent to some extent of the points I have mooted, but demanding solution before the subject of Wills can be exhausted. These are, how came an inheritance to be controlled in any case by the testator's volition, and what is the nature of the instrument by which it came to be controlled?

The first question relates to the *universitas juris*; that is, a university (or bundle) of rights and duties. A *universitas juris* is a collection of rights and duties united by the single circumstance of their having belonged at one time to some one person. It is, as it were, the legal clothing of some given individual. It is not formed by grouping together *any* rights and *any* duties. It can only be constituted by taking all the rights and all the duties of a particular person. The tie which so connects a number of rights of property, rights of way, rights to legacies, duties of specific performance, debts, obligations to compensate wrongs—which so connects all these legal privileges and duties together as to constitute them a *universitas juris*, is the *fact* of their having attached to some individual capable of exercising them. Without this *fact* there is no university of rights and duties. The expression *universitas juris* is not classical, but for the notion jurisprudence is exclusively indebted to Roman law; nor is it at all difficult to seize. We must endeavour to collect under one conception the whole set of legal relations in which each one of us stands to the rest of the world. These, whatever be their character and composition, make up together a *universitas juris*; and there is but little danger of mistake in forming the notion, if we are only careful to remember that duties enter into it quite as much as rights. Our duties may overbalance our rights. A man may owe more than he is worth, and therefore if a money value is set on his collective legal relations he may be what is called insolvent. But for all that the entire group of rights and duties which centres in him is not the less a "juris universitas."

We come next to a "universal succession." A universal succession is a succession to a *universitas juris*. It occurs when one man is invested with the legal clothing of another, becoming at the same moment subject to all his liabilities and entitled to all his rights. In order that the universal succession may be true and perfect, the devolution must take place *uno ictu*, as the jurists phrase it. It is of course possible to conceive one man acquiring the whole of the rights and duties of another at different periods, as for example by successive purchases; or he might acquire them in different capacities, part as

heir, part as purchaser, part as legatee.   But though
the group of rights and duties thus made up should
in fact amount to the whole legal personality of a
particular individual, the acquisition would not be a
universal succession.   In order that there may be a
true universal succession, the transmission must be
such as to pass the whole aggregate of rights and
duties at the *same* moment and in virtue of the *same*
legal capacity in the recipient.   The notion of a
universal succession, like that of a juris universitas,
is permanent in jurisprudence, though in the English
legal system it is obscured by the great variety of
capacities in which rights are acquired, and, above
all, by the distinction between the two great provinces
of English property, " realty " and " personalty."
The succession of an assignee in bankruptcy to the
entire property of the bankrupt is, however, a universal succession, though as the assignee only pays
debts to the extent of the assets this is only a modified
form of the primary notion.   Were it common among
us for persons to take assignments of *all* a man's property on condition of paying *all* his debts, such
transfers would exactly resemble the universal successions known to the oldest Roman Law.   When a
Roman citizen *adrogated* a son, i. e. took a man, not
already under Patria Potestas, as his adoptive child,
he succeeded *universally* to the adoptive child's estate,
i. e. he took all the property and became liable for all
the obligations.   Several other forms of universal

succession appear in the primitive Roman Law, but infinitely the most important and the most durable of all was that one with which we are more immediately concerned, Hæreditas or Inheritance. Inheritance was a universal succession occurring at a death. The universal successor was Hæres or Heir. He stepped at once into all the rights and all the duties of the dead man. He was instantly clothed with his entire legal person, and I need scarcely add that the special character of the Hæres remained the same, whether he was named by a Will or whether he took on an Intestacy. The term Hæres is no more emphatically used of the Intestate than of the Testamentary Heir, for the manner in which a man became Hæres had nothing to do with the legal character he sustained. The dead man's universal successor, however he became so, whether by Will or by Intestacy, was his Heir. But the Heir was not necessarily a single person. A group of persons, considered in law as a single unit, might succeed as *co-heirs* to the Inheritance.

Let me now quote the usual Roman definition of an Inheritance. The reader will be in a position to appreciate the full force of the separate terms. *Hæreditas est successio in universum jus quod defunctus habuit* ("an inheritance is a succession to the entire legal position of a deceased man"). The notion was that, though the physical person of the deceased had perished, his legal personality survived

and descended unimpared on his Heir or Co-hiers,
in whom his identity (so far as the law was concerned) was continued.   Our own law, in constituting the Executor or Aministrator the representative
of the deceased to the extent of his personal assets,
may serve as an illustration of the theory from which
it emanated, but, although it illustrates, it does not
explain it.   The view of even the later Roman Law
required a closeness of correspondence between the
position of the deceased and of his Heir which is no
feature of an English representation; and, in the
primitive jurisprudence everything turned on the
continuity of succession.   Unless provision was made
in the will for the instant devolution of the testator's
rights and duties on the Heir or Co-heirs, the testament lost all its effect.

In modern Testamentary jurisprudence, as in the
later Roman law, the object of first importance is
the execution of the testator's intentions.   In the
ancient law of Rome the subject of corresponding
carefulness was the bestowal of the Universal Succession.   One of these rules seems to our eyes a principle
dictated by common sense, while the other looks
very much like an idle crotchet.   Yet that without
the second of them the first would never have come
into being is as certain as any proposition of the
kind can be.

In order to solve this apparent paradox, and to

bring into greater clearness the train of ideas which I have been endeavouring to indicate, I must borrow the results of the inquiry which was attempted in the earlier portion of the preceding chapter. We saw one peculiarity invariably distinguishing the infancy of society. Men are regarded and treated, not as individuals, but always as members of a particular group. Everybody is first a citizen, and then, as a citizen, he is a member of his order—of an aristocracy or a democracy, of an order of patricians or plebeians ; or, in those societies which an unhappy fate has afflicted with a special perversion in their course of development, of a caste. Next, he is a member of a gens, house, or clan ; and lastly, he is a member of his *family*. This last was the narrowest and most personal relation in which he stood; nor, paradoxical as it may seem, was he ever regarded as *himself*, as a distinct individual. His individuality was swallowed up in his family. I repeat the definition of a primitive society given before. It has for its units, not individuals, but groups of men united by the reality or the fiction of blood-relationship.

It is in the peculiarities of an undeveloped society that we seize the first trace of a universal succession. Contrasted with the organisation of a modern state, the commonwealths of primitive times may be fairly described as consisting of a number of little despotic governments, each perfectly distinct from the rest, each absolutely controlled by the prerogative of a single monarch. But though the Patriarch, for we must not yet call him the Pater-familias, had rights thus extensive, it is impossible to doubt that he lay under an equal amplitude of obligations. If he governed the family, it was for its behoof. If he was lord of its possessions, he held them as trustee for his children and kindred. He had no privilege or position distinct from that conferred on him by his relation to the petty commonwealth which he governed. The Family, in fact, was a Corporation; and he was its representative or, we might almost say, its Public officer. He enjoyed rights and stood under duties, but the rights and the duties were, in the contemplation of his fellow-citizens and in the eye of the law, quite as much those of the collective body as his own. Let us consider for a moment, the effect which would be produced by the death of such a representative. In the eye of the law, in the view of the civil magistrate, the demise of the domestic authority would be a perfectly immaterial event. The person representing the collective body of the family and primarily responsible to municipal jurisdiction would bear a different name; and that would be all. The rights and obligations which attached to the deceased head of the house would attach, without breach of continuity, to his successor; for, in point of fact, they would be the rights and obligations of the family, and the family had the distinctive characteristic of a corporation—that it never died. Creditors would have the same remedies against the new chieftain as against the old, for the liability being that of the still existing family would be absolutely unchanged. All rights available to the family would be as available after the demise of the headship as before it—except that the Corporation would be obliged—if indeed language so precise and technical can be properly used of these early times—would be obliged to *sue* under a slightly modified name.

The history of jurisprudence must be followed in its whole course, if we are to understand how gradually and tardily society dissolved itself into the component atoms of which it is now constituted—by what insensible gradations the relation of man to man substituted itself for the relation of the individual to his family and of families to each other. The point now to be attended to is that even when the revolution had apparently quite accomplished itself, even when the magistrate had in great measure assumed the place of the Pater-familias, and the civil tribunal substituted itself for the domestic forum, nevertheless the whole scheme of rights and duties administered by the judicial authorities remained shaped by the influence of the obsolete privileges and coloured in every part by their reflection. There seems little question that the devolution of the Universitas Juris, so strenuously insisted upon by the Roman Law as the first condition of a testamentary or intestate succession, was a feature of the older form of society which men's minds have been unable to dissociate from the new, though with that newer phase it had no true or proper connection. It seems, in truth, that the prolongation of a man's legal existence in his heir, or in a group of co-heirs, is neither more nor less than a characteristic of *the family* transferred by a fiction to *the individual*. Succession in corporations is necessarily universal, and the family was a corporation. Corporations never die. The decease of individual members makes no difference to the collective existence of the aggregate body, and does not in any way affect its legal incidents, its faculties or liabilities. Now in the idea of a Roman universal succession all these qualities of a corporation seem to have been transferred to the individual citizen. His physical death is allowed to exercise no effect on the legal position which he filled, apparently on the principle that that position is to be adjusted as closely as possible to the analogies of a family, which, in its corporate character, was not of course liable to physical extinction.

I observe that not a few continental jurists have much difficulty in comprehending the nature of the connection between the conceptions blended in a universal succession, and there is perhaps no topic in the philosophy of jurisprudence on which their speculations, as a general rule, possess so little value. But the student of English law ought to be in no danger of stumbling at the analysis of the idea which we are examining. Much light is cast upon it by a fiction in our own system with which all lawyers are familiar. English lawyers classify corporations as Corporations aggregate and Corporations sole. A Corporation aggregrate is a true corporation, but a Corporation sole is an individual, being a member of a series of individuals, who is invested by a fiction with the qualities of a Corporation. I need hardly cite the King or the Parson of a Parish as instances of Corporations sole. The capacity or office is here considered apart from the particular person who from time to time may occupy it, and, this capacity being perpetual, the series of individuals who fill it are clothed with the leading attribute of Corporations— Perpetuity. Now in the older theory of Roman Law the individual bore to the family precisely the same relation which in the rationale of English jurisprudence a Corporation sole bears to a Corporation aggregate. The derivation and association of ideas are exactly the same. In fact, if we say to ourselves that for purposes of Roman Testamentary Jurisprudence each individual citizen was a Corporation sole, we shall not only realise the full conception of an inheritance, but have constantly at command the clue to the assumption in which it originated. It is an axiom with us that the King never dies, being a Corporation sole. His capacities are instantly filled by his successor, and the continuity of dominion is not deemed to have been interrupted. With the Romans it seemed an equally simple and natural process, to eliminate the fact of death from the devolution of rights and obligations. The testator lived on in his heir or in the group of his co-heirs. He was in law the same person with them, and if any one in his testamentary dispositions had even constructively violated the principle which united his actual and his posthumous existence, the law rejected the defective instrument, and gave the inheritance to the kindred in blood, whose capacity to fulfil the conditions of heirship, was conferred on them by the law itself, and not by any document which by possibility might be erroneously framed.

When a Roman citizen died intestate or leaving no valid Will, his descendants or kindred became his heirs according to a scale which will be presently described. The person or class of persons who succeeded did not simply *represent* the deceased, but, in conformity with the theory just delineated, they *continued* his civil life, his legal existence. The same results followed when the order of succession was determined by a Will, but the theory of the identity between the dead man and his heirs was certainly much older than any form of Testament or phase of Testamentary jurisprudence. This indeed is the proper moment for suggesting a doubt which will press on us with greater force the further we plumb the depths of this subject—whether *wills* would ever have come into being at all if it had not been for these remarkable ideas connected with universal succession. Testamentary law is the application of a principle which may be explained on a variety of philosophical hypotheses as plausible as they are gratuitous ; it is interwoven with every part of modern society, and it is defensible on the broadest grounds of general expediency. But the warning can never be too often repeated, that the grand source of mistake in questions of jurisprudence is the impression that those reasons which actuate us at the present moment, in the maintenance of an existing institution, have necessarily anything in common with the sentiment in which the institution originated. It is certain that, in the old Roman Law of Inheritance, the notion of a will or testament is inextricably mixed up, I might almost say confounded, with the theory of a man's posthumous existence in the person of his heir.

The conception of a universal succession, firmly as it has taken root in jurisprudence, has not occurred spontaneously to the framers of every body of laws. Wherever it is now found, it may be shown to have descended from Roman law ; and with it have come down a host of legal rules on the subject of Testaments and Testamentary gifts, which modern practitioners apply without discerning their relation to the parent theory. But, in the pure Roman jurisprudence, the principle that a man lives on in his Heir—the elimination, if we may so speak, of the fact of death —is too obviously for mistake the centre round which the whole Law of Testamentary and Intestate succession is circling. The unflinching sternness of the Roman law in enforcing compliance with the governing theory would in itself suggest that the theory grew out of something in the primitive constitution of Roman society ; but we may push the proof a good way beyond the presumption. It happens that several technical expressions, dating from the earliest institution of wills at Rome, have been accidentally preserved to us. We have in Gaius the formula of investiture by which the universal successor was created. We have the ancient name by which the person afterwards called Heir was at first designated. We have further the text of the celebrated clause in the Twelve Tables by which the Testamentary power was expressly recognised, and the clauses regulating Intestate Succession have also been preserved. All these archaic phrases have one salient peculiarity. They indicate that what passed from the Testator to the Heir was the *Family*, that is, the aggregate of rights and duties contained in the Patria Potestas and growing out of it. The material property is in three instances not mentioned at all ; in two others, it is visibly named as an adjunct or appendage of the Family.   The original Will or Testament was therefore an instrument, or (for it was probably not at first in writing) a proceeding, by which the devolution of the *Family* was regulated.   It was a mode of declaring who was to have the chieftainship, in succession to the Testator.   When Wills are understood to have this for their original object, we see at once how it is that they came to be connected with one of the most curious relics of ancient religion and law, the *sacra*, or Family Rites.   These *sacra* were the Roman form of an institution which shows itself wherever society has not wholly shaken itself free from its primitive clothing.   They are the sacrifices and ceremonies by which the brotherhood of the family is commemorated, the pledge and the witness of its perpetuity.   Whatever be their nature,— whether it be true or not that in all cases they are the worship of some mythical ancestor,—they are everywhere employed to attest the sacredness of the family relation ; and therefore they acquire prominent significance and importance, whenever the continuous existence of the Family is endangered by a change in the person of its chief.   Accordingly, we hear most about them in connection with demises of domestic sovereignty.   Among the Hindoos, the right to inherit a dead man's property is exactly co-extensive

with the duty of performing his obsequies. If the
rites are not properly performed or not performed by
the proper person, no relation is considered as established between the deceased and anybody surviving
him ; the Law of Succession does not apply, and
nobody can inherit the property. Every great event
in the life of a Hindoo seems to be regarded as
leading up to and bearing upon these solemnities.
If he marries, it is to have children who may celebrate
them after his death; if he has no children, he lies
under the strongest obligation to adopt them from
another family, "with a view," writes the Hindoo
doctor, "to the funeral cake, the water, and the
solemn sacrifice." The sphere preserved to the
Roman *sacra* in the time of Cicero, was not less in
extent. It embraced Inheritances and Adoptions.
No Adoption was allowed to take place without due
provision for the *sacra* of the family from which the
adoptive son was transferred, and no Testament was
allowed to distribute an Inheritance without a strict
apportionment of the expenses of these ceremonies
among the different co-heirs. The differences between
the Roman law at this epoch, when we obtain our
last glimpse of the *sacra*, and the existing Hindoo
system, are most instructive. Among the Hindoos,
the religious element in law has acquired a complete
predominance. Family sacrifices have become the
keystone of all the Law of Persons and much of the

Law of Things.   They have even received a monstrous extension, for it is a plausible opinion that the
self-immolation of the widow at her husband's funeral,
a practice continued to historical times by the Hindoos,
and commemorated in the traditions of several Indo-
European races, was an addition grafted on the primitive *sacra*, under the influence of the impression,
which always accompanies the idea of sacrifice, that
human blood is the most precious of all oblations.
With the Romans, on the contrary, the legal obligation and the religious duty have ceased to be blended.
The necessity of solemnising the *sacra* forms no part
of the theory of civil law, but they are under the
separate jurisdiction of the College of Pontiffs.   The
letters of Cicero to Atticus, which are full of allusions
to them, leave no doubt that they constituted an
intolerable burden on Inheritances; but the point of
development at which law breaks away from religion
has been passed, and we are prepared for their entire
disappearance from the later jurisprudence.

In Hindoo law there is no such thing as a true
Will.   The place filled by Wills is occupied by Adoptions.   We can now see the relation of the Testamentary Power to the Faculty of Adoption, and the
reason why the exercise of either of them could call
up a peculiar solicitude for the performance of the
sacra.   Both a Will and an Adoption threaten a distortion of the ordinary course of Family descent, but

they are obviously contrivances for preventing the
descent being wholly interrupted, when there is
no succession of kindred to carry it on.   Of the
two expedients Adoption, the factitious creation of
blood-relationship, is the only one which has suggested itself to the greater part of archaic societies.
The Hindoos have indeed advanced one point on
what was doubtless the antique practice, by allowing the widow to adopt when the father has neglected to do so, and there are in the local customs of
Bengal some faint traces of the Testamentary powers.
But to the Romans belongs pre-eminently the credit
of inventing the Will, the institution which, next to
the Contract, has exercised the greatest influence in
transforming human society.   We must be careful
not to attribute to it in its earliest shape the functions
which have attended it in more recent times.   It
was at first, not a mode of distributing a dead man's
goods, but one among several ways of transferring
the representation of the household to a new chief.
The goods descend no doubt to the Heir, but that is
only because the government of the family carries
with it in its devolution the power of disposing of
the common stock.   We are very far as yet from
that stage in the history of Wills in which they
become powerful instruments in modifying society
through the stimulus they give to the circulation
of property and the plasticity they produce in pro-

prietary rights.   No such consequences as these appear in fact to have been associated with the Testamentary power even by the latest Roman lawyers.
It will be found that Wills were never looked upon
in the Roman community as a contrivance for part-
ing Property and the Family, or for creating a
variety of miscellaneous interests, but rather as a
means of making a better provision for the members
of a household than could be secured through the
rules of Intestate succession.   We may suspect
indeed that the associations of a Roman with the
practice of will-making were extremely different
from those familiar to us nowadays.   The habit of
regarding Adoption and Testation as modes of con-
tinuing the Family cannot but have had something
to do with the singular laxity of Roman notions as
to the inheritance of sovereignty.   It is impossible
not to see that the succession of the early Roman
Emperors to each other was considered reasonably
regular, and that, in spite of all that had occurred,
no absurdity attached to the pretension of such
Princes as Theodosius or Justinian to style themselves Cæsar and Augustus.

When the phenomena of primitive societies emerge
into light, it seems impossible to dispute a proposition
which the jurists of the seventeenth century considered doubtful, that Intestate Inheritance is a more
ancient institution than Testamentary Succession.

As soon as this is settled, a question of much interest suggests itself, how and under what conditions were the directions of a will first allowed to regulate the devolution of authority over the household, and consequently the posthumous distribution of property.   The difficulty of deciding the point arises from the rarity of Testamentary power in archaic communities.   It is doubtful whether a true power of testation was known to any original society except the Roman.   Rudimentary forms of it occur here and there, but most of them are not exempt from the suspicion of a Roman origin.   The Athenian will was, no doubt, indigenous, but then, as will appear presently, it was only an inchoate Testament. As to the Wills which are sanctioned by the bodies of law which have descended to us as the codes of the barbarian conquerors of imperial Rome, they are almost certainly Roman.   The most penetrating German criticism has recently been directed to these *leges Barbarorum*, the great object of investigation being to detach those portions of each system which formed the customs of the tribe in its original home from the adventitious ingredients which were borrowed from the laws of the Romans.   In the course of this process, one result has invariably disclosed itself, that the ancient nucleus of the code contains no trace of a Will.   Whatever testamentary law exists, has been taken from Roman jurisprudence. Similarly, the rudimentary Testament which (as I

am informed) the Rabbinical Jewish law provides
for, has been attributed to contact with the Romans.
The only form of testament, not belonging to a Roman or Hellenic society, which can with any reason
be supposed indigenous, is that recognised by the
usages of the province of Bengal; and the testament
of Bengal, which some have even supposed to be an
invention of Anglo-Indian lawyers, is at most only a
rudimentary Will.

The evidence, however, such as it is, seems to
point to the conclusion that Testaments are at first
only allowed to take effect on failure of the persons
entitled to have the inheritance by right of blood
genuine or fictitious.   Thus, when Athenian citizens
were empowered for the first time by the Laws of
Solon to execute Testaments, they were forbidden to
disinherit their direct male descendants.   So, too,
the Will of Bengal is only permitted to govern the
succession so far as it is consistent with certain
overriding claims of the family.   Again, the original
institutions of the Jews having provided nowhere
for the privileges of Testatorship, the later Rabbinical jurisprudence, which pretends to supply the *casus
omissi* of the Mosaic law, allows the power of Testation to attach when all the kindred entitled under
the Mosaic system to succeed have failed or are
undiscoverable. The limitations by which the ancient
German codes hedge in the testamentary jurisprudence which has been incorporated with them are

also significant, and point in the same direction.   It
is the peculiarity of most of these German laws, in
the only shape in which we know them, that, besides
the *allod* or domain of each household, they recognise
several subordinate kinds or orders of property, each
of which probably represents a separate transfusion
of Roman principles into the primitive body of
Teutonic usage.   The primitive German or allodial
property is strictly reserved to the kindred.   Not
only is it incapable of being disposed of by testament, but it is scarcely capable of being alienated
by conveyance *inter vivos*.   The ancient German
law, like the Hindoo jurisprudence, makes the male
children co-proprietors with their father, and the
endowment of the family cannot be parted with
except by the consent of all its members.   But the
other sorts of property, of more modern origin and
lower dignity than the allodial possessions, are
much more easily alienated than they, and follow
much more lenient rules of devolution.   Women and
the descendants of women succeed to them, obviously
on the principle that they lie outside the sacred precinct of the Agnatic brotherhood.   Now, it is on
these last descriptions of property, and on these
only, that the Testaments borrowed from Rome were
at first allowed to operate.

These few indications may serve to lend additional
plausibility to that which in itself appears to be the

on the *gentiles*, that is, on the collective members of
the dead man's *gens* or *House*. The House, I have
explained already, was a fictitious extension of the
family, consisting of all Roman Patrician citizens
who bore the same name, and who, on the ground
of bearing the same name, were supposed to be descended from a Common ancestor. Now the Patrician Assembly called the Comitia Curiata was a
Legislature in which Gentes or Houses were exclusively represented. It was a representative assembly
of the Roman people, constituted on the assumption
that the constituent unit of the state was the Gens.
This being so, the inference seems inevitable, that the
cognisance of Wills by the Comitia was connected
with the rights of the Gentiles, and was intended to
secure them in their privilege of ultimate inheritance. The whole apparent anomaly is removed, if
we suppose that a Testament could only be made
when the Testator had no *gentiles* discoverable, or
when they waived their claims, and that every
Testament was submitted to the General Assembly
of the Roman Gentes, in order that those aggrieved
by its dispositions might put their veto upon it if
they pleased, or by allowing it to pass might be
presumed to have renounced their reversion. It is
possible that on the eve of the publication of the
Twelve Tables this vetoing power may have been
greatly curtailed or only occasionally and capriciously

exercised. It is much easier, however, to indicate the meaning and origin of the jurisdiction confided to the Comitia Calata, than to trace its gradual development or progressive decay.

The Testament to which the pedigree of all modern Wills may be traced is not, however, the Testament executed in the Calata Comitia, but another Testament designed to compete with it and destined to supersede it. The historical importance of this early Roman Will, and the light it casts on much of ancient thought, will excuse me for describing it at some length.

When the Testamentary power first discloses itself to us in legal history, there are signs that, like almost all the great Roman institutions, it was the subject of contention between the Patricians and the Plebeians. The effect of the political maxim, *Plebs Gentem non habet*, "a Plebeian cannot be a member of a house," was entirely to exclude the Plebeians from the Comitia Curiata. Some critics have accordingly supposed that a Plebeian could not have his Will read or recited to the Patrician Assembly, and was thus deprived of Testamentary privileges altogether. Others have been satisfied to point out the hardships of having to submit a proposed Will to the unfriendly jurisdiction of an assembly in which the Testator was not represented. Whatever be the true view, a form

of Testament came into use, which has all the characteristics of a contrivance intended to evade some
distasteful obligation. The Will in question was a
conveyance *inter vivos*, a complete and irrevocable
alienation of the Testator's family and substance to
the person whom he meant to be his heir. The
strict rules of Roman law must always have permitted such an alienation, but when the transaction
was intended to have a posthumous effect, there may
have been disputes whether it was valid for Testamentary purposes without the formal assent of the
Patrician Parliament. If a difference of opinion
existed on the point between the two classes of the
Roman population, it was extinguished, with many
other sources of heartburning, by the great Decemviral compromise. The text of the Twelve Tables
is still extant which says, "*Pater familias uti de
pecuniâ tutelâve rei suæ legâssit, ita jus esto*"—a law
which can hardly have had any other object than the
legalisation of the Plebeian Will.

It is well known to scholars that, centuries after
the Patrician Assembly had ceased to be the legislature of the Roman State, it still continued to hold
formal sittings for the convenience of private business. Consequently, at a period long subsequent
to the publication of the Decemviral Law, there is
reason to believe that the Comitia Calata still assembled for the validation of Testaments. Its pro-

bable functions may be best indicated by saying that it was a Court of Registration, with the understanding, however, that the Wills exhibited were not *enrolled*, but simply recited to the members, who were supposed to take note of their tenor and to commit them to memory. It is very likely that this form of Testament was never reduced to writing at all, but at all events if the Will had been originally written, the office of the Comitia was certainly confined to hearing it read aloud, the document being retained afterwards in the custody of the Testator, or deposited under the safeguard of some religious corporation. This publicity may have been one of the incidents of the Testament executed in the Comitia Calata which brought it into popular disfavour. In the early years of the Empire the Comitia still held its meetings, but they seem to have lapsed into the merest form, and few Wills, or none, were probably presented at the periodical sitting.

It is the ancient Plebeian Will—the alternative of the Testament just described—which in its remote effects has deeply modified the civilisation of the modern world. It acquired at Rome all the popularity which the Testament submitted to the Calata Comitia appears to have lost. The key to all its characteristics lies in its descent from the *mancipium*, or ancient Roman conveyance, a proceeding to

which we may unhesitatingly assign the parentage
of two great institutions without which modern
society can scarcely be supposed capable of holding
together, the Contract and the Will. The Mancipium,
or, as the word would exhibit itself in later Latinity,
the Mancipation, carries us back by its incidents
to the infancy of civil society. As it sprang from
times long anterior, if not to the invention, at all
events to the popularisation, of the art of writing,
gestures, symbolical acts, and solemn phrases take
the place of documentary forms, and a lengthy and
intricate ceremonial is intended to call the attention of the parties to the importance of the transaction, and to impress it on the memory of the witnesses. The imperfection, too, of oral, as compared
with written, testimony necessitates the multiplication of the witnesses and assistants beyond what
in later times would be reasonable or intelligible
limits.

The Roman Mancipation required the presence
first of all of the parties, the vendor and vendee,
or we should perhaps rather say, if we are to use
modern legal language, the grantor and grantee.
There were also no less than *five* witnesses; and an
anomalous personage, the Libripens, who brought
with him a pair of scales to weigh the uncoined copper money of ancient Rome. The Testament we are
considering—the Testament *per æs et libram,* " with

the copper and the scales," as it long continued to
be technically called—was an ordinary Mancipation with no change in the form and hardly any in
words. The Testator was the grantor ; the five
witnesses and the libripens were present; and the
place of grantee was taken by a person known
technically as the *familiæ emptor*, the Purchaser
of the Family. The ordinary ceremony of a Mancipation was then proceeded with. Certain formal
gestures were made and sentences pronounced. The
Emptor familiæ simulated the payment of a price
by striking the scales with a piece of money, and
finally the Testator ratified what had been done
in a set form of words called the "Nuncupatio" or
publication of the transaction, a phrase which, I
need scarcely remind the lawyer, has had a long
history in Testamentary jurisprudence. It is necessary to attend particularly to the character of
the person called *familiæ emptor*. There is no
doubt that at first he was the Heir himself. The
Testator conveyed to him outright his whole
"familia," that is, all the rights he enjoyed
over and through the family; his property, his
slaves, and all his ancestral privileges, together,
on the other hand, with all his duties and obligations.

With these data before us, we are able to note
several remarkable points in which the Mancipatory

Testament, as it may be called, differed in its primitive form from a modern will. As it amounted to a conveyance *out-and-out* of the Testator's estate, it was not *revocable.* There could be no new exercise of a power which had been exhausted.

Again, it was not secret. The Familiæ Emptor, being himself the Heir, knew exactly what his rights were, and was aware that he was irreversibly entitled to the inheritance ; a knowledge which the violences inseparable from the best-ordered ancient society rendered extremely dangerous. But perhaps the most surprising consequences of this relation of Testaments to Conveyances was the immediate vesting of the inheritance in the Heir. This has seemed so incredible to not a few civilians, that they have spoken of the Testator's estate as vesting conditionally on the Testator's death, or as granted to him from a time uncertain, i. e. the death of the grantor. But down to the latest period of Roman jurisprudence there was a certain class of transactions which never admitted of being directly modified by a condition, or of being limited to or from a point of time. In technical language they did not admit *conditio* or *dies.* Mancipation was one of them, and therefore, strange as it may seem, we are forced to conclude that the primitive Roman Will took effect at once, even though the Testator survived his act of Testation. It is indeed likely that Roman citizens originally

made their Wills only in the article of death, and that
a provision for the continuance of the Family effected
by a man in the flower of life would take the form
rather of an Adoption than of a Will.   Still we must
believe that, if the Testator did recover, he could only
continue to govern his household by the sufferance
of his Heir.

Two or three remarks should be made before I explain how these inconveniences were remedied, and
how Testaments came to be invested with the characteristics now universally associated with them.   The
Testament was not necessarily written : at first, it
seems to have been invariably oral, and, even in later
times, the instrument declaratory of the bequests was
only incidentally connected with the Will and formed
no essential part of it.   It bore in fact exactly the
same relation to the Testament, which the deed leading the uses bore to the Fines and Recoveries of old
English law, or which the charter of feoffment bore
to the feoffment itself.   Previously, indeed, to the
Twelve Tables, no writing would have been of the
slightest use, for the Testator had no power of giving
legacies, and the only persons who could be advan-
taged by a will were the Heir or Co-heirs.   But the
extreme generality of the clause in the Twelve Tables
soon produced the doctrine that the Heir must take
the inheritance burdened by any directions which the
Testator might give him, or, in other words, take it

subject to legacies. Written testamentary instruments assumed thereupon a new value, as a security
against the fraudulent refusal of the heir to satisfy
the legatees; but to the last it was at the Testator's
pleasure to rely exclusively on the testimony of the
witnesses, and to declare by word of mouth the
legacies which the *familiæ emptor* was commissioned
to pay.

The terms of the expression *Emptor familiæ* demand
notice. " Emptor" indicates that the Will was literally
a sale, and the word " familiæ," when compared with
the phraseology in the Testamentary clause in the
Twelve Tables, leads us to some instructive conclusions. "Familia," in classical Latinity, means always
a man's slaves. Here, however, and generally in the
language of ancient Roman law, it includes all persons under his Potestas, and the Testator's material
property or substance is understood to pass as an
adjunct or appendage of his household. Turning to
the law of the Twelve Tables, it will be seen that it
speaks of *tutela rei suæ*, "the guardianship of his substance," a form of expression which is the exact reverse
of the phrase just examined. There does not therefore
appear to be any mode of escaping from the conclusion, that even at an era so comparatively recent as
that of the Decemviral compromise, terms denoting
" household " and " property " were blended in the
current phraseology. If a man's household had been

spoken of as his property we might have explained the expression as pointing to the extent of the Patria Potestas, but, as the interchange is reciprocal, we must allow that the form of speech carries us back to that primeval period in which property is owned by the family, and the family is governed by the citizen, so that the members of the community do not own their property *and* their family, but rather own their property *through* their family.

At an epoch not easy to settle with precision, the Roman Prætors fell into the habit of acting upon Testaments solemnised in closer conformity with the spirit than the letter of the law. Casual dispensations became insensibly the established practice, till at length a wholly new form of Will was matured and regularly engrafted on the Edictal Jurisprudence. The new or *Prætorian* Testament derived the whole of its impregnability from the *Jus Honorarium* or Equity of Rome. The Prætor of some particular year must have inserted a clause in his Inaugural Proclamation declaratory of his intention to sustain all Testaments which should have been executed with such and such solemnities; and, the reform having been found advantageous, the article relating to it must have been again introduced by the Prætor's successor, and repeated by the next in office, till at length it formed a recognised portion of that body of jurisprudence which from these successive incorporations was styled the Perpetual or Continuous Edict. On examining the conditions of a valid Prætorian Will they will be plainly seen to have been determined by the requirements of the Mancipatory Testament, the innovating Prætor having obviously prescribed to himself the retention of the old formalities just so far as they were warrants of genuineness or securities against fraud. At the execution of the Mancipatory Testament seven persons had been present besides the Testator. Seven witnesses were accordingly essential to the Prætorian Will; two of them corresponding to the *libripens* and *familiæ emptor*, who were now stripped of their symbolical character, and were merely present for the purpose of supplying their testimony. No emblematic ceremony was gone through; the Will was merely recited; but then it is probable (though not absolutely certain) that a written instrument was necessary to perpetuate the evidence of the Testator's dispositions. At all events, whenever a writing was read or exhibited as a person's last Will, we know certainly that the Prætorian Court would not sustain it by special intervention, unless each of the seven witnesses had severally affixed his seal to the outside. This is the first appearance of *sealing* in the history of jurisprudence, considered as a mode of authentication. The use of seals, however, as mere fastenings, is doubtless of much higher antiquity; and it appears to have been known to the Hebrews. We may observe, that the seals of Roman

Wills, and other documents of importance, did not only serve as the index of the presence or assent of the signatary, but were also literally fastenings which had to be broken before the writing could be inspected.

The Edictal Law would therefore enforce the dispositions of a Testator, when, instead of being symbolised through the forms of mancipation, they were simply evidenced by the seals of seven witnesses. But it may be laid down as a general proposition, that the principal qualities of Roman property were incommunicable except through processes which were supposed to be coeval with the origin of the Civil Law. The Prætor therefore could not confer an *Inheritance* on anybody. He could not place the Heir or Co-heirs in that very relation in which the Testator had himself stood to his own rights and obligations. All he could do was to confer on the person designated as Heir the practical enjoyment of the property bequeathed, and to give the force of legal acquittances to his payments of the Testator's debts. When he exerted his powers to these ends, the Prætor was technically said to communicate the *Bonorum Possessio*. The Heir specially inducted under these circumstances, or *Bonorum Possessor*, had every proprietary privilege of the Heir by the Civil Law. He took the profits and he could alienate, but then, for all his remedies for redress against

wrong, he must go, as we should phrase it, not to the
Common Law, but to the Equity side of the Prætorian
Court.   No great chance of error would be incurred
by describing him as having an *equitable* estate in the
inheritance; but then, to secure ourselves against
being deluded by the analogy, we must always recollect that in one year the *Bonorum Possessio* was
operated upon by a principle of Roman Law known
as Usucapion, and the Possessor became Quiritarian
owner of all the property comprised in the inheritance.

We know too little of the older law of Civil Process to be able to strike the balance of advantage
and disadvantage between the different classes of
remedies supplied by the Prætorian Tribunal.   It is
certain, however, that, in spite of its many defects, the
Mancipatory Testament by which the *universitas juris*
devolved at once and unimpaired was never entirely
superseded by the new Will; and at a period less
bigoted to antiquarian forms, and perhaps not quite
alive to their significance, all the ingenuity of the
Jurisconsults seems to have been expended on the
improvement of the more venerable instrument.   At
the era of Gaius, which is that of the Antonine Cæsars,
the great blemishes of the Mancipatory Will had been
removed.   Originally, as we have seen, the essential
character of the formalities had required that the
Heir himself should be the Purchaser of the Family,
and the consequence was that he not only instantly

acquired a vested interest in the Testator's Property, but was formally made aware of his rights. But the age of Gaius permitted some unconcerned person to officiate as Purchaser of the Family. The Heir, therefore, was not necessarily informed of the succession to which he was destined ; and Wills thenceforward acquired the property of *secrecy*. The substitution of a stranger for the actual Heir in the functions of " Familiæ Emptor " had other ulterior consequences. As soon as it was legalised, a Roman Testament came to consist of two parts or stages,— a Conveyance, which was a pure form, and a Nuncupatio, or Publication. In this latter passage of the proceeding, the Testator either orally declared to the assistants the wishes which were to be executed after his death, or produced a written document in which his wishes were embodied. It was not probably till attention had been quite drawn off from the imaginary Conveyance, and concentrated on the Nuncupation as the essential part of the transaction, that Wills were allowed to become *revocable*.

I have thus carried the pedigree of Wills some way down in legal history. The root of it is the old Testament "with the copper and the scales," founded on a Mancipation or Conveyance. This ancient Will has, however, manifold defects, which are remedied, though only indirectly, by the Prætorian law. Meantime the ingenuity of the Jurisconsults effects, in the Common-Law Will or Mancipatory

Testament, the very improvements which the Prætor
may have concurrently carried out in Equity.   These
last ameliorations depend, however, on more legal dex-
terity, and we see accordingly that the Testamentary
Law of the day of Gaius or Ulpian is only transi-
tional.   What changes next ensued we know not;
but at length just before the reconstruction of the
jurisprudence by Justinian, we find the subjects of
the Eastern Roman Empire employing a form of Will
of which the pedigree is traceable to the Prætorian
Testament on one side, and to the Testament "with
the copper and the scales," on the other.   Like the
Testament of the Prætor, it required no Mancipation, and was invalid unless sealed by seven witnesses.
Like the Mancipatory Will, it passed the Inheritance
and not merely a *Bonorum Possessio*.   Several, however, of its most important features were annexed by
positive enactments, and it is out of regard to this
threefold derivation from the Prætorian Edict, from
the Civil Law, and from the Imperial Constitutions,
that Justinian speaks of the Law of Wills in his own
day as *Jus Tripertitum*.   The New Testament thus
described is the one generally known as the Roman
Will.   But it was the Will of the Eastern Empire
only; and the researches of Savigny have shown that
in Western Europe the old Mancipatory Testament,
with all its apparatus of conveyance, copper, and
scales, continued to be the form in use far down in
the Middle Ages.

CHAPTER VII.

ANCIENT AND MODERN IDEAS RESPECTING WILLS AND SUCCESSIONS.

ALTHOUGH there is much in the modern European Law of Wills which is intimately connected with the oldest rules of Testamentary disposition practised among men, there are nevertheless some important differences between ancient and modern ideas on the subject of Wills and Successions. Some of the points of difference 1 shall endeavour to illustrate in this chapter.

At a period, removed several centuries from the era of the Twelve Tables, we find a variety of rules engrafted on the Roman Civil Law with the view of limiting the disinherison of children ; we have the jurisdiction of the Prætor very actively exerted in the same interest ; and we are also presented with a new remedy, very anomalous in character and of uncertain origin, called the Querela Inofficiosi Testamenti, " the Plaint of an Unduteous Will," directed to the reinstatement of the issue in inheritances from which they had been unjustifiably excluded by a father's Testament. Comparing this condition of the law with the text of the Twelve Tables which concedes in terms the utmost liberty of Testation, several writers have been tempted to interweave a good deal of dramatic incident into their history of the Law Testamentary. They tell us of the boundless license of disinherison in which the heads of families instantly began to indulge, of the scandal and injury to public morals which the new practices engendered, and of the applause of all good men which hailed the courage of the Prætor in arresting the progress of paternal depravity. This story, which is not without some foundation for the principal fact it relates, is often so told as to disclose very serious misconceptions of the principles of legal history. The Law of the Twelve Tables is to be explained by the character of the age in which it was enacted. It does not license a tendency which a later era thought itself bound to counteract, but it proceeds on the assumption that no such tendency exists, or, perhaps we should say, in ignorance of the possibility of its existence. There is no likelihood that Roman citizens began immediately to avail themselves freely of the power to disinherit. It is against all reason and sound appreciation of history to suppose that the yoke of family bondage, still patiently submitted to, as we know, where its pressure galled most cruelly, would be cast off in the very particular in which its incidence in our own day is not otherwise than welcome. The Law of the Twelve Tables permitted the execution of Testaments in the only case in which it was thought possible that they could be executed, viz. on failure of children and proximate kindred. It did not forbid the disinherison of direct descendants, inasmuch as it did not legislate against a contingency which no Roman lawgiver of that era could have contemplated. No doubt, as the offices of family affection progressively lost the aspect of primary personal duties, the disinherison of children was occasionally attempted. But the interference of the Prætor, so far from being called for by the universality of the abuse, was doubtless first prompted by the fact that such instances of unnatural caprice were few and exceptional, and at conflict with the current morality.

The indications furnished by this part of Roman Testamentary Law are of a very different kind. It is remarkable that a Will never seems to have been regarded by the Romans as a means of *disinheriting* a Family, or of effecting the unequal distribution of a patrimony. The rules of law preventing its being turned to such a purpose, increase in number and stringency as the jurisprudence unfolds itself; and these rules correspond doubtless with the abiding sentiment of Roman society, as distinguished from occasional variations of feeling in individuals. It

would rather seem as if the Testamentary Power
were chiefly valued for the assistance it gave in
making provision for a Family, and in dividing the
inheritance more evenly and fairly than the Law of
Intestate Succession would have divided it.   If this
be the true reading of the general sentiment on the
point, it explains to some extent the singular horror
of Intestacy which always characterised the Roman.
No evil seems to have been considered a heavier
visitation than the forfeiture of Testamentary privileges; no curse appears to have been bitterer than
that which imprecated on an enemy that he might
die without a Will.   The feeling has no counterpart,
or none that is easily recognisable, in the forms of
opinion which exist at the present day.   All men at
all times will doubtless prefer chalking out the desti-
nation of their substance to having their office performed for them by the law; but the Roman passion
for Testacy is distinguished from the mere desire
to indulge caprice by its intensity; and it has, of
course, nothing whatever in common with that
pride of family, exclusively the creation of feudalism, which accumulates one description of property
in the hands of a single representative.   It is probable, *à priori*, that it was something in the rules of
Intestate Succession which caused this vehement preference for the distribution of property under a Testament over its distribution by law.   The difficulty,

however, is, that on glancing at the Roman law of
Intestate Succession, in the form which it wore for
many centuries before Justinian shaped it into that
scheme of inheritance which has been almost universally adopted by modern lawgivers, it by no means
strikes one as remarkably unreasonable or inequitable.
On the contrary, the distribution it prescribes is so
fair and rational, and differs so little from that with
which modern society has been generally contented,
that no reason suggests itself why it should have
been regarded with extraordinary distaste, especially
under a jurisprudence which pared down to a
narrow compass the testamentary privileges of persons who had children to provide for. We should
rather have expected that, as in France at this moment, the heads of families would generally save
themselves the trouble of executing a Will, and allow
the Law to do as it pleased with their assets. I
think, however, if we look a little closely at the pre-
Justinianean scale of Intestate Succession, we shall
discover the key to the mystery. The texture of the
law consists of two distinct parts. One department
of rules comes from the Jus Civile, the Common-Law
of Rome ; the other from the Edict of the Prætor.
The Civil Law, as I have already stated for another
purpose, calls to the inheritance only three orders of
successors in their turn ; the Unemancipated children,
the nearest class of Agnatic kindred, and the Gentiles.

Between these three orders, the Prætor interpolates various classes of relatives, of whom the Civil Law took no notice whatever. Ultimately, the combination of the Edict and of the Civil Law forms a table of succession not materially different from that which has descended to the generality of modern codes.

The point for recollection is, that there must anciently have been a time at which the rules of the Civil Law determined the scheme of Intestate Succession exclusively, and at which the arrangements of the Edict were non-existent, or not consistently carried out. We cannot doubt that, in its infancy, the Prætorian jurisprudence had to contend with formidable obstructions, and it is more than probable that, long after popular sentiment and legal opinion had acquiesced in it, the modifications which it periodically introduced were governed by no certain principles, and fluctuated with the varying bias of successive magistrates. The rules of Intestate Succession, which the Romans must at this period have practised, account, I think—and more than account —for that vehement distaste for an Intestacy to which Roman society during so many ages remained constant. The order of succession was this : on the death of a citizen, having no will or no valid will, his Unemancipated children became his Heirs. His *emancipated* sons had no share in the inheritance. If he left no direct descendants living at his death, the nearest grade of the Agnatic kindred succeeded, but no part of the inheritance was given to any relative united (however closely) with the dead man through female descents. All the other branches of the family were excluded, and the inheritance escheated to the *Gentiles*, or entire body of Roman citizens bearing the same name with the deceased. So that on failing to execute an operative Testament, a Roman of the era under examination left his emancipated children absolutely without provision, while, on the assumption that he died childless, there was imminent risk that his possessions would escape from the family altogether, and devolve on a number of persons with whom he was merely connected by the sacerdotal fiction that assumed all members of the same *gens* to be descended from a common ancestor. The prospect of such an issue is in itself a nearly sufficient explanation of the popular sentiment ; but, in point of fact, we shall only half understand it, if we forget that the state of things I have been describing is likely to have existed at the very moment when Roman society was in the first stage of its transition from its primitive organisation in detached families. The empire of the father had indeed received one of the earliest blows directed at it through the recognition of Emancipation as a legitimate usage, but the law, still considering the Patria Potestas to be the root of family connection, perse-

vered in looking on the emancipated children as
strangers to the rights of Kinship and aliens from
the blood. We cannot, however, for a moment suppose that the limitations of the family imposed by
legal pedantry had their counterpart in the natural
affection of parents. Family attachments must still
have retained that nearly inconceivable sanctity and
intensity which belonged to them under the Patriarchal system ; and so little are they likely to
have been extinguished by the act of emancipation,
that the probabilities are altogether the other way.
It may be unhesitatingly taken for granted that
enfranchisement from the father's power was a demonstration, rather than a severance, of affection—a
mark of grace and favour accorded to the best-beloved
and most esteemed of the children. If sons thus
honoured above the rest were absolutely deprived of
their heritage by an Intestacy, the reluctance to in-
cur it requires no farther explanation. We might
have assumed *à priori* that the passion for Testacy
was generated by some moral injustice entailed by
the rules of Intestate succession ; and here we find
them at variance with the very instinct by which
early society was cemented together. It is possible
to put all that has been urged in a very succinct
form. Every dominant sentiment of the primitive
Romans was entwined with the relations of the family.
But what was the Family? The Law defined it one

way—natural affection another. In the conflict between the two, the feeling we would analyse grew up,
taking the form of an enthusiasm for the institution
by which the dictates of affection were permitted to
determine the fortunes of its objects.

I regard, therefore, the Roman horror of Intestacy as a monument of a very early conflict between
ancient law and slowly changing ancient sentiment
on the subject of the Family. Some passages in
the Roman Statute-Law, and one statute in particular which limited the capacity for inheritance
possessed by women, must have contributed to keep
alive the feeling; and it is the general belief that
the system of creating Fidei-Commissa, or bequests
in trust, was devised to evade the disabilities imposed by those statutes. But the feeling itself, in
its remarkable intensity, seems to point back to some
deeper antagonism between law and opinion; nor
is it at all wonderful that the improvements of
jurisprudence by the Prætor should not have extinguished it. Everybody conversant with the philosophy of opinion is aware that a sentiment by no
means dies out, of necessity, with the passing away
of the circumstances which produced it. It may
long survive them; nay, it may afterwards attain
to a pitch and climax of intensity which it never
attained during their actual continuance.

The view of a Will which regards it as conferring

the power of diverting property from the Family,
or of distributing it in such uneven proportions as
the fancy or good sense of the Testator may dictate,
is not older than that later portion of the Middle
Ages in which Feudalism had completely consolidated itself. When modern jurisprudence first
shows itself in the rough, Wills are rarely allowed to
dispose with absolute freedom of a dead man's assets.
Wherever at this period the descent of property
was regulated by Will—and over the greater part
of Europe moveable or personal property was the
subject of Testamentary disposition—the exercise
of the Testamentary power was seldom allowed to
interfere with the right of the widow to a definite
share, and of the children to certain fixed proportions, of the devolving inheritance. The shares of
the children, as their amount shows, were determined by the authority of Roman law. The provision for the widow was attributable to the exer-
tions of the Church, which never relaxed its solicitude
for the interest of wives surviving their husbands—
winning, perhaps, one of the most arduous of its tri-
umphs when, after exacting for two or three centuries
an express promise from the husband at marriage to
endow his wife, it at length succeeded in engrafting
the principle of Dower on the Customary Law of
all Western Europe. Curiously enough, the dower
of lands proved a more stable institution than the

analogous and more ancient reservation of certain shares of the personal property to the widow and children. A few local customs in France maintained the right down to the Revolution, and there are traces of similar usages in England ; but on the whole the doctrine prevailed that moveables might be freely disposed of by Will, and, even when the claims of the widow continued to be respected, the privileges of the children were obliterated from jurisprudence. We need not hesitate to attribute the change to the influence of Primogeniture. As the Feudal law of land practically disinherited all the children in favour of one, the equal distribution even of those sorts of property which might have been equally divided ceased to be viewed as a duty. Testaments were the principal instruments employed in producing inequality, and in this condition of things originated the shade of difference which shows itself between the ancient and the modern conception of a Will. But, though the liberty of bequest, enjoyed through Testaments, was thus an accidental fruit of Feudalism, there is no broader distinction than that which exists between a system of free Testamentary disposition and a system, like that of the Feudal land-law, under which property descends compulsorily in prescribed lines of devolution. This truth appears to have been lost sight of by the authors of the French Codes. In the social

fabric which they determined to destroy, they saw
Primogeniture resting chiefly on Family settlements, but they also perceived that Testaments
were frequently employed to give the eldest son
precisely the same preference which was reserved
to him under the strictest of entails. In order,
therefore, to make sure of their work, they not
only rendered it impossible to prefer the eldest
son to the rest in marriage-arrangements, but they
almost expelled Testamentary succession from the
law, lest it should be used to defeat their fundamental principle of an equal distribution of property among children at the parent's death. The
result is that they have established a system of
small perpetual entails, which is infinitely nearer
akin to the system of feudal Europe than would be
a perfect liberty of bequest. The land-law of England, "the Herculaneum of Feudalism," is certainly
much more closely allied to the land-law of the Middle Ages than that of any Continental country, and
Wills with us are frequently used to aid or imitate
that preference of the eldest son and his line which
is a nearly universal feature in marriage settlements of real property. But nevertheless feeling and
opinion in this country have been profoundly affected
by the practice of free Testamentary disposition; and
it appears to me that the state of sentiment in a
great part of French society, on the subject of the

conservation of property in families, is much liker that which prevailed through Europe two or three centuries ago than are the current opinions of Englishmen.

The mention of Primogeniture introduces one of the most difficult problems of historical jurisprudence. Though I have not paused to explain my expressions, it may have been noticed that I have frequently spoken of a number of " co-heirs " as placed by the Roman Law of Succession on the same footing with a single Heir. In point of fact, we know of no period of Roman jurisprudence at which the place of the Heir, or Universal Successor, might not have been taken by a group of co-heirs. This group succeeded as a single unit, and the assets were afterwards divided among them in a separate legal proceeding. When the Succession was *ab intestato*, and the group consisted of the children of the deceased, they each took an equal share of the property; nor, though males had at one time some advantages over females, is there the faintest trace of Primogeniture. The mode of distribution is the same throughout archaic jurisprudence. It certainly seems that, when civil society begins and families cease to hold together through a series of generations, the idea which spontaneously suggests itself is to divide the domain equally among the members of each successive generation, and to reserve no

privilege to the eldest son or stock. Some peculiarly significant hints as to the close relation of this
phenomenon to primitive thought are furnished by
systems yet more archaic than the Roman. Among
the Hindoos, the instant a son is born, he acquires a
vested right in his father's property, which cannot
be sold without recognition of his joint-ownership.
On the son's attaining full age, he can sometimes
compel a partition of the estate even against the
consent of the parent; and, should the parent ac-
quiesce, one son can always have a partition even
against the will of the others. On such partition
taking place, the father has no advantage over his
children, except that he has two of the shares instead of one. The ancient law of the German
tribes was exceedingly similar. The *allod* or domain
of the family was the joint property of the father
and his sons. It does not, however, appear to have
been habitually divided even at the death of the
parent, and in the same way the possessions of a
Hindoo, however divisible theoretically, are so rarely
distributed in fact, that many generations constantly
succeed each other without a partition taking place,
and thus the Family in India has a perpetual tendency
to expand into the Village Community, under conditions which I shall hereafter attempt to elucidate.
All this points very clearly to the absolutely equal
division of assets among the male children at death as

the practice most usual with society at the period
when family-dependency is in the first stages of
disintegration.   Here then emerges the historical
difficulty of Primogeniture.   The more clearly we
perceive that, when the Feudal institutions were in
process of formation, there was no source in the
world whence they could derive their elements but
the Roman law of the provincials on the one hand
and the archaic customs of the barbarians on the
other, the more are we perplexed at first sight by
our knowledge that neither Roman nor barbarian
was accustomed to give any preference to the eldest
son or his line in the succession to property.

Primogeniture did not belong to the Customs which
the barbarians practised on their first establishment
within the Roman Empire.   It is known to have had
its origin in the *benefices* or beneficiary gifts of the
invading chieftains.   These benefices, which were occasionally conferred by the earlier immigrant kings,
but were distributed on a great scale by Charlemagne,
were grants of Roman provincial land to be holden
by the beneficiary on condition of military service.
The *allodial* proprietors do not seem to have followed
their sovereign on distant or difficult enterprises, and
all the grander expeditions of the Frankish chiefs and
of Charlemagne were accomplished with forces composed of soldiers either personally dependent on the
royal house or compelled to serve it by the tenure of

their land. The benefices, however, were not at
first in any sense hereditary. They were held at
the pleasure of the grantor, or at most for the
life of the grantee; but still, from the very outset,
no effort seems to have been spared by the beneficiaries to enlarge the tenure, and to continue their
lands in their family after death. Through the feebleness of Charlemagne's successors these attempts
were universally successful, and the Benefice gradually transformed itself into the hereditary Fief. But,
though the fiefs were hereditary, they did not necessarily descend to the eldest son. The rules of succession which they followed were entirely determined
by the terms agreed upon between the grantor
and the beneficiary, or imposed by one of them
on the weakness of the other. The original tenures
were therefore extremely various; not indeed so
capriciously various as is sometimes asserted, for all
which have hitherto been described present some
combination of the modes of succession familiar to
Romans and to barbarians, but still exceedingly miscellaneous. In some of them, the eldest son and his
stock undoubtedly succeeded to the fief before the
others, but such successions, so far from being universal, do not even appear to have been general.
Precisely the same phenomena recur during that
more recent transmutation of European society which
entirely substituted the feudal form of property for

the domainial (or Roman) and the allodial (or German). The allods were wholly absorbed by the fiefs. The greater allodial proprietors transformed themselves into feudal lords by conditional alienations of portions of their land to dependants ; the smaller sought an escape from the oppressions of that terrible time by surrendering their property to some powerful chieftain, and receiving it back at his hands on condition of service in his wars. Meantime, that vast mass of the population of Western Europe whose condition was servile or semi-servile—the Roman and German personal slaves, the Roman *coloni* and the German *lidi*—were concurrently absorbed by the feudal organisation, a few of them assuming a menial relation to the lords, but the greater part receiving land on terms which in those centuries were considered degrading. The tenures created during this era of universal infeudation were as various as the conditions which the tenants made with their new chiefs or were forced to accept from them. As in the case of the benefices, the succession to some, but by no means to all, of the estates followed the rule of Primogeniture. No sooner, however, has the feudal system prevailed throughout the West, than it becomes evident that Primogeniture has some great advantage over every other mode of succession. It spread over Europe with remarkable rapidity, the principal instrument of diffusion being Family Settle-

ments, the Pactes de Famille of France and Haus-
Gesetze of Germany, which universally stipulated
that lands held by knightly service should descend
to the eldest son. Ultimately the law resigned itself
to follow inveterate practice, and we find that in all
the bodies of Customary Law, which were gradually
built up, the eldest son and stock are preferred in the
succession to estates of which the tenure is free and
military. As to lands held by servile tenures (and
originally all tenures were servile which bound the
tenant to pay money or bestow manual labour), the
system of succession prescribed by custom differed
greatly in different countries and different provinces.
The more general rule was that such lands were
divided equally at death among all the children, but
still in some instances the eldest son was preferred,
in some the youngest. But Primogeniture usually
governed the inheritance of that class of estates, in
some respects the most important of all, which were
held by tenures that, like the English Socage, were
of later origin than the rest, and were neither altogether free nor altogether servile.

The diffusion of Primogeniture is usually accounted
for by assigning what are called Feudal reasons for
it. It is asserted that the feudal superior had a better security for the military service he required when
the fief descended to a single person, instead of being
distributed among a number on the decease of the

last holder.   Without denying that this consideration
may partially explain the favour gradually acquired
by Primogeniture, I must point out that Primogeniture became a custom of Europe much more through
its popularity with the tenants than through any
advantage it conferred on the lords.   For its origin,
moreover, the reason given does not account at all.
Nothing in law springs entirely from a sense of convenience.   There are always certain ideas existing
antecedently on which the sense of convenience works,
and of which it can do no more than form some new
combination; and to find these ideas in the present
case is exactly the problem.

A valuable hint is furnished to us from a quarter
fruitful of such indications.   Although in India the
possessions of a parent are divisible at his death, and
may be divisible during his life, among all his male
children in equal shares, and though this principle of
the equal distribution of *property* extends to every
part of the Hindoo institutions, yet wherever *public
office* or *political power* devolves at the decease of the
last Incumbent, the succession is nearly universally
according to the rules of Primogeniture.   Sovereign-
ties descend therefore to the eldest son, and where
the affairs of the Village Community, the corporate
unit of Hindoo society, are confided to a single
manager, it is generally the eldest son who takes up
the administration at his parent's death.   All offices,

indeed, in India, tend to become hereditary, and, when their nature permits it, to vest in the eldest member of the oldest stock.   Comparing these Indian successions with some of the ruder social organisations which have survived in Europe almost to our own day, the conclusion suggests itself that, when Patriarchal power is not only *domestic* but *political*, it is not distributed among all the issue at the parent's death, but is the birthright of the eldest son.   The chieftainship of a Highland clan, for example, followed the order of Primogeniture.   There seems, in truth, to be a form of family-dependency still more archaic than any of those which we know from the primitive records of organised civil societies.   The Agnatic Union of the kindred in ancient Roman law, and a multitude of similar indications, point to a period at which all the ramifying branches of the family tree held together in one organic whole; and it is no presumptuous conjecture, that, when the corporation thus formed by the kindred was in itself an independent society, it was governed by the eldest male of the oldest line.   It is true that we have no actual knowledge of any such society.   Even in the most elementary communities, family-organisations, as we know them, are at most *imperia in imperio*.   But the position of some of them, of the Celtic clans in particular, was sufficiently near independence within historical times to force on us the conviction that they

were once separate *imperia*, and that Primogeniture
regulated the succession to the chieftainship. It
is, however, necessary to be on our guard against
modern associations with the term of law. We are
speaking of a family-connection still closer and more
stringent than any with which we are made acquainted
by Hindoo society or ancient Roman law. If the
Roman Paterfamilias was visibly steward of the family possessions, if the Hindoo father is only joint-
sharer with his sons, still more emphatically must the
true patriarchal chieftain be merely the administrator
of a common fund.

The examples of succession by Primogeniture
which were found among the Benefices may, therefore, have been imitated from a system of family-
government known to the invading races, though
not in general use. Some ruder tribes may have still
practised it, or, what is still more probable, society
may have been so slightly removed from its more
archaic condition that the minds of some men spontaneously recurred to it, when they were called upon
to settle the rules of inheritance for a new form of
property. But there is still the question, Why did
Primogeniture gradually supersede every other principle of succession? The answer, I think, is, that
European society decidedly retrograded during the
dissolution of the Carlovingian empire. It sank a
point or two back even from the miserably low degree

which it had marked during the early barbarian
monarchies. The great characteristic of the period
was the feebleness, or rather the abeyance, of kingly
and therefore of civil authority; and hence it seems
as if, civil society no longer cohering, men universally flung themselves back on a social organisation
older than the beginnings of civil communities. The
lord with his vassals, during the ninth and tenth
centuries, may be considered as a patriarchal household, recruited, not as in the primitive times by
Adoption, but by Infeudation; and to such a con-
federacy, succession by Primogeniture was a source
of strength and durability. So long as the land was
kept together on which the entire organisation rested,
it was powerful for defence and attack; to divide
the land was to divide the little society, and volun-
tarily to invite aggression in an era of universal
violence. We may be perfectly certain that into this
preference for Primogeniture there entered no idea
of disinheriting the bulk of the children in favour of
one. Everybody would have suffered by the division
of the fief. Everybody was a gainer by its consolidation. The Family grew stronger by the concentra-
tion of power in the same hands; nor is it likely that
the lord who was invested with the inheritance had
any advantage over his brethren and kinsfolk in occupations, interests, or indulgences. It would be a singular anachronism to estimate the privileges succeeded

to by the heir of a fief, by the situation in which the eldest son is placed under an English strict settlement.

I have said that I regard the early feudal confederacies as descended from an archaic form of the Family, and as wearing a strong resemblance to it. But then in the ancient world, and in the societies which have not passed through the crucible of feudalism, the Primogeniture which seems to have prevailed never transformed itself into the Primogeniture of the later feudal Europe. When the group of kinsmen ceased to be governed through a series of generations by a hereditary chief, the domain which had been managed for all appears to have been equally divided among all. Why did this not occur in the feudal world? If during the confusions of the first feudal period the eldest son held the land for the behoof of the whole family, why was it that when feudal Europe had consolidated itself, and regular communities were again established, the whole family did not resume that capacity for equal inheritance which had belonged to Roman and German alike? The key which unlocks this difficulty has rarely been seized by the writers who occupy themselves in tracing the genealogy of Feudalism. They perceive the materials of the feudal institutions, but they miss the cement. The ideas and social forms which contributed to the formation of the system were unquestionably barbarian and archaic, but, as soon as Courts and lawyers

were called in to interpret and define it, the principles
of interpretation which they applied to it were those
of the latest Roman jurisprudence, and were therefore
excessively refined and matured.   In a patriarchally
governed society, the eldest son may succeed to the
government of the Agnatic group, and to the absolute
disposal of its property.   But he is not therefore a
true proprietor.   He has correlative duties not involved in the conception of proprietorship, but quite
undefined and quite incapable of definition.   The
later Roman jurisprudence, however, like our own
law, looked upon uncontrolled power over property
as equivalent to ownership, and did not, and, in fact,
could not, take notice of liabilities of such a kind,
that the very conception of them belonged to a period
anterior to regular law.   The contact of the refined
and the barbarous notion had inevitably for its effect
the conversion of the eldest son into legal proprietor
of the inheritance.   The clerical and secular lawyers
so defined his position from the first; but it was only
by insensible degrees that the younger brother, from
participating on equal terms in all the dangers and
enjoyments of his kinsman, sank into the priest, the
soldier of fortune, or the hanger-on of the mansion.
The legal revolution was identical with that which
occurred on a smaller scale, and in quite recent times,
through the greater part of the Highlands of Scotland.
When called in to determine the legal powers of the

chieftain over the domains which gave sustenance to
the clan, Scottish jurisprudence had long since passed
the point at which it could take notice of the vague
limitations on completeness of dominion imposed by
the claims of the clansmen, and it was inevitable
therefore that it should convert the patrimony of
many into the estate of one.

For the sake of simplicity, I have called the mode
of succession Primogeniture whenever a single son
or descendant succeeds to the authority over a household or society.   It is remarkable, however, that in
the few very ancient examples which remain to us of
this sort of succession, it is not always the eldest son,
in the sense familiar to us, who takes up the representation.   The form of Primogeniture which has
spread over Western Europe has also been perpetuated among the Hindoos, and there is every
reason to believe that it is the normal form.   Under
it, not only the eldest son, but the eldest line is always
preferred.   If the eldest son fails, his eldest son has
precedence not only over brothers but over uncles;
and, if he too fails, the same rule is followed in the
next generation.   But when the succession is not
merely to *civil* but to *political* power, a difficulty may
present itself which will appear of greater magnitude
according as the cohesion of society is less perfect.
The chieftain who last exercised authority may have
outlived his eldest son, and the grandson who is

primarily entitled to succeed may be too young and immature to undertake the actual guidance of the community, and the administration of its affairs. In such an event, the expedient which suggests itself to the more settled societies is to place the infant heir under guardianship till he reaches the age of fitness for government. The guardianship is generally that of the male Agnates; but it is remarkable that the contingency supposed is one of the rare cases in which ancient societies have consented to the exercise of power by women, doubtless out of respect to the overshadowing claims of the mother. In India, the widow of a Hindoo sovereign governs in the name of her infant son, and we cannot but remember that the custom regulating succession to the throne of France —which, whatever be its origin, is doubtless of the highest antiquity—preferred the queen-mother to all other claimants for the Regency, at the same time that it rigorously excluded all females from the throne. There is, however, another mode of obviating the inconvenience attending the devolution of sovereignty on an infant heir, and it is one which would doubtless occur spontaneously to rudely organised communities. This is to set aside the infant heir altogether, and confer the chieftainship on the eldest surviving male of the first generation. The Celtic clan-associations, among the many phenomena which they have preserved of an age in which civil and political society were not yet even rudimentarily separated, have brought down this rule of succession to historical times. With them, it seems to have existed in the form of a positive canon, that, failing the eldest son, his next brother succeeds in priority to all grandsons, whatever be their age at the moment when the sovereignty devolves. Some writers have explained the principle by assuming that the Celtic customs took the last chieftain as a sort of root or stock, and then gave the succession to the descendant who should be least remote from him; the uncle thus being preferred to the grandson as being nearer to the common root. No objection can be taken to this statement if it be merely intended as a description of the system of succession; but it would be a serious error to conceive the men who first adopted the rule as applying a course of reasoning which evidently dates from the time when feudal schemes of succession began to be debated among lawyers. The true origin of the preference of the uncle to the grandson is doubtless a simple calculation on the part of rude men in a rude society that it is better to be governed by a grown chieftain than by a child, and that the younger son is more likely to have come to maturity than any of the eldest son's descendants. At the same time, we have some evidence that the form of Primogeniture with which we are best acquainted is the primary form, in the tradition that the assent of the clan was asked when an infant heir was passed over in favour of his uncle. There is a tolerably well authenticated instance of this ceremony in the annals of the Scottish Macdonalds; and Irish Celtic antiquities, as interpreted by recent inquirers, are said to disclose many traces of similar practices. The substitution, by means of election, of a "worthier" Agnatic relative for an elder is not unknown, too, in the system of the Indian Village Communities.

Under Mahometan law, which has probably preserved an ancient Arabian custom, inheritances of property are divided equally among sons, the daughters taking a half share; but if any of the children die before the division of the inheritance, leaving issue behind, these grandchildren are entirely excluded by their uncles and aunts. Consistently with this principle, the succession, when political authority devolves, is according to the form of Primogeniture which appears to have obtained among the Celtic societies. In the two great Mahometan families of the West, the rule is believed to be, that the uncle succeeds to the throne in preference to the nephew, though the latter be the son of an elder brother; but though this rule has been followed quite recently both in Egypt and in Turkey, I am informed that there has always been some doubt as to its governing the devolution of the Turkish sovereignty. The policy of the Sultans has in fact generally prevented cases for its application from occurring, and it is possible that their wholesale massacres of their younger brothers may have been perpetrated quite as much in the interest of their children as for the sake of making away with dangerous competitors for the throne. It is evident, however, that in polygamous societies the form of Primogeniture will always tend to vary. Many considerations may constitute a claim on the succession, the rank of the mother, for example, or her degree in the affections of the father. Accordingly, some of the Indian Mahometan sovereigns, without pretending to any distinct testamentary power, claim the right of nominating the son who is to succeed. The *blessing* mentioned in the Scriptural history of Isaac and his sons has sometimes been spoken of as a will, but it seems rather to have been a mode of naming an eldest son.

CHAPTER VIII.

THE EARLY HISTORY OF PROPERTY.

THE Roman Institutional Treatises, after giving their definition of the various forms and modifications of ownership, proceed to discuss the Natural Modes of Acquiring Property. Those who are unfamiliar with the history of jurisprudence are not likely to look upon these "natural modes" of acquisition as possessing, at first sight, either much speculative or much practical interest. The wild animal which is snared or killed by the hunter, the soil which is added to our field by the imperceptible deposits of a river, the tree which strikes its roots into our ground, are each said by the Roman lawyers to be acquired by us *naturally*. The older jurisconsults had doubtless observed that such acquisitions were universally sanctioned by the usages of the little societies around them, and thus the lawyers of a later age, finding them classed in the ancient Jus Gentium, and perceiving them to be of the simplest description, allotted them a place among the ordinances of Nature. The dignity with which they were invested has gone on increasing in modern times till it is quite out of proportion to their original importance. Theory has made them its favourite food, and has enabled them to exercise the most serious influence on practice.

It will be necessary for us to attend to one only among these "natural modes of acquisition," Occupatio or Occupancy. Occupancy is the advisedly taking possession of that which at the moment is the property of no man, with the view (adds the technical definition) of acquiring property in it for yourself. The objects which the Roman lawyers called *res nullius*—things which have not or have never had an owner—can only be ascertained by enumerating them. Among things which *never had* an owner are wild animals, fishes, wild fowl, jewels disinterred for the first time, and lands newly discovered or never before cultivated. Among things which *have not* an owner are moveables which have been abandoned, lands which have been deserted, and (an anomalous but most formidable item) the property of an enemy. In all these objects the full rights of dominion were acquired by the *Occupant*, who first took possession of them with the intention of keeping them as his own—an intention which, in certain cases, had to be manifested by specific acts. It is not difficult, I think, to understand the universality which caused the practice of Occupancy to be placed by one generation of Roman lawyers in the Law common to all Nations, and the simplicity which occasioned its being attributed by another to the Law of Nature. But for its fortunes in modern legal history we are less prepared by *à priori* considerations. The Roman principle of Occupancy, and the rules into which the jurisconsults expanded it, are the source of all modern International Law on the subject of Capture in War and of the acquisition of sovereign rights in newly discovered countries. They have also supplied a theory of the Origin of Property, which is at once the popular theory, and the theory which, in one form or another, is acquiesced in by the great majority of speculative jurists.

I have said that the Roman principle of Occupancy has determined the tenor of that chapter of International Law which is concerned with Capture in War. The Law of Warlike Capture derives its rules from the assumption that communities are remitted to a state of nature by the outbreak of hostilities, and that, in the artificial natural condition thus produced, the institution of private property falls into abeyance so far as concerns the belligerents. As the later writers on the Law of Nature have always been anxious to maintain that private property was in some sense sanctioned by the system which they were expounding, the hypothesis that an enemy's property is *res nullius* has seemed to them perverse and shocking, and they are careful to stigmatise it as a mere fiction of jurisprudence. But, as soon as the Law of Nature is traced to its source in the Jus Gentium, we see at once how the goods of an enemy came to be looked upon as nobody's property, and therefore as capable of being acquired by the first occupant. The idea would occur spontaneously to persons practising the ancient forms of Warfare, when victory dissolved the organisation of the conquering army and dismissed the soldiers to indiscriminate plunder. It is probable, however, that originally it was only moveable property which was thus permitted to be acquired by the Captor. We know on independent authority that a very different rule prevailed in ancient Italy as to the acquisition of ownership in the soil of a conquered country, and we may therefore suspect that the application of the principle of occupancy to land (always a matter of difficulty) dates from the period when the Jus Gentium was becoming the Code of Nature, and that it is the result of a generalisation effected by the jurisconsults of the golden age. Their dogmas on the point are preserved in the Pandects of Justinian, and amount to an unqualified assertion that enemy's property of every sort is *res nullius* to the other belligerent, and that Occupancy, by which the Captor makes it his own, is an institution of Natural Law. The rules which International jurisprudence derives from these positions have sometimes been stigmatised as needlessly indulgent to the ferocity and cupidity of combatants, but the charge has been made, I think, by persons who are unacquainted with the history of wars, and who are consequently ignorant how great an exploit it is to command obedience for a rule of any kind. The Roman principle of Occupancy, when it was admitted into the modern law of Capture in War, drew with it a number of subordinate canons, limiting and giving precision to its operation, and if the contests which have been waged since the treatise of Grotius became an authority, are compared with those of an earlier date, it will be seen that, as soon as the Roman maxims were received, Warfare instantly assumed a more tolerable complexion. If the Roman law of Occupancy is to be taxed with having had pernicious influence on any part of the modern Law of Nations, there is another chapter in it which may be said, with some reason, to have been injuriously affected. In applying to the discovery of new countries the same principles which the Romans had applied to the finding of a jewel, the Publicists forced into their service a doctrine altogether unequal to the task expected from it. Elevated into extreme importance by the discoveries of the great navigators of the 15th and 16th centuries, it raised more disputes than it solved. The greatest uncertainty was very shortly found to exist on the very two points on which certainty was most required, the extent of the territory which was acquired for his sovereign by the discoverer, and the

nature of the acts which were necessary to complete
the *adprehensio* or assumption of sovereign possession.   Moreover, the principle itself, conferring as it
did such enormous advantages as the consequence of
a piece of good luck, was instinctively mutinied
against by some of the most adventurous nations
in Europe, the Dutch, the English, and the Portuguese.   Our own countrymen, without expressly denying the rule of International Law, never did, in
practice, admit the claim of the Spaniards to engross
the whole of America south of the Gulf of Mexico, or
that of the King of France to monopolise the valleys
of the Ohio and the Mississippi.   From the accession
of Elizabeth to the accession of Charles the Second,
it cannot be said that there was at any time thorough
peace in the American waters, and the encroach-
ments of the New England Colonists on the territory
of the French King continued for almost a century
longer.   Bentham was so struck with the confusion
attending the application of the legal principle, that
he went out of his way to eulogise the famous Bull
of Pope Alexander the Sixth, dividing the undis-
covered countries of the world between the Spaniards
and Portuguese by a line drawn one hundred leagues
West of the Azores; and, grotesque as his praises may
appear at first sight, it may be doubted whether the
arrangement of Pope Alexander is absurder in principle than the rule of Public law, which gave half a

continent to the monarch whose servants had fulfilled
the conditions required by Roman jurisprudence for
the acquisition of property in a valuable object which
could be covered by the hand.

To all who pursue the inquiries which are the
subject of this volume, Occupancy is pre-eminently
interesting on the score of the service it has been
made to perform for speculative jurisprudence, in
furnishing a supposed explanation of the origin of
private property. It was once universally believed
that the proceeding implied in Occupancy was identical with the process by which the earth and its
fruits, which were at first in common, became the
allowed property of individuals. The course of
thought which led to this assumption is not difficult
to understand, if we seize the shade of difference
which separates the ancient from the modern conception of Natural Law. The Roman lawyers had
laid down that Occupancy was one of the Natural
modes of acquiring property, and they undoubtedly
believed that, were mankind living under the institutions of Nature, Occupancy would be one of their
practices. How far they persuaded themselves that
such a condition of the race had ever existed, is a
point, as I have already stated, which their language
leaves in much uncertainty; but they certainly do
seem to have made the conjecture, which has at all
times possessed much plausibility, that the institution

of property was not so old as the existence of mankind. Modern jurisprudence, accepting all their dogmas without reservation, went far beyond them in the eager curiosity with which it dwelt on the supposed state of Nature. Since then it had received the position that the earth and its fruits were once *res nullius,* and since its peculiar view of Nature led it to assume without hesitation that the human race had actually practised the Occupancy of *res nullius* long before the organisation of civil societies, the inference immediately suggested itself that Occupancy was the process by which the "no man's goods" of the primitive world became the private property of individuals in the world of history. It would be wearisome to enumerate the jurists who have subscribed to this theory in one shape or another, and it is the less necessary to attempt it because Blackstone, who is always a faithful index of the average opinions of his day, has summed them up in his 2nd book and 1st chapter.

"The earth," he writes, "and all things therein were the general property of mankind from the immediate gift of the Creator. Not that the communion of goods seems ever to have been applicable, even in the earliest ages, to aught but the substance of the thing; nor could be extended to the use of it. For, by the law of nature and reason, he who first began to use it acquired therein a kind of transient property that lasted so long as he was using it, and no longer; or to speak with greater precision, the right of possession continued for the same time only that the act of possession lasted. Thus the ground was in common, and no part was the permanent property of any man in particular; yet whoever was in the occupation of any determined spot of it, for rest, for shade, or the like, acquired for the time a sort of ownership, from which it would have been unjust and contrary to the law of nature to have driven him by force, but the instant that he quitted the use or occupation of it, another might seize it without injustice." He then proceeds to argue that " when mankind increased in number, it became necessary to entertain conceptions of more permanent dominion, and to appropriate to individuals not the immediate use only, but the very substance of the thing to be used."

Some ambiguities of expression in this passage lead to the suspicion that Blackstone did not quite understand the meaning of the proposition which he found in his authorities, that property in the earth's surface was first acquired, under the law of Nature, by the *occupant*; but the limitation which designedly or through misapprehension he has imposed on the theory brings it into a form which it has not infrequently assumed. Many writers more famous than Blackstone for precision of language have laid down that, in the beginning of things, Occupancy first gave a right against the world to an exclusive but temporary enjoyment, and that afterwards this right, while it remained exclusive, became perpetual. Their object in so stating their theory was to reconcile the doctrine that in the state of Nature *res nullius* became property through Occupancy, with the inference which they drew from the Scriptural history that the Patriarchs did not at first permanently appropriate the soil which had been grazed over by their flocks and herds.

The only criticism which could be directly applied to the theory of Blackstone would consist in inquiring whether the circumstances which make up his picture of a primitive society are more or less probable than other incidents which could be imagined with equal readiness. Pursuing this method of examination, we might fairly ask whether the man who had *occupied* (Blackstone evidently uses this word with its ordinary English meaning) a particular spot of ground for rest or shade would be permitted to retain it without disturbance. The chances surely are that his right to possession would be exactly coextensive with his power to keep it, and that he would be constantly liable to disturbance by the first comer who coveted the spot and thought himself strong enough to drive away the possessor But the truth is that all such cavil at these positions is perfectly idle from the very baselessness of the positions themselves. What mankind did in the primitive state may not be a hopeless subject of inquiry, but of their motives for doing it it is impossible to know anything. These sketches of the plight of human beings in the first ages of the world are effected by first supposing mankind to be divested of a great part of the circumstances by which they are now surrounded, and by then assuming that, in the condition thus imagined, they would preserve the same sentiments and prejudices by which they are now actuated,—although, in fact, these sentiments may have been created and engendered by those very circumstances of which, by the hypothesis, they are to be stripped.

There is an aphorism of Savigny which has been sometimes thought to countenance a view of the origin of property somewhat similar to the theories epitomised by Blackstone. The great German jurist has laid down that all Property is founded on Adverse Possession ripened by Prescription. It is only with respect to Roman law that Savigny makes this statement, and before it can fully be appreciated much labour must be expended in explaining and defining the expressions employed. His meaning will, however, be indicated with sufficient accuracy if we consider him to assert that, how far soever we carry our inquiry into the ideas of property received

among the Romans, however closely we approach in
tracing them to the infancy of law, we can get no
farther than a conception of ownership involving the
three elements in the canon—Possession, Adverse-
ness of Possession, that is, a holding not permissive
or subordinate, but exclusive against the world, and
Prescription, or a period of time during which the
Adverse Possession has uninterruptedly continued.
It is exceedingly probable that this maxim might
be enunciated with more generality than was allowed
to it by its author, and that no sound or safe conclusion can be looked for from investigations into
any system of laws which are pushed farther back
than the point at which these combined ideas constitute the notion of proprietary right.   Meantime,
so far from bearing out the popular theory of the
origin of property, Savigny's canon is particularly
valuable as directing our attention to its weakest
point.   In the view of Blackstone and those whom
he follows, it was the mode of assuming the exclusive
enjoyment which mysteriously affected the minds of
the fathers of our race.   But the mystery does not
reside here.   It is not wonderful that property began
in adverse possession.   It is not surprising that the
first proprietor should have been the strong man
armed who kept his goods in peace.   But why it was
that lapse of time created a sentiment of respect for
his possession—which is the exact source of the

universal reverence of mankind for that which has
for a long period *de facto* existed—are questions really
deserving the profoundest examination, but lying far
beyond the boundary of our present inquiries.

Before pointing out the quarter in which we may
hope to glean some information, scanty and uncertain at best, concerning the early history of
proprietary right, I venture to state my opinion that
the popular impression in reference to the part
played by Occupancy in the first stages of civilisation directly reverses the truth. Occupancy is the
advised assumption of physical possession ; and the
notion that an act of this description confers a title
to "res nullius," so far from being characteristic
of very early societies, is in all probability the
growth of a refined jurisprudence and of a settled
condition of the laws. It is only when the rights of
property have gained a sanction from long practical inviolability, and when the vast majority of
the objects of enjoyment have been subjected to
private ownership, that mere possession is allowed
to invest the first possessor with dominion over
commodities in which no prior proprietorship has
been asserted. The sentiment in which this doctrine
originated is absolutely irreconcilable with that
infrequency and uncertainty of proprietary rights
which distinguish the beginnings of civilisation.
Its true basis seems to be, not an instinctive bias

towards the institution of Property, but a presumption, arising out of the long continuance of that
institution, that *everything ought to have an owner.*
When possession is taken of a "res nullius," that is,
of an object which *is* not, or has *never* been, reduced
to dominion, the possessor is permitted to become
proprietor from a feeling that all valuable things
are naturally the subjects of an exclusive enjoyment,
and that in the given case there is no one to invest
with the right of property except the Occupant.
The Occupant, in short, becomes the owner, because
all things are presumed to be somebody's property
and because no one can be pointed out as having
a better right than he to the proprietorship of this
particular thing.

Even were there no other objection to the descriptions of mankind in their natural state which
we have been discussing, there is one particular in
which they are fatally at variance with the authentic
evidence possessed by us.   It will be observed, that
the acts and motives which these theories suppose
are the acts and motives of Individuals.   It is each
Individual who for himself subscribes the Social
Compact.   It is some shifting sandbank in which
the grains are Individual men, that according to
the theory of Hobbes is hardened into the social
rock by the wholesome discipline of force.   It is an
Individual who in the picture drawn by Blackstone,

" is in the occupation of a determined spot of ground for rest, for shade, or the like." The vice is one which necessarily afflicts all the theories descended from the Natural Law of the Romans, which differed principally from their Civil Law in the account which it took of Individuals, and which has rendered precisely its greatest service to civilisation in enfranchising the individual from the authority of archaic society. But Ancient Law, it must again be repeated, knows next to nothing of Individuals. It is concerned not with Individuals, but with Families, not with single human beings, but groups. Even when the law of the State has succeeded in permeating the small circles of kindred into which it had originally no means of penetrating, the view it takes of Individuals is curiously different from that taken by jurisprudence in its maturest stage. The life of each citizen is not regarded as limited by birth and death; it is but a continuation of the existence of his forefathers, and it will be prolonged in the existence of his descendants.

The Roman distinction between the Law of Persons and the Law of Things, which though extremely convenient is entirely artificial, has evidently done much to divert inquiry on the subject before us from the true direction. The lessons learned in discussing the Jus Personarum have been forgotten where the Jus Rerum is reached, and Property, Contract, and

Delict, have been considered as if no hints concerning their original nature were to be gained from the facts ascertained respecting the original condition of Persons. The futility of this method would be manifest if a system of pure archaic law could be brought before us, and if the experiment could be tried of applying to it the Roman classifications. It would soon be seen that the separation of the Law of Persons from that of Things has no meaning in the infancy of law, that the rules belonging to the two departments are inextricably mingled together, and that the distinctions of the later jurists are appropriate only to the later jurisprudence. From what has been said in the earlier portions of this treatise, it will be gathered that there is a strong *à priori* improbability of our obtaining any clue to the early history of property, if we confine our notice to the proprietary rights of individuals. It is more than likely that joint-ownership, and not separate ownership, is the really archaic institution, and that the forms of property which will afford us instruction will be those which are associated with the rights of families and of groups of kindred. The Roman jurisprudence will not here assist in enlightening us, for it is exactly the Roman jurisprudence which, transformed by the theory of Natural Law, has bequeathed to the moderns the impression that individual ownership is the normal state of proprietary right, and that ownership in common by groups of men is only the exception to a general rule. There is, however, one community which will always be carefully examined by the inquirer who is in quest of any lost institution of primeval society. How far soever any such institution may have undergone change among the branch of the Indo-European family which has been settled for ages in India, it will seldom be found to have entirely cast aside the shell in which it was originally reared. It happens that, among the Hindoos, we do find a form of ownership which ought at once to rivet our attention from its exactly fitting in with the ideas which our studies in the Law of Persons would lead us to entertain respecting the original condition of property. The Village Community of India is at once an organised patriarchal society and an assemblage of co-proprietors. The personal relations to each other of the men who compose it are indistinguishably confounded with their proprietary rights, and to the attempts of English functionaries to separate the two may be assigned some of the most formidable miscarriages of Anglo-Indian administration. The Village Community is known to be of immense antiquity. In whatever direction research has been pushed into Indian history, general or local, it has always found the Community in existence at the farthest point of its progress. A great number of intelligent and observant writers, most of whom had no theory of any sort to support concerning its nature and origin, agree in considering it the least destructible institution of a society which never willingly surrenders any one of its usages to innovation. Conquests and revolutions seem to have swept over it without disturbing or displacing it, and the most beneficent systems of government in India have always been those which have recognised it as the basis of administration.

The mature Roman law, and modern jurisprudence following in its wake, look upon co-ownership as an exceptional and momentary condition of the rights of property. This view is clearly indicated in the maxim which obtains universally in Western Europe, *Nemo in communione potest invitus detineri* ("No one can be kept in co-proprietorship against his will"). But in India this order of ideas is reversed, and it may be said that separate proprietorship is always on its way to become proprietorship in common. The process has been adverted to already. As soon as a son is born, he acquires a vested interest in his father's substance, and on attaining years of discretion he is even, in certain contingencies, permitted by the letter of the law to call for a partition of the family estate. As a fact, however, a division rarely takes place even at the death of the father, and the property constantly remains undivided for several

generations, though every member of every generation has a legal right to an undivided share in it.
The domain thus held in common is sometimes administered by an elected manager, but more generally,
and in some provinces always, it is managed by the
eldest agnate, by the eldest representative of the
eldest line of the stock.   Such an assemblage of
joint proprietors, a body of kindred holding a domain
in common, is the simplest form of an Indian Village
Community, but the Community is more than a
brotherhood of relatives and more than an association
of partners.   It is an organised society, and besides
providing for the management of the common fund,
it seldom fails to provide, by a complete staff of
functionaries, for internal government, for police, for
the administration of justice, and for the apportionment of taxes and public duties.

The process which I have described as that under
which a Village Community is formed, may be regarded as typical.   Yet it is not to be supposed that
every Village Community in India drew together in
so simple a manner.   Although, in the North of India,
the archives, as I am informed, almost invariably
show that the Community was founded by a single
assemblage of blood-relations, they also supply information that men of alien extraction have always,
from time to time, been engrafted on it, and a mere
purchaser of a share may generally, under certain
conditions, be admitted to the brotherhood.   In the

South of the Peninsula there are often Communities which appear to have sprung not from one but from two or more families: and there are some whose composition is known to be entirely artificial; indeed, the occasional aggregation of men of different castes in the same society is fatal to the hypothesis of a common descent. Yet in all these brotherhoods either the tradition is preserved, or the assumption made, of an original common parentage. Mountstuart Elphinstone, who writes more particularly of the Southern Village Communities, observes of them (*History of India*, i. 126): "The popular notion is that the Village landholders are all descended from one or more individuals who settled the Village; and that the only exceptions are formed by persons who have derived their rights by purchase or otherwise from members of the original stock. The supposition is confirmed by the fact that, to this day, there are only single families of landholders in small villages and not many in large ones; but each has branched out into so many members that it is not uncommon for the whole agricultural labour to be done by the landholders, without the aid either of tenants or of labourers. The rights of the landholders are theirs collectively, and, though they almost always have a more or less perfect partition of them, they never have an entire separation. A landholder, for instance, can sell or mortgage his rights; but he must first have the consent of the Village, and the purchaser steps exactly into his place and takes up all his obligations. If a family becomes extinct, its share returns to the common stock."

Some considerations which have been offered in the fifth chapter of this volume will assist the reader, I trust, in appreciating the significance of Elphinstone's language. No institution of the primitive world is likely to have been preserved to our day, unless it has acquired an elasticity foreign to its original nature through some vivifying legal fiction. The Village Community then is not necessarily an assemblage of blood-relations, but it is *either* such an assemblage *or* a body of co-proprietors formed on the model of an association of kinsmen. The type with which it should be compared is evidently not the Roman Family, but the Roman Gens or House. The Gens was also a group on the model of the family; it was the family extended by a variety of fictions of which the exact nature was lost in antiquity. In historical times, its leading characteristics were the very two which Elphinstone remarks in the Village Community. There was always the assumption of a common origin, an assumption sometimes notoriously at variance with fact: and, to repeat the historian's words, "if a family became extinct, its share returned to the common stock." In old Roman law, unclaimed inheritances escheated to the Gentiles. It is further suspected by all who have examined their history that the

Communities, like the Gentes, have been very generally adulterated by the admission of strangers, but
the exact mode of absorption cannot now be ascertained.   At present, they are recruited, as Elphinstone tells us, by the admission of purchasers, with
the consent of the brotherhood.   The acquisition of
the adopted member is, however, of the nature of a
universal succession; together with the share he has
bought, he succeeds to the liabilities which the vendor
had incurred towards the aggregate group.   He is an
Emptor Familiæ, and inherits the legal clothing of
the person whose place he begins to fill.   The consent
of the whole brotherhood required for his admission
may remind us of the consent which the Comitia
Curiata, the Parliament of that larger brotherhood
of self-styled kinsmen, the ancient Roman commonwealth, so strenuously insisted on as essential to the
legislation of an Adoption or the confirmation of a
Will.

The tokens of an extreme antiquity are discoverable in almost every single feature of the Indian
Village Communities.   We have so many independent
reasons for suspecting that the infancy of law is distinguished by the prevalence of co-ownership, by
the intermixture of personal with proprietary rights,
and by the confusion of public with private duties,
that we should be justified in deducing many important conclusions from our observation of these

proprietary brotherhoods, even if no similarly com-
pounded societies could be detected in any other
part of the world. It happens, however, that much
earnest curiosity has been very recently attracted to
a similar set of phenomena in those parts of Europe
which have been most slightly affected by the feudal
transformation of property, and which in many
important particulars have as close an affinity with
the Eastern as with the Western world. The researches of M. de Haxthausen, M. Tengoborski, and
others, have shown us that the Russian villages are
not fortuitous assemblages of men, nor are they
unions founded on contract; they are naturally organised communities like those of India. It is true
that these villages are always in theory the patrimony
of some noble proprietor, and the peasants have within historical times been converted into the predial,
and to a great extent into the personal, serfs of the
seignior. But the pressure of this superior ownership
has never crushed the ancient organisation of the
village, and it is probable that the enactment of the
Czar of Russia, who is supposed to have introduced
serfdom, was really intended to prevent the peasants
from abandoning that co-operation without which the
old social order could not long be maintained. In
the assumption of an agnatic connection between the
villagers, in the blending of personal rights with privileges of ownership, and in a variety of spontaneous

provisions for internal administration, the Russian village appears to be a nearly exact repetition of the Indian Community ; but there is one important difference which we note with the greatest interest. The co-owners of an Indian village, though their property is blended, have their rights distinct, and this separation of rights is complete and continues indefinitely. The severance of rights is also theoretically complete in a Russian village, but there it is only temporary. After the expiration of a given, but not in all cases of the same, period, separate ownerships are extinguished, the land of the village is thrown into a mass, and then it is re-distributed among the families composing the community, according to their number. This repartition having been effected, the rights of families and of individuals are again allowed to branch out into various lines, which they continue to follow till another period of division comes round. An even more curious variation from this type of ownership occurs in some of those countries which long formed a debateable land between the Turkish Empire and the possessions of the House of Austria. In Servia, in Croatia, and the Austrian Sclavonia, the villages are also brotherhoods of persons who are at once co-owners and kinsmen ; but there the internal arrangements of the community differ from those adverted to in the last two examples. The substance of the common property is in this case neither divided in practice nor considered in theory as divisible, but the entire land is cultivated by the combined labour of all the villagers, and the produce is annually distributed among the households, sometimes according to their supposed wants, sometimes according to rules which give to particular persons a fixed share of the usufruct. All these practices are traced by the jurists of the East of Europe to a principle which is asserted to be found in the earliest Sclavonian laws, the principle that the property of families cannot be divided for a perpetuity.

The great interest of these phenomena in an inquiry like the present arises from the light they throw on the development of distinct proprietary rights *inside* the groups by which property seems to have been originally held. We have the strongest reason for thinking that property once belonged not to individuals nor even to isolated families, but to larger societies composed on the patriarchal model; but the mode of transition from ancient to modern ownerships, obscure at best, would have been infinitely obscurer if several distinguishable forms of Village Communities had not been discovered and examined. It is worth while to attend to the varieties of internal arrangement within the patriarchal groups which are, or were till recently, observable among races of Indo-European blood. The chiefs of the ruder Highland clans used, it is said, to dole out

food to the heads of the households under their jurisdiction at the very shortest intervals, and sometimes
day by day. A periodical distribution is also made
to the Sclavonian villagers of the Austrian and
Turkish provinces by the elders of their body, but
then it is a distribution once for all of the total
produce of the year. In the Russian villages, however, the substance of the property ceases to be looked
upon as indivisible, and separate proprietary claims
are allowed freely to grow up, but then the progress
of separation is peremptorily arrested after it has
continued a certain time. In India, not only is there
no indivisibility of the common fund, but separate
proprietorship in parts of it may be indefinitely
prolonged and may branch out into any number of
derivative ownerships, the *de facto* partition of the
stock being, however, checked by inveterate usage,
and by the rule against the admission of strangers
without the consent of the brotherhood. It is not of
course intended to insist that these different forms of
the Village Community represent distinct stages in a
process of transmutation which has been everywhere
accomplished in the same manner. But, though the
evidence does not warrant our going so far as this, it
renders less presumptuous the conjecture that private
property, in the shape in which we know it, was
chiefly formed by the gradual disentanglement of the
separate rights of individuals from the blended rights

of a community. Our studies in the Law of Persons
seemed to show us the Family expanding into the
Agnatic group of kinsmen, then the Agnatic group
dissolving into separate households; lastly, the household supplanted by the individual; and it is now
suggested that each step in the change corresponds to
an analogous alteration in the nature of Ownership.
If there be any truth in the suggestion, it is to be
observed that it materially affects the problem which
theorists on the origin of Property have generally
proposed to themselves. The question—perhaps an
insoluble one—which they have mostly agitated is,
what were the motives which first induced men to
respect each other's possessions ? It may still be put,
without much hope of finding an answer to it, in the
form of an inquiry into the reasons which led one
composite group to keep aloof from the domain of
another. But, if it be true that far the most important passage in the history of Private Property is
its gradual separation from the co-ownership of
kinsmen, then the great point of inquiry is identical with that which lies on the threshold of all
historical law—what were the motives which originally prompted men to hold together in the family
union? To such a question, Jurisprudence, unassisted by other sciences, is not competent to give a
reply. The fact can only be noted.

The undivided state of property in ancient

societies is consistent with a peculiar sharpness of division, which shows itself as soon as any single share is completely separated from the patrimony of the group. This phenomenon springs, doubtless, from the circumstance that the property is supposed to become the domain of a new group, so that any dealing with it, in its divided state, is a transaction between two highly complex bodies. I have already compared Ancient Law to Modern International Law, in respect of the size and complexity of the corporate associations, whose rights and duties it settles. As the contracts and conveyances known to ancient law are contracts and conveyances to which not single individuals, but organised companies of men, are parties, they are in the highest degree ceremonious; they require a variety of symbolical acts and words intended to impress the business on the memory of all who take part in it; and they demand the presence of an inordinate number of witnesses. From these peculiarities, and others allied to them, springs the universally unmalleable character of the ancient forms of property. Sometimes the patrimony of the family is absolutely inalienable, as was the case with the Sclavonians, and still oftener, though alienations may not be entirely illegitimate, they are virtually impracticable, as among most of the Germanic tribes, from the necessity of having the consent of a large number of persons to the transfer.

Where these impediments do not exist, or can be surmounted, the act of conveyance itself is generally burdened with a perfect load of ceremony, in which not one iota can be safely neglected. Ancient law uniformly refuses to dispense with a single gesture, however grotesque; with a single syllable, however its meaning may have been forgotten; with a single witness, however superfluous may be his testimony. The entire solemnities must be scrupulously completed by persons legally entitled to take part in it, or else the conveyance is null, and the seller is re-established in the rights of which he had vainly attempted to divest himself.

These various obstacles to the free circulation of the objects of use and enjoyment, begin of course to make themselves felt as soon as society has acquired even a slight degree of activity, and the expedients by which advancing communities endeavour to overcome them form the staple of the history of Property. Of such expedients there is one which takes precedence of the rest from its antiquity and universality. The idea seems to have spontaneously suggested itself to a great number of early societies, to classify property into kinds. One kind or sort of property is placed on a lower footing of dignity than the others, but at the same time is relieved from the fetters which antiquity has imposed on them. Subsequently, the superior convenience of the rules from various rights to which they have a close affinity. Thus, the Res Mancipi of Roman Law included not only land but slaves, horses, and oxen. Scottish law ranks with land a certain class of securities, and Hindoo law associates it with slaves. English law, on the other hand, parts leases of land for years from other interests in the soil, and joins them to personalty under the name of chattels real. Moreover, the classifications of Ancient Law are classifications implying superiority and inferiority; while the distinction between moveables and immoveables, so long at least as it was confined to Roman jurisprudence, carried with it no suggestion whatever of a difference in dignity. The Res Mancipi, however, did certainly at first enjoy a precedence over the Res Nec Mancipi, as did heritable property in Scotland, and realty in England, over the personalty to which they were opposed. The lawyers of all systems have spared no pains in striving to refer these classifications to some intelligible principle; but the reasons of the severance must ever be vainly sought for in the philosophy of law: they belong not to its philosophy, but to its history. The explanation which appears to cover the greatest number of instances is, that the objects of enjoyment honoured above the rest were the forms of property known first and earliest to each particular community, and dignified therefore emphatically with the designation of *Property*. On the other hand, the articles not enumerated among the favoured objects seem to have been placed on a lower standing, because the knowledge of their value was posterior to the epoch at which the catalogue of superior property was settled. They were at first unknown, rare, limited in their uses, or else regarded as mere appendages to the privileged objects. Thus, though the Roman Res Mancipi included a number of moveable articles of great value, still the most costly jewels were never allowed to take rank as Res Mancipi, because they were unknown to the early Romans. In the same way chattels real in England are said to have been degraded to the footing of personalty, from the infrequency and valuelessness of such estates under the feudal land-law. But the grand point of interest is, the continued degradation of these commodities when their importance had increased and their number had multiplied. Why were they not successively included among the favoured objects of enjoyment? One reason is found in the stubbornness with which Ancient Law adheres to its classifications. It is a characteristic both of uneducated minds and of early societies, that they are little able to conceive a general rule apart from the particular applications of it with which they are practically familiar. They cannot dissociate a general term or maxim from the special examples which meet them in daily experience; and in this way the designation covering the

best-known forms of property is denied to articles
which exactly resemble them in being objects of
enjoyment and subjects of right.   But to these influences, which exert peculiar force in a subject-matter
so stable as that of law, are afterwards added others
more consistent with progress in enlightenment and
in the conceptions of general expediency.   Courts
and lawyers become at last alive to the inconvenience
of the embarrassing formalities required for the
transfer, recovery, or devolution of the favoured
commodities, and grow unwilling to fetter the
newer descriptions of property with the technical
trammels which characterised the infancy of law.
Hence arises a disposition to keep these last on a
lower grade in the arrangements of Jurisprudence,
and to permit their transfer by simpler processes
than those which, in archaic conveyances, serve as
stumbling-blocks to good faith and stepping-stones
to fraud.   We are perhaps in some danger of under-
rating the inconveniences of the ancient modes of
transfer.   Our instruments of conveyance are written, so that their language, well pondered by the
professional draftsman, is rarely defective in accuracy.   But an ancient conveyance was not written,
but *acted*. Gestures and words took the place of
written technical phraseology, and any formula mis-
pronounced, or symbolical act omitted, would have
vitiated the proceeding as fatally as a material mis-

take in stating the uses or setting out the remainders would, two hundred years ago, have vitiated an English deed. Indeed, the mischiefs of the archaic ceremonial are even thus only half stated. So long as elaborate conveyances, written or acted, are required for the alienation of *land* alone, the chances of mistake are not considerable in the transfer of a description of property which is seldom got rid of with much precipitation. But the higher class of property in the ancient world comprised not only land but several of the commonest and several of the most valuable moveables. When once the wheels of society had begun to move quickly, there must have been immense inconvenience in demanding a highly intricate form of transfer for a horse or an ox, or for the most costly chattel of the old world—the Slave. Such commodities must have been constantly and even ordinarily conveyed with incomplete forms, and held, therefore, under imperfect titles.

The Res Mancipi of old Roman law were, land,— in historical times, land on Italian soil,—slaves and beasts of burden, such as horses and oxen. It is impossible to doubt that the objects which make up the class are the instruments of agricultural labour, the commodities of first consequence to a primitive people. Such commodities were at first, I imagine, called emphatically Things or Property, and the mode of conveyance by which they were transferred was

called a Mancipium or Mancipation; but it was not
probably till much later that they received the distinctive appellation of Res Mancipi, "Things which
require a Mancipation." By their side there may
have existed or grown up a class of objects, for which
it was not worth while to insist upon the full ceremony of Mancipation. It would be enough if, in
transferring these last from owner to owner, a part
only of the ordinary formalities were proceeded with,
namely, that actual delivery, physical transfer, or
tradition, which is the most obvious index of a change
of proprietorship. Such commodities were the Res
Nec Mancipi of the ancient jurisprudence, "things
which did not require a Mancipation," little prized
probably at first, and not often passed from one group
of proprietors to another. While, however, the list of
the Res Mancipi was irrevocably closed, that of the
Res Nec Mancipi admitted of indefinite expansion;
and hence every fresh conquest of man over material
nature added an item to the Res Nec Mancipi, or
effected an improvement in those already recognised.
Insensibly, therefore, they mounted to an equality
with the Res Mancipi, and the impression of an intrinsic inferiority being thus dissipated, men began
to observe the manifold advantages of the simple
formality which accompanied their transfer over the
more intricate and more venerable ceremonial. Two
of the agents of legal amelioration, Fictions and
Equity, were assiduously employed by the Roman

property are first, from disdain and disregard, released from the perplexed ceremonies in which primitive law delights, and then afterwards, in another state of intellectual progress, the simple methods of transfer and recovery which have been allowed to come into use serve as a model which condemns by its convenience and simplicity the cumbrous solemnities inherited from ancient days.   But in some societies, the trammels in which Property is tied up are much too complicated and stringent to be relaxed in so easy a manner.   Whenever male children have been born to a Hindoo, the law of India, as I have stated, gives them all an interest in his property, and makes their consent a necessary condition of its alienation.   In the same spirit, the general usage of the old Germanic peoples—it is remarkable that the Anglo-Saxon customs seem to have been an exception—forbade alienations without the consent of the male children; and the primitive law of the Sclavonians even prohibited them altogether.   It is evident that such impediments as these cannot be overcome by a distinction between kinds of property, inasmuch as the difficulty extends to commodities of all sorts; and accordingly, Ancient Law, when once launched on a course of improvement, encounters them with a distinction of another character, a distinction classifying property, not according to its nature but according to its origin.   In India, where there are traces of both systems of classifica-

tion, the one which we are considering is exemplified in the difference which Hindoo law establishes
between Inheritances and Acquisitions. The inherited
property of the father is shared by the children as
soon as they are born; but according to the custom
of most provinces, the acquisitions made by him
during his lifetime are wholly his own, and can be
transferred by him at pleasure. A similar distinction
was not unknown to Roman law, in which the earliest
innovation on the Parental Powers took the form of
a permission given to the son to keep for himself
whatever he might have acquired in military service.
But the most extensive use ever made of this mode of
classification appears to have been among the Germans. I have repeatedly stated that the *allod*, though
not inalienable, was commonly transferable with the
greatest difficulty; and moreover, it descended exclusively to the agnatic kindred. Hence an extraordinary variety of distinctions came to be recognised,
all intended to diminish the inconveniences inseparable from allodial property. The *wehrgeld*, for example, or composition for the homicide of a relative,
which occupies so large a space in German jurisprudence, formed no part of the family domain, and
descended according to rules of succession altogether
different. Similarly, the *reipus*, or fine leviable on
the re-marriage of a widow, did not enter into the
allod of the person to whom it was paid, and followed

a line of devolution in which the privileges of the
agnates were neglected. The law, too, as among
the Hindoos, distinguished the Acquisitions of the
chief of the household from his Inherited property,
and permitted him to deal with them under much more
liberal conditions. Classifications of the other sort
were also admitted, and the familiar distinction
drawn between land and moveables ; but moveable
property was divided into several subordinate categories, to each of which different rules applied. This
exuberance of classification, which may strike us as
strange in so rude a people as the German conquerors
of the Empire, is doubtless to be explained by the
presence in their systems of a considerable element
of Roman law, absorbed by them during their long
sojourn on the confines of the Roman dominion. It
is not difficult to trace a great number of the rules
governing the transfer and devolution of the commodities which lay outside the *allod*, to their source in
Roman jurisprudence, from which they were probably borrowed at widely distant epochs, and in
fragmentary importations. How far the obstacles to
the free circulation of property were surmounted by
such contrivances, we have not the means even of
conjecturing, for the distinctions adverted to have no
modern history. As I before explained, the allodial
form of property was entirely lost in the feudal, and
when the consolidation of feudalism was once com-

pleted, there was practically but one distinction left standing of all those which had been known to the western world—the distinction between land and goods, immoveables and moveables. Externally this distinction was the same with that which Roman law had finally accepted, but the law of the middle ages differed from that of Rome in distinctly consider-ing immoveable property to be more dignified than moveable. Yet this one sample is enough to show the importance of the class of expedients to which it belongs. In all the countries governed by systems based on the French codes, that is, through much the greatest part of the Continent of Europe, the law of moveables, which was always Roman law, has superseded and annulled the feudal law of land. England is the only country of import-ance in which this transmutation, though it has gone some way, is not nearly accomplished. Our own, too, it may be added, is the only considerable European country in which the separation of moveables from immoveables has been somewhat disturbed by the same influences which caused the ancient classifications to depart from the only one which is countenanced by nature. In the main, the English distinction has been between land and goods; but a certain class of goods have gone as heir-looms with the land, and a certain description of interests in land have from historical causes been ranked with personalty. This is not the

only instance in which English jurisprudence, standing apart from the main current of legal modification,
has reproduced phenomena of archaic law.

I proceed to notice one or two more contrivances
by which the ancient trammels of proprietary right
were more or less successfully relaxed, premising that
the scheme of this treatise only permits me to mention those which are of great antiquity. On one of
them in particular it is necessary to dwell for a moment or two, because persons unacquainted with the
early history of law will not be easily persuaded that
a principle, of which modern jurisprudence has very
slowly and with the greatest difficulty obtained the
recognition, was really familiar to the very infancy of
legal science.   There is no principle in all law which
the moderns, in spite of its beneficial character, have
been so loath to adopt and to carry to its legitimate
consequences as that which was known to the Romans
as Usucapion, and which has descended to modern
jurisprudence under the name of Prescription.   It
was a positive rule of the oldest Roman law, a rule
older than the Twelve Tables, that commodities
which had been uninterruptedly possessed for a certain period became the property of the possessor.
The period of possession was exceedingly short—
one or two years, according to the nature of the
commodities—and in historical times Usucapion
was only allowed to operate when possession had

commenced in a particular way; but I think it
likely that at a less advanced epoch possession was
converted into ownership under conditions even less
severe than we read of in our authorities. As I
have said before, I am far from asserting that the
respect of men for *de facto* possession is a phenomenon which jurisprudence can account for by itself,
but it is very necessary to remark that primitive
societies, in adopting the principle of Usucapion,
were not beset with any of the speculative doubts
and hesitations which have impeded its reception
among the moderns. Prescriptions were viewed by
the modern lawyers, first with repugnance, afterwards
with reluctant approval. In several countries, including our own, legislation long declined to advance
beyond the rude device of barring all actions based
on a wrong which had been suffered earlier than
a fixed point of time in the past, generally the first
year of some preceding reign; nor was it till the
middle ages had finally closed, and James the First
had ascended the throne of England, that we obtained a true statute of limitation of a very imperfect kind. This tardiness in copying one of the
most famous chapters of Roman law, which was no
doubt constantly read by the majority of European
lawyers, the modern world owes to the influence of
the Canon Law. The ecclesiastical customs out of
which the Canon Law grew, concerned as they were

with sacred or quasi-sacred interests, very naturally
regarded the privileges which they conferred as incapable of being lost through disuse however prolonged; and in accordance with this view, the spiritual jurisprudence, when afterwards consolidated, was
distinguished by a marked leaning against Prescriptions.   It was the fate of the Canon Law, when held
up by the clerical lawyers as a pattern to secular legislation, to have a peculiar influence on first principles.
It gave to the bodies of custom which were formed
throughout Europe far fewer express rules than did
the Roman law, but then it seems to have communi-
cated a bias to professional opinion on a surprising
number of fundamental points, and the tendencies
thus produced progressively gained strength as each
system was developed.   One of the dispositions it
produced was a disrelish for Prescriptions; but I do
not know that this prejudice would have operated as
powerfully as it has done, if it had not fallen in
with the doctrine of the scholastic jurists of the
realist sect, who taught that, whatever turn actual
legislation might take, a *right*, how long soever neglected, was in point of fact indestructible.   The
remains of this state of feeling still exist.   Wherever
the philosophy of law is earnestly discussed, questions respecting the speculative basis of Prescription
are always hotly disputed; and it is still a point of
the greatest interest in France and Germany, whether

a person who has been out of possession for a series
of years is deprived of his ownership as a penalty
for his neglect, or loses it through the summary interposition of the law in its desire to have a *finis litium*.
But no such scruples troubled the mind of early
Roman society. Their ancient usages directly took
away the ownership of everybody who had been out
of possession, under certain circumstances, during
one or two years. What was the exact tenor of the
rule of Usucapion in its earliest shape, it is not
easy to say; but, taken with the limitations which
we find attending it in the books, it was a most useful security against the mischiefs of a too cumbrous
system of conveyance. In order to have the benefit
of Usucapion, it was necessary that the adverse possession should have begun in good faith, that is, with
belief on the part of the possessor that he was law-
fully acquiring the property, and it was further required that the commodity should have been transferred to him by some mode of alienation which,
however unequal to conferring a complete title in the
particular case, was at least recognised by the law.
In the case therefore of a Mancipation, however
slovenly the performance might have been, yet if it
had been carried so far as to involve a Tradition or
Delivery, the vice of the title would be cured by
Usucapion in two years at most. I know nothing in
the practice of the Romans which testifies so strongly

to their legal genius as the use which they made of Usucapion. The difficulties which beset them were nearly the same with those which embarrassed and still embarrass the lawyers of England. Owing to the complexity of their system, which as yet they had neither the courage nor the power to reconstruct, actual right was constantly getting divorced from technical right, the equitable ownership from the legal. But Usucapion, as manipulated by the jurisconsults, supplied a self-acting machinery, by which the defects of titles to property were always in course of being cured, and by which the ownerships that were temporarily separated were again rapidly cemented together with the briefest possible delay. Usucapion did not lose its advantages till the reforms of Justinian. But as soon as law and equity had been completely fused, and when Mancipation ceased to be the Roman conveyance, there was no further necessity for the ancient contrivance, and Usucapion, with its periods of time considerably lengthened, became the Prescription which has at length been adopted by nearly all systems of modern law.

I· pass by with brief mention another expedient having the same object with the last, which, though it did not immediately make its appearance in English legal history, was of immemorial antiquity in Roman law; such indeed is its apparent age that some

German civilians, not sufficiently aware of the light
thrown on the subject by the analogies of English
law, have thought it even older than the Mancipation. I speak of the Cessio in Jure, a collusive
recovery, in a Court of Law, of property sought to
be conveyed. The plaintiff claimed the subject of
this proceeding with the ordinary forms of a litigation; the defendant made default; and the commodity
was of course adjudged to the plaintiff. I need
scarcely remind the English lawyer that this expedient suggested itself to our forefathers, and produced those famous Fines and Recoveries which did
so much to undo the harshest trammels of the feudal
land-law. The Roman and English contrivances
have very much in common and illustrate each other
most instructively, but there is this difference between them, that the object of the English lawyers
was to remove complications already introduced into
the title, while the Roman jurisconsults sought to
prevent them by substituting a mode of transfer
necessarily unimpeachable for one which too often
miscarried. The device is in fact one which suggests itself as soon as Courts of Law are in steady
operation, but are nevertheless still under the empire of primitive notions. In an advanced state of
legal opinion, tribunals regard collusive litigation
as an abuse of their procedure; but there has
always been a time when, if their forms were

scrupulously complied with, they never dreamed of looking further.

The influence of Courts of Law and of their proce-dure upon Property has been most extensive, but the subject is too large for the dimensions of this treatise, and would carry us further down the course of legal history than is consistent with its scheme. It is desirable, however, to mention, that to this influence we must attribute the importance of the distinction between Property and Possession—not, indeed, the distinction itself, which (in the language of an eminent English civilian) is the same thing as the distinction between the legal right to act upon a thing and the physical power to do so—but the extraordinary im-portance which the distinction has obtained in the philosophy of law. Few educated persons are so little versed in legal literature as not to have heard that the language of the Roman jurisconsults on the subject of Possession long occasioned the greatest possible perplexity, and that the genius of Savigny is supposed to have chiefly proved itself by the solu-tion which he discovered for the enigma. Possession, in fact, when employed by the Roman lawyers, ap-pears to have contracted a shade of meaning not easily accounted for. The word, as appears from its etymology, must have originally denoted physical contact or physical contact resumeable at pleasure; but as actually used, without any qualifying epithet, it signifies not simply physical detention, but physical detention coupled with the intention to hold the thing detained as one's own.   Savigny, following Niebuhr, perceived that for this anomaly there could only be a historical origin.   He pointed out that the Patrician burghers of Rome, who had become tenants of the greatest part of the public domain at nominal rents, were, in the view of the old Roman law, mere possessors, but then they were possessors intending to keep their land against all comers.   They, in truth, put forward a claim almost identical with that which has recently been advanced in England by the lessees of Church lands.   Admitting that in theory they were the tenants-at-will of the state, they contended that time and undisturbed enjoyment had ripened their holding into a species of ownership, and that it would be unjust to eject them for the purpose of redistributing the domain.   The association of this claim with the Patrician tenancies, permanently influenced the sense of " possession."   Meanwhile the only legal remedies of which the tenants could avail themselves, if ejected or threatened with disturbance, were the Possessory Interdicts, summary processes of Roman law which were either expressly devised by the Prætor for their protection, or else, according to another theory, had in older times been employed for the provisional maintenance of possessions pending the settlement of questions of legal right.   It came, therefore, to be understood that everybody who possessed property *as his own* had the power of demanding the Interdicts, and, by a system of highly artificial pleading, the Interdictal process was moulded into a shape fitted for the trial of conflicting claims to a disputed possession. Then commenced a movement which, as Mr. John Austin pointed out, exactly reproduced itself in English law. Proprietors, *domini*, began to prefer the simpler forms or speedier course of the Interdict to the lagging and intricate formalities of the Real Action, and for the purpose of availing themselves of the possessory remedy fell back upon the possession which was supposed to be involved in their proprietorship. The liberty conceded to persons who were not true Possessors, but Owners, to vindicate their rights by possessory remedies, though it may have been at first a boon, had ultimately the effect of seriously deteriorating both English and Roman jurisprudence. The Roman law owes to it those subtleties on the subject of Possession which have done so much to discredit it, while English law, after the actions which it appropriated to the recovery of real property had fallen into the most hopeless confusion, got rid at last of the whole tangled mass by a heroic remedy. No one can doubt that the virtual abolition of the English real actions which took place nearly thirty years since was a public benefit, but still persons sensitive to the harmonies of jurisprudence will lament that, instead of cleansing, improving, and simplifying the true proprietary actions, we sacrificed them all to the possessory action of ejectment, thus basing our whole system of land recovery upon a legal fiction.

Legal tribunals have also powerfully assisted to shape and modify conceptions of proprietary right by means of the distinction between Law and Equity, which always makes its first appearance as a distinction between jurisdictions. Equitable property in England is simply property held under the jurisdiction of the Court of Chancery. At Rome, the Prætor's Edict introduced its novel principles in the guise of a promise that under certain circumstances a particular action or a particular plea would be granted; and, accordingly, the property *in bonis*, or Equitable Property, of Roman law was property exclusively protected by remedies which had their source in the Edict. The mechanism by which equitable rights were saved from being overridden by the claims of the legal owner was somewhat different in the two systems. With us their independence is secured by the Injunction of the Court of Chancery. Since however Law and Equity, while not as yet consolidated, were administered under the Roman system by the same Court, nothing like the Injunction was required, and the Magistrate took the simpler course of refusing to grant to the Civil Law Owner those actions and pleas by which alone he could obtain the

property that belonged in equity to another. But
the practical operation of both systems was nearly
the same. Both, by means of a distinction in procedure, were able to preserve new forms of property in
a sort of provisional existence, until the time should
come when they were recognised by the whole law.
In this way, the Roman Prætor gave an immediate
right of property to the person who had acquired a
Res Mancipi by mere delivery, without waiting for
the ripening of Usucapion. Similarly he in time recognised an ownership in the Mortgagee, who had at
first been a mere "bailee" or depositary, and in the
Emphyteuta, or tenant of land which was subject to
a fixed perpetual rent. Following a parallel line of
progress, the English Court of Chancery created a
special proprietorship for the Mortgagor, for the
Cestui que Trust, for the Married Woman who had
the advantage of a particular kind of settlement, and
for the Purchaser who had not yet acquired a complete legal ownership. All these are examples in
which forms of proprietary right, distinctly new,
were recognised and preserved. But indirectly Property has been affected in a thousand ways by equity,
both in England and at Rome. Into whatever corner
of jurisprudence its authors pushed the powerful instrument in their command, they were sure to meet,
and touch, and more or less materially modify the
law of property. When in the preceding pages I have

spoken of certain ancient legal distinctions and expedients as having powerfully affected the history of ownership, I must be understood to mean that the greatest part of their influence has arisen from the hints and suggestions of improvement infused by them into the mental atmosphere which was breathed by the fabricators of equitable systems.

But to describe the influence of Equity on Ownership would be to write its history down to our own days. I have alluded to it principally because several esteemed contemporary writers have thought that in the Roman severance of Equitable from Legal property we have the clue to that difference in the conception of Ownership, which apparently distinguishes the law of the middle ages from the law of the Roman Empire. The leading characteristic of the feudal conception is its recognition of a double proprietorship, the superior ownership of the lord of the fief coexisting with the inferior property or estate of the tenant. Now, this duplication of proprietary right looks, it is urged, extremely like a generalised form of the Roman distribution of rights over property into *Quiritarian* or legal, and (to use a word of late origin) *Bonitarian* or equitable. Gaius himself observes upon the splitting of *dominion* into two parts as a singularity of Roman law, and expressly contrasts it with the entire or allodial ownership to which other nations were accustomed. Justinian, it is true, reconsolidated dominion into one, but then it was the partially reformed system of the Western Empire, and not Justinian's jurisprudence, with which the barbarians were in contact during so many centuries. While they remained poised on the edge of the Empire, it may well be that they learned this distinction, which afterwards bore remarkable fruit. In favour of this theory, it must at all events be admitted that the element of Roman law in the various bodies of barbarian custom has been very imperfectly examined. The erroneous or insufficient theories which have served to explain Feudalism resemble each other in their tendency to draw off attention from this particular ingredient in its texture. The older investigators, who have been mostly followed in this country, attached an exclusive importance to the circumstances of the turbulent period during which the Feudal system grew to maturity; and in later times a new source of error has been added to those already existing, in that pride of nationality which has led German writers to exaggerate the completeness of the social fabric which their forefathers had built up before their appearance in the Roman world. One or two English inquirers who looked in the right quarter for the foundations of the feudal system, failed nevertheless to conduct their investigations to any satisfactory result, either from searching too exclusively for analogies in the compilations of Justinian, or from confining their attention to the compendia of Roman law which are found appended to some of the extant barbarian codes. But, if Roman jurisprudence had any influence on the barbarous societies, it had probably produced the greatest part of its effects before the legislation of Justinian, and before the preparation of these compendia. It was not the reformed and purified jurisprudence of Justinian, but the undigested system which prevailed in the Western Empire, and which the Eastern *Corpus Juris* never succeeded in displacing, that I conceive to have clothed with flesh and muscle the scanty skeleton of barbarous usage. The change must be supposed to have taken place before the Germanic tribes had distinctly appropriated, as conquerors, any portion of the Roman dominions, and therefore long before Germanic monarchs had ordered breviaries of Roman law to be drawn up for the use of their Roman subjects. The necessity for some such hypothesis will be felt by everybody who can appreciate the difference between archaic and developed law. Rude as are the *Leges Barbarorum* which remain to us, they are not rude enough to satisfy the theory of their purely barbarous origin; nor have we any reason for believing that we have received, in written records, more than a fraction of the fixed rules which were practised among themselves by the members of the conquering tribes. If we can once persuade

ourselves that a considerable element of debased
Roman law already existed in the barbarian systems,
we shall have done something to remove a grave
difficulty. The German law of the conquerors and
the Roman law of their subjects would not have combined if they had not possessed more affinity for each
other than refined jurisprudence has usually for the
customs of savages. It is extremely likely that the
codes of the barbarians, archaic as they seem, are
only a compound of true primitive usage with half-
understood Roman rules, and that it was the foreign
ingredient which enabled them to coalesce with a
Roman jurisprudence that had already receded
somewhat from the comparative finish which it
had acquired under the Western Emperors.

But, though all this must be allowed, there are
several considerations which render it unlikely that
the feudal form of ownership was directly suggested
by the Roman duplication of domainial rights. The
distinction between legal and equitable property
strikes one as a subtlety little likely to be appreciated by barbarians; and, moreover, it can scarcely
be understood unless Courts of Law are contemplated in regular operation. But the strongest reason
against this theory is the existence in Roman law of
a form of property—a creation of Equity, it is true
—which supplies a much simpler explanation of the
transition from one set of ideas to the other. This

is the Emphyteusis, upon which the Fief of the middle ages has often been fathered, though without much knowledge of the exact share which it had in bringing feudal ownership into the world. The truth is that the Emphyteusis, not probably as yet known by its Greek designation, marks one stage in a current of ideas which led ultimately to feudalism. The first mention in Roman history of estates larger than could be farmed by a Paterfamilias, with his household of sons and slaves, occurs when we come to the holdings of the Roman patricians. These great proprietors appear to have had no idea of any system of farming by free tenants. Their *latifundia* seem to have been universally cultivated by slave-gangs, under bailiffs who were themselves slaves or freedmen ; and the only organisation attempted appears to have consisted in dividing the inferior slaves into small bodies, and making them the *peculium* of the better and trustier sort, who thus acquired a kind of interest in the efficiency of their labour. This system was, however, especially disadvantageous to one class of estated proprietors, the Municipalities. Functionaries in Italy were changed with the rapidity which often surprises us in the administration of Rome herself; so that the superintendence of a large landed domain by an Italian corporation must have been excessively imperfect. Accordingly, we are told that with the municipalities began the practice

feudal structure, they continued in many countries to render to the landlord precisely the same dues which they had paid to the Roman *dominus*, and from a particular class among them, the *coloni medietarii*, who reserved half the produce for the owner, are descended the *metayer* tenantry, who still conduct the cultivation of the soil in almost all the South of Europe. On the other hand, the Emphyteusis, if we may so interpret the allusions to it in the *Corpus Juris*, became a favourite and beneficial modification of property; and it may be conjectured that wherever free farmers existed, it was this tenure which regulated their interest in the land. The Prætor, as has been said, treated the Emphyteuta as a true proprietor. When ejected, he was allowed to reinstate himself by a Real Action, the distinctive badge of proprietary right, and he was protected from disturbance by the author of his lease so long as the *canon*, or quit-rent, was punctually paid. But at the same time it must not be supposed that the ownership of the author of the lease was either extinct or dormant. It was kept alive by a power of re-entry on non-payment of the rent, a right of pre-emption in case of sale, and a certain control over the mode of cultivation. We have, therefore, in the Emphyteusis a striking example of the double ownership which characterised feudal property, and one, moreover, which is much simpler and much more easily imitated than the juxtaposition of legal and equitable rights. The history of the Roman tenure does not end, however, at this point. We have clear evidence that between the great fortresses which, disposed along the line of the Rhine and Danube, long secured the frontier of the Empire against its barbarian neighbours, there extended a succession of strips of land, the *agri limitrophi*, which were occupied by veteran soldiers of the Roman army on the terms of an Emphyteusis. There was a double ownership. The Roman State was landlord of the soil, but the soldiers cultivated it without disturbance so long as they held themselves ready to be called out for military service whenever the state of the border should require it. In fact, a sort of garrison-duty, under a system closely resembling that of the military colonies on the Austro-Turkish border, had taken the place of the quit-rent which was the service of the ordinary Emphyteuta. It seems impossible to doubt that this was the precedent copied by the barbarian monarchs who founded feudalism. It had been within their view for some hundred years, and many of the veterans who guarded the border were, it is to be remembered, themselves of barbarian extraction, who probably spoke the Germanic tongues. Not only does the proximity of so easily followed a model explain whence the Frankish and Lombard Sovereigns got the idea of securing the military service of their followers

by granting away portions of their public domain;
but it perhaps explains the tendency which immediately showed itself in the Benefices to become hereditary, for an Emphyteusis, though capable of being
moulded to the terms of the original contract, nevertheless descended as a general rule to the heirs of the
grantee.   It is true that the holder of a benefice, and
more recently the lord of one of those fiefs into which
the benefices were transformed, appears to have owed
certain services which were not likely to have been
rendered by the military colonist, and were certainly
not rendered by the Emphyteuta.. The   duty   of
respect and gratitude to the feudal superior, the
obligation to assist in endowing his daughter and
equipping his son, the liability to his guardianship
in minority, and many other similar incidents of
tenure, must have been literally borrowed from the
relations of Patron and Freedman under Roman law,
that is, of quondam-master and quondam-slave.   But
then it is known that the earliest beneficiaries were
the personal companions of the sovereign, and it is
indisputable that this position, brilliant as it seems,
was at first attended by some shade of servile debasement.   The person who ministered to the Sovereign
in his Court had given up something of that absolute
personal freedom which was the proudest privilege of
the allodial proprietor.

CHAPTER IX.

THE EARLY HISTORY OF CONTRACT.

THERE are few general propositions concerning the age to which we belong which seem at first sight likely to be received with readier concurrence than the assertion that the society of our day is mainly distinguished from that of preceding generations by the largeness of the sphere which is occupied in it by Contract. Some of the phenomena on which this proposition rests are among those most frequently singled out for notice, for comment, and for eulogy. Not many of us are so unobservant as not to perceive that in innumerable cases where old law fixed a man's social position irreversibly at his birth, modern law allows him to create it for himself by convention; and indeed several of the few exceptions which remain to this rule are constantly denounced with passionate indignation. The point, for instance, which is really debated in the vigorous controversy still carried on upon the subject of negro servitude, is whether the status of the slave does not belong to by-gone institutions, and whether the only relation between employer and labourer which commends

itself to modern morality be not a relation determined exclusively by contract.   The recognition of
this difference between past ages and the present
enters into the very essence of the most famous
contemporary speculations.   It is certain that the
science of Political Economy, the only department
of moral inquiry which has made any considerable
progress in our day, would fail to correspond with
the facts of life if it were not true that Imperative
Law had abandoned the largest part of the field
which it once occupied, and had left men to settle
rules of conduct for themselves with a liberty never
allowed to them till recently.   The bias indeed of most
persons trained in political economy is to consider
the general truth on which their science reposes as
entitled to become universal, and, when they apply
it as an art, their efforts are ordinarily directed to
enlarging the province of Contract and to curtailing
that of Imperative Law, except so far as law is
necessary to enforce the performance of Contracts.
The impulse given by thinkers who are under the
influence of these ideas is beginning to be very
strongly felt in the Western world.   Legislation has
nearly confessed its inability to keep pace with the
activity of man in discovery, in invention, and in the
manipulation of accumulated wealth; and the law
even of the least advanced communities tends more
and more to become a mere surface-stratum, having

under it an ever-changing assemblage of contractual rules with which it rarely interferes except to compel compliance with a few fundamental principles, or unless it be called in to punish the violation of good faith.

Social inquiries, so far as they depend on the consideration of legal phenomena, are in so backward a condition that we need not be surprised at not finding these truths recognised in the commonplaces which pass current concerning the progress of society. These commonplaces answer much more to our prejudices than to our convictions. The strong disinclination of most men to regard morality as advancing seems to be especially powerful when the virtues on which Contract depends are in question, and many of us have an almost instinctive reluctance to admitting that good faith and trust in our fellows are more widely diffused than of old, or that there is anything in contemporary manners which parallels the loyalty of the antique world. From time to time, these prepossessions are greatly strengthened by the spectacle of frauds, unheard of before the period at which they were observed, and astonishing from their complication as well as shocking from criminality. But the very character of these frauds shows clearly that, before they became possible, the moral obligations of which they are the breach must have been more than proportionately developed. It is the confidence reposed and deserved by the many which affords facilities for the bad faith of the few, so that, if colossal examples of dishonesty occur, there is no surer conclusion than that scrupulous honesty is displayed in the average of the transactions which, in the particular case, have supplied the delinquent with his opportunity. If we insist on reading the history of morality as reflected in jurisprudence, by turning our eyes not on the law of Contract but on the law of Crime, we must be careful that we read it aright. The only form of dishonesty treated of in the most ancient Roman law is Theft. At the moment at which I write, the newest chapter in the English criminal law is one which attempts to prescribe punishment for the frauds of Trustees. The proper inference from this contrast is not that the primitive Romans practised a higher morality than ourselves. We should rather say that, in the interval between their days and ours, morality has advanced from a very rude to a highly refined conception — from viewing the rights of property as exclusively sacred, to looking upon the rights growing out of the mere unilateral reposal of confidence as entitled to the protection of the penal law.

The definite theories of jurists are scarcely nearer the truth in this point than the opinions of the multitude. To begin with the views of the Roman lawyers, we find them inconsistent with the true history of moral and legal progress. One class of contracts, in which the plighted faith of the contracting parties was the only material ingredient, they specifically denominated Contracts *juris gentium*, and though these contracts were undoubtedly the latest born into the Roman system, the expression employed implies, if a definite meaning be extracted from it, that they were more ancient than certain other forms of engagement treated of in Roman law, in which the neglect of a mere technical formality was as fatal to the obligation as misunderstanding or deceit.   But then the antiquity to which they were referred was vague, shadowy, and only capable of being understood through the Present ; nor was it until the language of the Roman lawyers became the language of an age which had lost the key to their mode of thought that a "Contract of the Law of Nations" came to be distinctly looked upon as a Contract known to man in a state of Nature. Rousseau adopted both the juridical and the popular error.   In the Dissertation on the effects of Art and Science upon Morals, the first of his works which attracted attention and the one in which he states most unreservedly the opinions which made him the founder of a sect, the veracity and good faith attributed to the ancient Persians are repeatedly pointed out as traits of primitive innocence which have been gradually

obliterated by civilisation; and at a later period
he found a basis for all his speculations in the
doctrine of an original Social Contract. The Social Contract or Compact is the most systematic
form which has ever been assumed by the error
we are discussing. It is a theory which, though
nursed into importance by political passions, derived all its sap from the speculations of lawyers.
True it certainly is that the famous Englishmen, for
whom it had first had attraction, valued it chiefly
for its political serviceableness, but, as I shall presently attempt to explain, they would never have
arrived at it, if politicians had not long conducted
their controversies in legal phraseology. Nor were
the English authors of the theory blind to that
speculative amplitude which recommended it so
strongly to the Frenchmen who inherited it from
them. Their writings show they perceived that it
could be made to account for all social, quite as well
as for all political phenomena. They had observed
the fact, already striking in their day, that of the
positive rules obeyed by men, the greater part were
created by Contract, the lesser by Imperative Law.
But they were ignorant or careless of the historical
relation of these two constituents of jurisprudence.
It was for the purpose, therefore, of gratifying their
speculative tastes by attributing all jurisprudence
to a uniform source, as much as with the view of

eluding the doctrines which claimed a divine parentage for Imperative Law, that they devised the theory that all Law had its origin in Contract.   In another stage of thought, they would have been satisfied to leave their theory in the condition of an ingenious hypothesis or a convenient verbal formula.   But that age was under the dominion of legal superstitions. The State of Nature had been talked about till it had ceased to be regarded as paradoxical, and hence it seemed easy to give a fallacious reality and definiteness to the contractual origin of Law by insisting on the Social Compact as a historical fact.

Our own generation has got rid of these erroneous juridical theories, partly by outgrowing the intellectual state to which they belong, and partly by almost ceasing to theorise on such subjects altogether. The favourite occupation of active minds at the present moment, and the one which answers to the speculations of our forefathers on the origin of the social state, is the analysis of society as it exists and moves before our eyes; but, through omitting to call in the assistance of history, this analysis too often degenerates into an idle exercise of curiosity, and is especially apt to incapacitate the inquirer for comprehending states of society which differ considerably from that to which he is accustomed.   The mistake of judging the men of other periods by the morality of our own day has its parallel in the mistake of supposing that every wheel and bolt in the modern social machine had its counterpart in more rudimentary societies. Such impressions ramify very widely, and masque themselves very subtly, in historical works written in the modern fashion; but I find the trace of their presence in the domain of jurisprudence in the praise which is frequently bestowed on the little apologue of Montesquieu concerning the Troglodytes, inserted in the *Lettres Persanes*. The Troglodytes were a people who systematically violated their Contracts, and so perished utterly. If the story bears the moral which its author intended, and is employed to expose an anti-social heresy by which this century and the last have been threatened, it is most unexceptionable; but if the inference be obtained from it that society could not possibly hold together without attaching a sacredness to promises and agreements which should be on something like a par with the respect that is paid to them by a mature civilisation, it involves an error so grave as to be fatal to all sound understanding of legal history. The fact is that the Troglodytes have flourished and founded powerful states with very small attention to the obligations of Contract. The point which before all others has to be apprehended in the constitution of primitive societies is that the individual creates for himself few or no rights, and few or no duties. The rules which he obeys are derived first from the

station into which he is born, and next from the imperative commands addressed to him by the chief of
the household of which he forms part.   Such a system leaves the very smallest room for Contract.   The
members of the same family (for so we may interpret
the evidence) are wholly incapable of contracting
with each other, and the family is entitled to disregard the engagements by which any one of its subordinate members has attempted to bind it.   Family, it
is true, may contract with family, chieftain with
chieftain, but the transaction is one of the same nature, and encumbered by as many formalities, as the
alienation of property, and the disregard of one iota
of the performance is fatal to the obligation.   The
positive duty resulting from one man's reliance on
the word of another is among the slowest conquests
of advancing civilisation.

Neither Ancient Law nor any other source of evidence discloses to us society entirely destitute of the
conception of Contract.   But the conception, when
it first shows itself, is obviously rudimentary.   No
trustworthy primitive record can be read without
perceiving that the habit of mind which induces us
to make good a promise is as yet imperfectly developed, and that acts of flagrant perfidy are often
mentioned without blame and sometimes described
with approbation.   In the Homeric literature, for instance, the deceitful cunning of Ulysses appears as a

virtue of the same rank with the prudence of Nestor, the constancy of Hector, and the gallantry of Achilles. Ancient law is still more suggestive of the distance which separates the crude form of Contract from its maturity. At first, nothing is seen like the interposition of law to compel the performance of a promise. That which the law arms with its sanctions is not a promise, but a promise accompanied with a solemn ceremonial. Not only are the formalities of equal importance with the promise itself, but they are, if anything, of greater importance; for that delicate analysis which mature jurisprudence applies to the conditions of mind under which a particular verbal assent is given appears, in ancient law, to be transferred to the words and gestures of the accompanying performance. No pledge is enforced if a single form be omitted or misplaced, but, on the other hand, if the forms can be shown to have been accurately proceeded with, it is of no avail to plead that the promise was made under duress or deception. The transmutation of this ancient view into the familiar notion of a Contract is plainly seen in the history of jurisprudence. First one or two steps in the ceremonial are dispensed with; then the others are simplified or permitted to be neglected on certain conditions; lastly, a few specific contracts are separated from the rest and allowed to be entered into without form, the selected contracts being those on which the activity and energy of social intercourse depend. Slowly, but most distinctly, the mental engagement isolates itself amid the technicalities, and gradually becomes the sole ingredient on which the interest of the juris-consult is concentrated. Such a mental engagement, signified through external acts, the Romans called a Pact or Convention; and when the Convention has once been conceived as the nucleus of a Contract, it soon becomes the tendency of advancing jurisprudence to break away the external shell of form and ceremony. Forms are thenceforward only retained so far as they are guarantees of authenticity, and securities for caution and deliberation. The idea of a Contract is fully developed, or, to employ the Roman phrase, Contracts are absorbed in Pacts.

The history of this course of change in Roman law is exceedingly instructive. At the earliest dawn of the jurisprudence, the term in use for a Contract was one which is very familiar to the students of historical Latinity. It was *nexum*, and the parties to the contract were said to be *nexi*, expressions which must be carefully attended to on account of the singular durableness of the metaphor on which they are founded. The notion that persons under a contractual engagement are connected together by a strong *bond* or *chain*, continued till the last to influence the Roman jurisprudence of Contract; and flowing thence it has mixed itself with modern ideas. What then was involved in this nexum or bond? A definition which has descended to us from one of the Latin antiquarians describes *nexum* as *omne quod geritur per æs et libram*, " every transaction with the copper and the balance," and these words have occasioned a good deal of perplexity. The copper and the balance are the well-known accompaniments of the Mancipation, the ancient solemnity described in a former chapter, by which the right of ownership in the highest form of Roman Property was transferred from one person to another. Mancipation was a *conveyance*, and hence has arisen the difficulty, for the definition thus cited appears to confound Contracts and Conveyances, which in the philosophy of jurisprudence are not simply kept apart, but are actually opposed to each other. The *jus in re*, right *in rem*, right " availing against all the world," or Proprietary Right, is sharply distinguished by the analyst of mature jurisprudence from the *jus ad rem*, right *in personam*, right " availing against a single individual or group," or Obligation. Now Conveyances transfer Proprietary Rights, Contracts create Obligations—how then can the two be included under the same name or same general conception? This, like many similar embarrassments, has been occasioned by the error of ascribing to the mental condition of an unformed society a faculty which pre-eminently belongs to an advanced stage of intellectual development, the faculty of distinguishing in speculation ideas which are blended in practice. We have indications not to be mistaken of a state of social affairs in which Conveyances and Contracts were practically confounded; nor did the discrepance of the conceptions become perceptible till men had begun to adopt a distinct practice in contracting and conveying.

It may here be observed that we know enough of ancient Roman law to give some idea of the mode of transformation followed by legal conceptions and by legal phraseology in the infancy of Jurisprudence. The change which they undergo appears to be a change from general to special; or, as we might otherwise express it, the ancient conceptions and the ancient terms are subjected to a process of gradual specialisation. An ancient legal conception corresponds not to one but to several modern conceptions. An ancient technical expression serves to indicate a variety of things which in modern law have separate names allotted to them. If, however, we take up the history of Jurisprudence at the next stage, we find that the subordinate conceptions have gradually disengaged themselves, and that the old general names are giving way to special appellations. The old general conception is not obliterated, but it has ceased to cover more than one or a few of the notions which it first included. So too the old technical name remains, but it discharges only one of the functions which it once performed. We may exemplify this phenomenon in various ways. Patriarchal Power of all sorts appears, for instance, to have been once conceived as identical in character, and it was doubtless distinguished by one name. The Power exercised by the ancestor was the same whether it was exercised over the family or the material property—over flocks, herds, slaves, children, or wife. We cannot be absolutely certain of its old Roman name, but there is very strong reason for believing, from the number of expressions indicating shades of the notion of *power* into which the word *manus* enters, that the ancient general term was *manus*. But, when Roman law has advanced a little, both the name and the idea have become specialised. Power is discriminated, both in word and in conception, according to the object over which it is exerted. Exercised over material commodities or slaves, it has become *dominium*—over children it is *Potestas*—over free persons whose services have been made away to another by their own ancestor, it is *mancipium*—over a wife, it is still *manus*. The old word, it will be perceived, has not altogether fallen into desuetude, but is confined to one very special exercise of the authority it had formerly denoted. This example will enable us to comprehend the nature of the historical alliance between Contracts and Conveyances. There seems to have

been one solemn ceremonial at first for all solemn
transactions, and its name at Rome appears to have
been *nexum*.   Precisely the same forms which were
in use when a conveyance of property was effected
seem to have been employed in the making of a contract.   But we have not very far to move onwards
before we come to a period at which the notion of a
Contract has disengaged itself from the notion of a
Conveyance.   A double change has thus taken place.
The transaction " with the copper and the balance,"
when intended to have for its office the transfer of
property, is known by the new and special name of
Mancipation.   The ancient Nexum still designates
the same ceremony, but only when it is employed for
the special purpose of solemnising a contract.

When two or three legal conceptions are spoken of
as anciently blended in one, it is not intended to
imply that some one of the included notions may
not be older than the others, or, when those others
have been formed, may not greatly predominate over
and take precedence over them.   The reason why
one legal conception continues so long to cover
several conceptions, and one technical phrase to do
instead of several, is doubtless that practical changes
are accomplished in the law of primitive societies
long before men see occasion to notice or name them.
Though I have said that Patriarchal Power was not
at first distinguished according to the objects over

which it was exercised, I feel sure that Power over Children was the root of the old conception of Power; and I cannot doubt that the earliest use of the Nexum, and the one primarily regarded by those who resorted to it, was to give proper solemnity to the alienation of property.   It is likely that a very slight perversion of the Nexum from its original functions first gave rise to its employment in Contracts, and that the very slightness of the change long prevented its being appreciated or noticed.   The old name remained because men had not become conscious that they wanted a new one; the old notion clung to the mind because nobody had seen reason to be at the pains of examining it.   We have had the process clearly exemplified in the history of Testaments.   A Will was at first a simple conveyance of Property.   It was only the enormous practical difference that gradually showed itself between this particular conveyance and all others which caused it to be regarded separately, and even as it was, centuries elapsed before the ameliorators of law cleared away the useless encumbrance of the nominal mancipation, and consented to care for nothing in the Will but the expressed intentions of the Testator.   It is unfortunate that we cannot track the early history of Contracts with the same absolute confidence as the early history of Wills, but we are not quite without hints that contracts first showed themselves through

right of property was transmitted, and the personal obligation of the debtor for the unpaid purchase-money. We may still go forward, and picture to ourselves a proceeding wholly formal, in which *nothing* is handed over and *nothing* paid; we are brought at once to a transaction indicative of much higher commercial activity, an *executory Contract of Sale*.

If it be true that, both in the popular and in the professional view, a *Contract* was long regarded as an *incomplete Conveyance*, the truth has importance for many reasons. The speculations of the last century concerning mankind in a state of nature, are not unfairly summed up in the doctrine that " in the primitive society property was nothing, and obligation everything;" and it will now be seen that, if the proposition were reversed, it would be nearer the reality. On the other hand, considered historically, the primitive association of Conveyances and Contracts explains something which often strikes the scholar and jurist as singularly enigmatical, I mean the extraordinary and uniform severity of very ancient systems of law to *debtors*, and the extravagant powers which they lodge with *creditors*. When once we understand that the *nexum* was artificially prolonged to give time to the debtor, we can better comprehend his position in the eye of the public and of the law. His indebtedness was doubtless regarded as an anomaly, and suspense of payment in general as an artifice and a distortion of strict rule. The person who had duly consummated his part in the transaction must, on the contrary, have stood in peculiar favour ; and nothing would seem more natural than to arm him with stringent facilities for enforcing the completion of a proceeding which, of strict right, ought never to have been extended or deferred.

Nexum, therefore, which originally signified a Conveyance of property, came insensibly to denote a Contract also, and ultimately so constant became the association between this word and the notion of a Contract, that a special term, Mancipium or Mancipatio, had to be used for the purpose of designating the true nexum or transaction in which the property was really transferred. Contracts are therefore now severed from Conveyances, and the first stage in their history is accomplished, but still they are far enough from that epoch of their development when the promise of the contractor has a higher sacredness than the formalities with which it is coupled. In attempting to indicate the character of the changes passed through in this interval, it is necessary to trespass a little on a subject which lies properly beyond the range of these pages, the analysis of Agreement effected by the Roman jurisconsults. Of this analysis, the most beautiful monument of their sagacity, I need not say more than that it is based on the theoretical separation of the Obligation from the

Convention or Pact.   Bentham and Mr. Austin have
laid down that the " two main essentials of a contract
are these : first, a signification by the promising
party of his *intention* to do the acts or to observe the
forbearances which he promises to do or to observe.
Secondly, a signification by the promisee that he
expects the promising party will fulfil the proferred
promise." This is virtually identical with the doctrine
of the Roman lawyers, but then, in their view, the
result of these " significations" was not a Contract,
but a Convention or Pact.   A Pact was the utmost
product of the engagements of individuals agreeing
among themselves, and it distinctly fell short of a
Contract.   Whether it ultimately became a Contract
depended on the question whether the law annexed
an Obligation to it.   A Contract was a Pact (or Convention) *plus* an Obligation.   So long as the Pact
remained unclothed with the Obligation, it was called
nude or *naked.*

What was an Obligation ?   It is defined by the
Roman lawyers as " Juris vinculum, quo necessitate
adstringimur alicujus solvendæ rei."   This definition
connects the Obligation with the Nexum through the
common metaphor on which they are founded, and
shows us with much clearness the pedigree of a peculiar conception.   The Obligation is the " bond " or
" chain," with which the law joins together persons or groups of persons, in consequence of certain

voluntary acts. The acts which have the effect of attracting an Obligation are chiefly those classed under the heads of Contract and Delict, of Agreement and Wrong; but a variety of other acts have a similar consequence which are not capable of being comprised in an exact classification. It is to be remarked, however, that the Pact does not draw to itself the Obligation in consequence of any moral necessity; it is the law which annexes it in the plenitude of its power, a point the more necessary to be noted, because a different doctrine has sometimes been propounded by modern interpreters of the Civil Law who had moral or metaphysical theories of their own to support. The image of a *vinculum juris* colours and pervades every part of the Roman law of Contract and Delict. The law bound the parties together, and the *chain* could only be undone by the process called *solutio*, an expression still figurative, to which our word "payment" is only occasionally and incidentally equivalent. The consistency with which the figurative image was allowed to present itself, explains an otherwise puzzling peculiarity of Roman legal phraseology, the fact that "Obligation" signifies rights as well as duties, the right, for example, to have a debt paid as well as the duty of paying it. The Romans kept, in fact, the entire picture of the "legal chain" before their eyes, and regarded one end of it no more and no less than the other.

In the developed Roman law, the Convention, as soon as it was completed, was, in almost all cases, at once crowned with the Obligation, and so became a Contract; and this was the result to which contract-law was surely tending. But for the purpose of this inquiry, we must attend particularly to the intermediate stage—that in which something more than a perfect agreement was required to attract the Obligation. This epoch is synchronous with the period at which the famous Roman classification of Contracts into four sorts—the Verbal, the Literal, the Real, and the Consensual—had come into use, and during which these four orders of Contract constituted the only descriptions of engagement which the law would enforce. The meaning of the fourfold distribution is readily understood as soon as we apprehend the theory which severed the Obligation from the Convention. Each class of contracts was in fact named from certain formalities which were required over and above the mere agreement of the contracting parties. In the Verbal Contract, as soon as the Convention was effected, a form of words had to be gone through before the vinculum juris was attached to it. In the Literal Contract, an entry in a ledger or table-book had the effect of clothing the Convention with the Obligation, and the same result followed, in the case of the Real Contract, from the delivery of the Res or Thing which was the subject of the preliminary engagement.   The Contracting parties came, in short, to an understanding in each case; but, if they went no further, they were not *obliged* to one another, and could not compel performance or ask redress for a breach of faith.   But let them comply with certain prescribed formalities, and the Contract was immediately complete, taking its name from the particular form which it had suited them to adopt.   The exceptions to this practice will be noticed presently.

I have enumerated the four Contracts in their historical order, which order, however, the Roman Institutional writers did not invariably follow.   There can be no doubt that the Verbal Contract was the most ancient of the four, and that it is the eldest known descendant of the primitive Nexum.   Several species of Verbal Contract were anciently in use, but the most important of all, and the only one treated of by our authorities, was effected by means of a *stipulation*, that is, a Question and Answer; a question addressed by the person who exacted the promise, and an answer given by the person who made it.   This question and answer constituted the additional ingredient which, as I have just explained, was demanded by the primitive notion over and above the mere agreement of the persons interested.   They formed the agency by which the Obligation was annexed. The old Nexum has now bequeathed to maturer jurisprudence first of all the conception of a chain uniting the contracting parties, and this has become the Obligation. It has further transmitted the notion of a ceremonial accompanying and consecrating the engagement, and this ceremonial has been transmuted into the Stipulation. The conversion of the solemn conveyance, which was the prominent feature of the original Nexum, into a mere question and answer, would be more of a mystery than it is if we had not the analogous history of Roman Testaments to enlighten us. Looking at that history, we can understand how the formal conveyance was first separated from the part of the proceeding which had immediate reference to the business in hand, and how afterwards it was omitted altogether. As then the question and answer of the Stipulation were unquestionably the Nexum in a simplified shape, we are prepared to find that they long partook of the nature of a technical form. It would be a mistake to consider them as exclusively recommending themselves to the older Roman lawyers through their usefulness in furnishing persons meditating an agreement with an opportunity for consideration and reflection. It is not to be disputed that they had a value of this kind, which was gradually recognised; but there is proof that their function in respect to Contracts was at first formal and ceremonial in the statement of our authorities, that not every question and answer was of old sufficient to constitute a Stipulation, but only a question and answer couched in technical phraseology specially appropriated to the particular occasion.

But although it is essential for the proper appreciation of the history of contract-law that the Stipulation should be understood to have been looked upon as a solemn form before it was recognised as a useful security, it would be wrong on the other hand to shut our eyes to its real usefulness. The Verbal Contract, though it had lost much of its ancient importance, survived to the latest period of Roman jurisprudence; and we may take it for granted that no institution of Roman law had so extended a longevity unless it served some practical advantage. I observe in an English writer some expressions of surprise that the Romans even of the earliest times were content with so meagre a protection against haste and irreflection. But on examining the Stipulation closely, and remembering that we have to do with a state of society in which written evidence was not easily procurable, I think we must admit that this Question and Answer, had it been expressly devised to answer the purpose which it served, would have been justly designated a highly ingenious expedient. It was the *promisee* who, in the character of stipulator, put all the terms of the contract into the form of a question, and the answer was given by the *promisor*. " Do you promise that you will deliver me such and such a slave, at such and such a place, on such and such a

day?"   "I do promise."   Now, if we reflect for a
moment, we shall see that this obligation to put the
promise interrogatively inverts the natural position
of the parties, and, by effectually breaking the tenor
of the conversation, prevents the attention from
gliding over a dangerous pledge.   With us, a verbal
promise is, generally speaking, to be gathered exclusively from the words of the promisor.   In old Roman
law, another step was absolutely required; it was
necessary for the promisee, after the agreement had
been made, to sum up all its terms in a solemn interrogation; and it was of this interrogation, of course,
and of the assent to it, that proof had to be given at
the trial—*not* of the promise, which was not in itself
binding.   How great a difference this seemingly insignificant peculiarity may make in the phraseology
of contract-law is speedily realised by the beginner in
Roman jurisprudence, one of whose first stumbling-
blocks is almost universally created by it.   When we
in English have occasion, in mentioning a contract,
to connect it for convenience' sake with one of the
parties,—for example, if we wished to speak generally
of a contractor,—it is always the promis*or* at whom
our words are pointing.   But the general language of
Roman law takes a different turn; it always regards
the contract, if we may so speak, from the point of
view of the promis*ee*; in speaking of a party to a
contract, it is always the Stipulator, the person who

asks the question, who is primarily alluded to. But
the serviceableness of the stipulation is most vividly
illustrated by referring to the actual examples in the
pages of the Latin comic dramatists. If the entire
scenes are read down in which these passages occur
(ex. gra. Plautus, *Pseudolus*, Act I. sc. 1; Act IV.
sc. 6; *Trinummus*, Act V. sc. 2), it will be perceived
how effectually the attention of the person meditating
the promise must have been arrested by the question,
and how ample was the opportunity for withdrawal
from an improvident undertaking.

In the Literal or Written Contract, the formal act
by which an Obligation was superinduced on the Convention, was an entry of the sum due, where it could
be specifically ascertained, on the debit side of a
ledger. The explanation of this contract turns on a
point of Roman domestic manners, the systematic
character and exceeding regularity of book-keeping
in ancient times. There are several minor difficulties
of old Roman law, as, for example, the nature of the
Slave's Peculium, which are only cleared up when we
recollect that a Roman household consisted of a number of persons strictly accountable to its head, and
that every single item of domestic receipt and expen-
diture, after being entered in waste books, was transferred at stated periods to a general household ledger.
There are some obscurities, however, in the descriptions we have received of the Literal Contract, the

fact being that the habit of keeping books ceased to
be universal in later times, and the expression
" Literal Contract " came to signify a form of engagement entirely different from that originally understood.   We are not, therefore, in a position to say,
with respect to the primitive Literal Contract, whether
the obligation was created by a simple entry on the
part of the creditor, or whether the consent of the
debtor or a correspondent entry in his own books was
necessary to give it legal effect.   The essential point
is however established, that, in the case of this
Contract, all formalities were dispensed with on a
condition being complied with.   This is another step
downwards in the history of contract-law.

The Contract which stands next in historical succession, the Real Contract, shows a great advance in
ethical conceptions.   Whenever any agreement had
for its object the delivery of a specific thing—and this
is the case with the large majority of simple engagements—the Obligation was drawn down as soon as
the delivery had actually taken place.   Such a result
must have involved a serious innovation on the oldest
ideas of Contract; for doubtless, in the primitive times,
when a contracting party had neglected to clothe his
agreement in a stipulation, nothing done in pursuance
of the agreement would be recognised by the law.
A person who had paid over money on loan would
be unable to sue for its repayment unless he had

formally *stipulated* for it. But, in the Real Contract, performance on one side is allowed to impose a legal duty on the other—evidently on ethical grounds. For the first time then moral considerations appear as an ingredient in Contract-law, and the Real Contract differs from its two predecessors in being founded on these, rather than on respect for technical forms or on deference to Roman domestic habits.

We now reach the fourth class, or Consensual Contracts, the most interesting and important of all. Four specified Contracts were distinguished by this name: Mandatum, *i.e.* Commission or Agency; Societas or Partnership; Emtio Venditio or Sale; and Locatio Conductio or Letting and Hiring. A few pages back, after stating that a Contract consisted of a Pact or Convention to which an Obligation had been superadded, I spoke of certain acts or formalities by which the law permitted the Obligation to be attracted to the Pact. I used this language on account of the advantage of a general expression, but it is not strictly correct unless it be understood to include the negative as well as the positive. For, in truth, the peculiarity of these Consensual Contracts is that *no* formalities are required to create them out of the Pact. Much that is indefensible, and much more that is obscure, has been written about the Consensual Contracts, and it has even been asserted that in them the *consent* of the Parties is more emphatically given than in any other species of agreement. But the term Consensual merely indicates that the Obligation is here annexed at once to the *Consensus*. The Consensus, or mutual assent of the parties, is the final and crowning ingredient in the Convention, and it is the special characteristic of agreements falling under one of the four heads of Sale, Partnership, Agency, and Hiring, that, as soon as the assent of the parties has supplied this ingredient, there is *at once* a Contract. The Consensus draws with it the Obligation, performing, in transactions of the sort specified, the exact functions which are discharged, in the other contracts, by the *Res* or Thing, by the *Verba* stipulationis, and by the *Literæ* or written entry in a ledger. Consensual is therefore a term which does not involve the slightest anomaly, but is exactly analogous to Real, Verbal, and Literal.

In the intercourse of life the commonest and most important of all the contracts are unquestionably the four styled Consensual. The larger part of the collective existence of every community is consumed in transactions of buying and selling, of letting and hiring, of alliances between men for purposes of business, of delegation of business from one man to another; and this is no doubt the consideration which led the Romans, as it has led most societies, to relieve these transactions from technical incumbrance, to abstain as much as possible from clogging the most efficient springs of social movement. Such motives were not of course confined to Rome, and the commerce of the Romans with their neighbours must have given them abundant opportunities for observing that the contracts before us tended everywhere to become *Consensual*, obligatory on the mere signification of mutual assent. Hence, following their usual practice, they distinguished these contracts as contracts *Juris Gentium*. Yet I do not think that they were so named at a very early period. The first notions of a Jus Gentium may have been deposited in the minds of the Roman lawyers long before the appointment of a Prætor Peregrinus, but it would only be through extensive and regular trade that they would be familiarised with the contractual system of other Italian communities, and such a trade would scarcely attain considerable proportions before Italy had been thoroughly pacified, and the supremacy of Rome conclusively assured. Although, however, there is strong probability that the Consensual Contracts were the latest-born into the Roman system, and though it is likely that the qualification, *Juris Gentium*, stamps the recency of their origin, yet this very expression, which attributes them to the " Law of Nations," has in modern times produced the notion of their extreme antiquity. For, when the " Law of Nations" had been converted into the " Law of

Nature," it seemed to be implied that the Consensual Contracts were the type of the agreements most congenial to the natural state; and hence arose the singular belief that the younger the civilisation, the simpler must be its forms of contract.

The Consensual Contracts, it will be observed, were extremely limited in number. But it cannot be doubted that they constituted the stage in the history of Contract-law from which all modern conceptions of contract took their start. The motion of the will which constitutes agreement was now completely insulated, and became the subject of separate contemplation; forms were entirely eliminated from the notion of contract, and external acts were only regarded as symbols of the internal act of volition. The Consensual Contracts had, moreover, been classed in the Jus Gentium, and it was not long before this classification drew with it the inference that they were the species of agreement which represented the engagements approved of by Nature and included in her code. This point once reached, we are prepared for several celebrated doctrines and distinctions of the Roman lawyers. One of them is the distinction between Natural and Civil Obligations. When a person of full intellectual maturity had deliberately bound himself by an engagement, he was said to be under a *natural obligation*, even though he had omitted some necessary formality, and even though

through some technical impediment he was devoid
of the formal capacity for making a valid contract.
The law (and this is what the distinction implies)
would not enforce the obligation, but it did not
absolutely refuse to recognise it ; and *natural obligations* differed in many respects from obligations
which were merely null and void, more particularly
in the circumstance that they could be civilly confirmed, if the capacity for contract were subsequently
acquired.   Another very peculiar doctrine of the
jurisconsults could not have had its origin earlier than
the period at which the Convention was severed from
the technical ingredients of Contract.   They taught
that though nothing but a Contract could be the
foundation of an *action*, a mere Pact or Convention
could be the basis of a *plea*.   It followed from this,
that though nobody could sue upon an agreement
which he had not taken the precaution to mature into
a Contract by complying with the proper forms, nevertheless a claim arising out of a valid contract could
be rebutted by proving a counter-agreement which
had never got beyond the state of a simple convention.   An action for the recovery of a debt could be
met by showing a mere informal agreement to waive
or postpone the payment.

The doctrine just stated indicates the hesitation of
the Prætors in making their advances towards the
greatest of their innovations.   Their theory of Natural

law must have led them to look with especial favour on the Consensual Contracts and on those Pacts or Conventions of which the Consensual Contracts were only particular instances; but they did not at once venture on extending to all Conventions the liberty of the Consensual Contracts. They took advantage of that special superintendence over procedure which had been confided to them since the first beginnings of Roman law, and, while they still declined to permit a suit to be launched which was not based on a formal contract, they gave full play to their new theory of agreement in directing the ulterior stages of the proceeding. But, when they had proceeded thus far, it was inevitable that they should proceed farther. The revolution of the ancient law of Contract was consummated when the Prætor of some one year announced in his Edict that he would grant equitable actions upon Pacts which had never been matured at all into Contracts, provided only that the Pacts in question had been founded on a consideration (*causa*). Pacts of this sort are always enforced under the advanced Roman jurisprudence. The principle is merely the principle of the Consensual Contract carried to its proper consequence; and, in fact, if the technical language of the Romans had been as plastic as their legal theories, these Pacts enforced by the Prætor would have been styled new Contracts, new Consensual Contracts. Legal phraseology is, how-

ever, the part of the law which is the last to alter,
and the Pacts equitably enforced continued to be
designated simply Prætorian Pacts.   It will be remarked that unless there were consideration for the
Pact, it would continue *nude* so far as the new jurisprudence was concerned; in order to give it effect,
it would be necessary to convert it by a stipulation
into a Verbal Contract.

The extreme importance of this history of Contract, as a safeguard against almost innumerable
delusions, must be my justification for discussing it
at so considerable a length.   It gives a complete
account of the march of ideas from one great land-
mark of jurisprudence to another.   We begin with
the Nexum, in which a Contract and a Conveyance
are blended, and in which the formalities which ac-
company the agreement are even more important
than the agreement itself.   From the Nexum we pass
to the Stipulation, which is a simplified form of the
older ceremonial.   The Literal Contract comes next,
and here all formalities are waived, if proof of the
agreement can be supplied from the rigid observances
of a Roman household.   In the Real Contract a
moral duty is for the first time recognised, and
persons who have joined or acquiesced in the partial
performance of an engagement are forbidden to
repudiate it on account of defects in form.   Lastly,
the Consensual Contracts emerge, in which the

mental attitude of the contractors is solely regarded, and external circumstances have no title to notice except as evidence of the inward undertaking.   It is of course uncertain how far this progress of Roman ideas from a gross to a refined conception exemplifies the necessary progress of human thought on the subject of Contract.   The Contract-law of all other ancient societies but the Roman is either too scanty to furnish information, or else is entirely lost; and modern jurisprudence is so thoroughly leavened with the Roman notions that it furnishes us with no contrasts or parallels from which instruction can be gleaned.   From the absence, however, of everything violent, marvellous, or unintelligible in the changes I have described, it may be reasonably believed that the history of Ancient Roman Contracts is, up to a certain point, typical of the history of this class of legal conceptions in other ancient societies.   But it is only up to a certain point that the progress of Roman law can be taken to represent the progress of other systems of jurisprudence.   The theory of Natural law is exclusively Roman.   The notion of the *vinculum juris*, so far as my knowledge extends, is exclusively Roman.   The many peculiarities of the mature Roman law of Contract and Delect which are traceable to these two ideas, whether singly or in combination, are therefore among the exclusive products of one particular society.   These later legal

conceptions are important, not because they typify
the necessary results of advancing thought under all
conditions, but because they have exercised perfectly
enormous influence on the intellectual diathesis of the
modern world.

I know nothing more wonderful than the variety
of sciences to which Roman law, Roman Contract-
law more particularly, has contributed modes of
thought, courses of reasoning, and a technical language.   Of the subjects which have whetted the
intellectual appetite of the moderns, there is scarcely
one, except Physics, which has not been filtered
through Roman jurisprudence.   The science of pure
Metaphysics had, indeed, rather a Greek than a Roman
parentage, but Politics, Moral Philosophy, and even
Theology, found in Roman law not only a vehicle of
expression, but a nidus in which some of their profoundest enquiries were nourished into maturity.   For
the purpose of accounting for this phenomenon, it is
not absolutely necessary to discuss the mysterious
relation between words and ideas, or to explain how
it is that the human mind has never grappled with
any subject of thought, unless it has been provided
beforehand with a proper store of language and with
an apparatus of appropriate logical methods.   It is
enough to remark, that, when the philosophical interests of the Eastern and Western worlds were separated, the founders of Western thought belonged to

a society which spoke Latin and reflected in Latin. But in the Western provinces the only language which retained sufficient precision for philosophical purposes was the language of Roman law, which by a singular fortune had preserved nearly all the purity of the Augustan age, while vernacular Latin was degenerating into a dialect of portentous barbarism. And if Roman jurisprudence supplied the only means of exactness in speech, still more emphatically did it furnish the only means of exactness, subtlety, or depth in thought. For at least three centuries, philosophy and science were without a home in the West ; and though metaphysics and metaphysical theology were engrossing the mental energies of multitudes of Roman subjects, the phraseology employed in these ardent enquiries was exclusively Greek, and their theatre was the Eastern half of the Empire. Sometimes, indeed, the conclusions of the Eastern disputants became so important that every man's assent to them, or dissent from them, had to be recorded, and then the West was introduced to the results of Eastern controversy, which it generally acquiesced in without interest and without resistance. Meanwhile, one department of enquiry, difficult enough for the most laborious, deep enough for the most subtile, delicate enough for the most refined, had never lost its attractions for the educated classes of the Western provinces.   To the cultivated citizen of Africa, of Spain, of Gaul, and of Northern Italy, it was jurisprudence, and jurisprudence only, which stood in the place of poetry and history, of philosophy and science. So far then from there being anything mysterious in the palpably legal complexion of the earliest efforts of Western thought, it would rather be astonishing if it had assumed any other hue. I can only express my surprise at the scantiness of the attention which has been given to the difference between Western ideas and Eastern, between Western theology and Eastern, caused by the presence of a new ingredient. It is precisely because the influence of jurisprudence begins to be powerful that the foundation of Constantinople and the subsequent separation of the Western empire from the Eastern, are epochs in philosophical history. But continental thinkers are doubtless less capable of appreciating the importance of this crisis by the very intimacy with which notions derived from Roman law are mingled up with their every-day ideas. Englishmen, on the other hand, are blind to it through the monstrous ignorance to which they condemn themselves of the most plentiful source of the stream of modern knowledge, of the one intellectual result of the Roman civilisation. At the same time, an Englishman who will be at the pains to familiarise himself with the classical Roman law, is perhaps, from the very slightness of the interest which his countrymen have hitherto taken in the subject, a better judge than a Frenchman or a German of the value of the assertions I have ventured to make. Anybody who knows what Roman jurisprudence is, as actually practised by the Romans, and who will observe in what characteristics the earliest Western theology and philosophy differ from the phases of thought which preceded them, may be safely left to pronounce what was the new element which had begun to pervade and govern speculation.

The part of Roman law which has had most extensive influence on foreign subjects of enquiry has been the law of Obligation, or, what comes nearly to the same thing, of Contract and Delict. The Romans themselves were not unaware of the offices which the copious and malleable terminology belonging to this part of their system might be made to discharge, and this is proved by their employment of the peculiar adjunct *quasi* in such expressions as Quasi-Contract and Quasi-Delict. " Quasi," so used, is exclusively a term of classification. It has been usual with English critics to identify the Quasi-contracts with *implied* contracts, but this is an error, for implied contracts are true contracts, which quasi-contracts are not. In implied contracts, acts and circumstances are the symbols of the same ingredients which are symbolised, in express contracts, by words; and whether a man employs one set of symbols or the other must be a matter of indifference so far as concerns the theory of agreement. But a Quasi-Contract is not a contract at all. The commonest sample of the class is the relation subsisting between two persons, one of whom has paid money to the other through mistake. The law, consulting the interests of morality, imposes an obligation on the receiver to refund, but the very nature of the transaction indicates that it is not a contract, inasmuch as the Convention, the most essential ingredient of Contract, is wanting. This word "quasi," prefixed to a term of Roman law, implies that the conception to which it serves as an index is connected with the conception with which the comparison is instituted by a strong superficial analogy or resemblance. It does not denote that the two conceptions are the same, or that they belong to the same genus. On the contrary, it negatives the notion of an identity between them; but it points out that they are sufficiently similar for one to be classed as the sequel to the other, and that the phraseology taken from one department of law may be transferred to the other, and employed without violent straining in the statement of rules which would otherwise be imperfectly expressed.

It has been shrewdly remarked, that the confusion between Implied Contracts, which are true contracts, and Quasi-Contracts, which are not contracts at all, has much in common with the famous error which attributed political rights and duties to an Original Compact between the governed and the governor. Long before this theory had clothed itself in definite shape, the phraseology of Roman contract-law had been largely drawn upon to describe that reciprocity of rights and duties which men had always conceived as existing between sovereigns and subjects. While the world was full of maxims setting forth with the utmost positiveness the claims of kings to implicit obedience—maxims which pretended to have had their origin in the New Testament, but which were really derived from indelible recollections of the Cæsarian despotism— the consciousness of correlative rights possessed by the governed would have been entirely without the means of expression if the Roman law of Obligation had not supplied a language capable of shadowing forth an idea which was as yet imperfectly developed. The antagonism between the privileges of kings and their duties to their subjects was never, I believe, lost sight of since Western history began, but it had interest for few except speculative writers so long as feudalism continued in vigour, for feudalism effectually controlled by express customs the exorbitant theoretical pretensions of most European sovereigns. It is notorious, however, that as soon as the decay of the Feudal System had thrown the mediæval constitutions out of working order, and when

the Reformation had discredited the authority of the
Pope, the doctrine of the divine right of Kings rose
immediately into an importance which had never
before attended it.   The vogue which it obtained entailed still more constant resort to the phraseology of
Roman law, and a controversy which had originally
worn a theological aspect assumed more and more
the air of a legal disputation.   A phenomenon then
appeared which has repeatedly shown itself in the
history of opinion.   Just when the argument for
monarchical authority rounded itself into the definite
doctrine of Filmer, the phraseology, borrowed from
the Law of Contract, which had been used in defence
of the rights of subjects, crystallised into the theory
of an actual original compact between king and
people, a theory which, first in English and afterwards, and more particularly, in French hands, expanded into a comprehensive explanation of all the
phenomena of society and law.   But the only real
connection between political and legal science had
consisted in the last giving to the first the benefit
of its peculiarly plastic terminology.   The Roman
jurisprudence of Contract had performed for the
relation of sovereign and subject precisely the same
service which, in a humbler sphere, it rendered to
the relation of persons bound together by an obligation of "quasi-contract."   It had furnished a body of
words and phrases which approximated with sufficient

accuracy to the ideas which then were from time to time forming on the subject of political obligation. The doctrine of an Original Compact can never be put higher than it is placed by Dr. Whewell, when he suggests that, though unsound, " it may be a *convenient* form for the expression of moral truths."

The extensive employment of legal language on political subjects previously to the invention of the Original Compact, and the powerful influence which that assumption has exercised subsequently, amply account for the plentifulness in political science of words and conceptions, which were the exclusive creation of Roman jurisprudence.   Of their plentifulness in Moral Philosophy a rather different explanation must be given, inasmuch as ethical writings have laid Roman law under contribution much more directly than political speculations, and their authors have been much more conscious of the extent of their obligation.   In speaking of moral philosophy as extraordinarily indebted to Roman jurisprudence, I must be understood to intend moral philosophy as understood previously to the break in its history effected by Kant, that is, as the science of the rules governing human conduct, of their proper interpre·tation and of the limitations to which they are subject.   Since the rise of the Critical Philosophy, moral science has almost wholly lost its older meaning, and, except where it is preserved under a debased

form in the casuistry still cultivated by Roman
Catholic theologians, it seems to be regarded nearly
universally as a branch of ontological enquiry. I do
not know that there is a single contemporary English
writer, with the exception of Dr. Whewell, who un-
derstands moral philosophy as it was understood
before it was absorbed by metaphysics and before the
groundwork of its rules came to be a more important
consideration than the rules themselves. So long,
however, as ethical science had to do with the
practical regimen of conduct, it was more or less
saturated with Roman law. Like all the great
subjects of modern thought, it was originally incorporated with theology. The science of Moral Theology, as it was at first called, and as it is still
designated by the Roman Catholic divines, was undoubtedly constructed, to the full knowledge of its
authors, by taking principles of conduct from the
system of the Church, and by using the language and
methods of jurisprudence for their expression and
expansion. While this process went on, it was inevitable that jurisprudence, though merely intended
to be the vehicle of thought, should communicate its
colour to the thought itself. The tinge received
through contact with legal conceptions is perfectly
perceptible in the earliest ethical literature of the
modern world, and it is evident, I think, that the Law
of Contract, based as it is on the complete reciprocity

and indissoluble connection of rights and duties, has acted as a wholesome corrective to the predispositions of writers who, if left to themselves, might have exclusively viewed a moral obligation as the public duty of a citizen in the Civitas Dei. But the amount of Roman Law in moral theology becomes sensibly smaller at the time of its cultivation by the great Spanish moralists. Moral theology, developed by the juridical method of doctor commenting on doctor, provided itself with a phraseology of its own, and Aristotelian peculiarities of reasoning and expression, imbibed doubtless in great part from the Disputations on Morals in the academical schools, take the place of that special turn of thought and speech which can never be mistaken by any person conversant with the Roman law. If the credit of the Spanish school of moral theologians had continued, the juridical ingredient in ethical science would have been insignificant, but the use made of their conclusions by the next generation of Roman Catholic writers on these subjects almost entirely destroyed their influence. Moral Theology, degraded into Casuistry, lost all interest for the leaders of European speculation; and the new science of Moral Philosophy, which was entirely in the hands of the Protestants, swerved greatly aside from the path which the moral theologians had followed. The effect was vastly to increase the influence of Roman law on ethical enquiry.

" Shortly* after the Reformation, we find two great schools of thought dividing this class of subjects between them. The most influential of the two was at first the sect or school known to us as the Casuists, all of them in spiritual communion with the Roman Catholic Church, and nearly all of them affiliated to one or other of her religious orders. On the other side were a body of writers connected with each other by a common intellectual descent from the great author of the treatise *De Jure Belli et Pacis*, Hugo Grotius. Almost all of the latter were adherents of the Reformation; and though it cannot be said that they were formally and avowedly at conflict with the Casuists, the origin and object of their system were nevertheless essentially different from those of Casuistry. It is necessary to call attention to this difference, because it involves the question of the influence of Roman law on that department of thought with which both systems are concerned. The book of Grotius, though it touches questions of pure Ethics in every page, and though it is the parent immediate or remote of innumerable volumes of formal morality, is not, as is well known, a professed treatise on Moral Philosophy; it is an attempt to determine the Law of Nature, or Natural Law. Now, without entering upon the question, whether the con-

---

* The passage quoted is transcribed, with slight alterations, from a paper contributed by the author to the *Cambridge Essays* for 1856.

ception of a Law Natural be not exclusively a creation of the Roman jurisconsults, we may lay down
that, even on the admission of Grotius himself, the
dicta of the Roman jurisprudence as to what parts of
known positive law must be taken to be parts of the
Law of Nature, are, if not infallible, to be received
at all events with the profoundest respect.   Hence
the system of Grotius is implicated with Roman law
at its very foundation, and this connection rendered
inevitable—what the legal training of the writer
would perhaps have entailed without it—the free
employment in every paragraph of technical phraseology, and of modes of reasoning, defining, and illus-
trating, which must sometimes conceal the sense, and
almost always the force and cogency, of the argument
from the reader who is unfamiliar with the sources
whence they have been derived.   On the other hand,
Casuistry borrows little from Roman law, and the
views of morality contended for have nothing whatever in common with the undertaking of Grotius.
All that philosophy of right and wrong which has
become famous, or infamous, under the name of
Casuistry, had its origin in the distinction between
Mortal and Venial sin.   A natural anxiety to escape
the awful consequences of determining a particular act
to be mortally sinful, and a desire, equally intelligible,
to assist the Roman Catholic Church in its conflict
with Protestantism by disburthening it of an incon-

venient theory, were the motives which impelled the authors of the Casuistical philosophy to the invention of an elaborate system of criteria, intended to remove immoral actions, in as many cases as possible, out of the category of mortal offences, and to stamp them as venial sins. The fate of this experiment is matter of ordinary history. We know that the distinctions of Casuistry, by enabling the priesthood to adjust spiritual control to all the varieties of human character, did really confer on it an influence with princes, statesmen, and generals, unheard of in the ages before the Reformation, and did really contribute largely to that great reaction which checked and narrowed the first successes of Protestantism. But beginning in the attempt, not to establish, but to evade—not to discover a principle, but to escape a postulate—not to settle the nature of right and wrong, but to determine what was not wrong of a particular nature,—Casuistry went on with its dexterous refinements till it ended in so attenuating the moral features of actions, and so belying the moral instincts of our being, that at length the conscience of mankind rose suddenly in revolt against it, and consigned to one common ruin the system and its doctors. The blow, long pending, was finally struck in the *Provincial Letters* of Pascal, and since the appearance of those memorable Papers, no moralist of the smallest influence or credit has ever avowedly conducted his speculations in the footsteps of the Casuists. The whole field of ethical science was thus left at the exclusive command of the writers who followed Grotius; and it still exhibits in an extraordinary degree the traces of that entanglement with Roman law which is sometimes imputed as a fault, and sometimes the highest of its recommendations, to the Grotian theory. Many inquirers since Grotius's day have modified his principles, and many, of course, since the rise of the critical philosophy, have quite deserted them; but even those who have departed most widely from his fundamental assumptions have inherited much of his method of statement, of his train of thought, and of his mode of illustration; and these have little meaning and no point to the person ignorant of Roman jurisprudence."

I have already said that, with the exception of the physical sciences, there is no walk of knowledge which has been so slightly affected by Roman law as Metaphysics. The reason is that discussion on metaphysical subjects has always been conducted in Greek, first in pure Greek, and afterwards in a dialect of Latin expressly constructed to give expression to Greek conceptions. The modern languages have only been fitted to metaphysical inquiries by adopting this Latin dialect, or by imitating the process which was originally followed in its formation. The source of the phraseology which has been always employed for metaphysical discussion in modern times was the Latin translations of Aristotle, in which, whether derived or not from Arabic versions, the plan of the translator was not to seek for analogous expressions in any part of Latin literature, but to construct anew from Latin roots a set of phrases equal to the expression of Greek philosophical ideas. Over such a process the terminology of Roman law can have exercised little influence; at most, a few Latin law terms in a transmuted shape have made their way into metaphysical language. At the same time it is worthy of remark that whenever the problems of metaphysics are those which have been most strongly agitated in Western Europe, the thought, if not the language, betrays a legal parentage. Few things in the history of speculation are more impressive than the fact that no Greek-speaking people has ever felt itself seriously perplexed by the great question of Free-will and Necessity. I do not pretend to offer any summary explanation of this, but it does not seem an irrelevant suggestion that neither the Greeks, nor any society speaking and thinking in their language, ever showed the smallest capacity for producing a philosophy of law. Legal science is a Roman creation, and the problem of Free-will arises when we contemplate a metaphysical conception under a legal aspect. How came it to be a question whether invariable sequence was identical with necessary connection ? I can only say that the tendency of Roman law, which became stronger as it advanced, was to look upon legal consequences as united to legal causes by an inexorable necessity, a tendency most markedly exemplified in the definition of Obligation which I have repeatedly cited, " Juris vinculum quo necessitate adstringimur alicujus solvendæ rei."

But the problem of Free-will was theological before it became philosophical, and, if its terms have been affected by jurisprudence, it will be because Jurisprudence has made itself felt in Theology. The great point of inquiry which is here suggested has never been satisfactorily elucidated. What has to be determined, is whether jurisprudence has ever served as the medium through which theological principles have been viewed ; whether, by supplying a peculiar language, a peculiar mode of reasoning, and a peculiar solution of many of the problems of life, it has ever opened new channels in which theological speculation could flow out and expand itself. For the purpose of giving an answer it is necessary to recollect what is already agreed upon by the best writers as to the intellectual food which theology first assimilated. It is conceded on all sides that the earliest language of the Christian Church was Greek, and that the problems to which it first addressed itself were those for which Greek philosophy in its later forms had prepared the way. Greek metaphysical literature contained the sole stock of words and ideas out of which the human mind could provide itself with the means of engaging in the profound controversies as to the Divine Persons, the Divine Substance, and the Divine Natures. The Latin language and the meagre Latin philosophy were quite unequal to the undertaking, and accordingly the Western or Latin-speaking provinces of the Empire adopted the conclusions of the East without disputing or reviewing them. "Latin Christianity," says Dean Milman, "accepted the creed which its narrow and barren vocabulary could hardly express in adequate terms. Yet, throughout, the adhesion of Rome and the West was a passive acquiescence in the dogmatic system which had been wrought out by the profounder theology of the Eastern divines, rather than a vigorous and original examination on her part of those mysteries. The Latin Church was the scholar as well as the loyal partizan of Athanasius." But when the separation of East and West became wider, and the Latin-speaking Western Empire began to live with an intellectual life of its own, its deference to the East was all at once exchanged for the agitation of a number of questions entirely foreign to Eastern speculation. "While Greek theology (Milman, *Latin Christianity*, Preface, 5) went on defining with still more exquisite subtlety the Godhead and the nature of Christ"—"while the interminable controversy still lengthened out and cast forth sect after sect from the enfeebled community"—the Western Church threw itself with passionate ardour into a new order of disputes, the same which from those days to this have never lost their interest for any family of mankind at any time included in the Latin communion. The nature of Sin and its transmission by inheritance—the debt owed by man and its vicarious satisfaction—the necessity and sufficiency of the Atonement—above all the apparent antagonism between Free-will and the Divine Providence—these were the points which the West began to debate as ardently as ever the East had discussed the articles of its more special creed. Why is it then that on the two sides of the line which divides the Greek-speaking from the Latin-speaking provinces there lie two classes of theological problems so strikingly different from one another? The historians of the Church have come close upon the solution when they remark that the new problems were more " practical," less absolutely speculative, than those which had torn Eastern Christianity asunder, but none of them, so far as I am aware, has quite reached it. I affirm without hesitation that the difference between the two theological systems is accounted for by the fact that, in passing from the East to the West, theological speculation had passed from a climate of Greek metaphysics to a climate of Roman law. For some centuries

before these controversies rose into overwhelming
importance, all the intellectual activity of the Western
Romans had been expended on jurisprudence exclusively.   They had been occupied in applying a peculiar set of principles to all the combinations in which
the circumstances of life are capable of being arranged.
No foreign pursuit or taste called off their attention
from this engrossing occupation, and for carrying it
on they possessed a vocabulary as accurate as it was
copious, a strict method of reasoning, a stock of
general propositions on conduct more or less verified
by experience, and a rigid moral philosophy.   It was
impossible that they should not select from the questions indicated by the Christian records those which
had some affinity with the order of speculations to
which they were accustomed, and that their manner
of dealing with them should borrow something from
their forensic habits.   Almost everybody who has
knowledge enough of Roman law to appreciate the
Roman penal system, the Roman theory of the obligations established by Contract or Delict, the Roman
view of Debts and of the modes of incurring, extin-
guishing, and transmitting them, the Roman notion of
the continuance of individual existence by Universal
Succession, may be trusted to say whence arose the
frame of mind to which the problems of Western
theology proved so congenial, whence came the phraseology in which these problems were stated, and

whence the description of reasoning employed in their solution.   It must only be recollected that the Roman law which had worked itself into Western thought was neither the archaic system of the ancient city, nor the pruned and curtailed jurisprudence of the Byzantine Emperors ; still less, of course, was it the mass of rules, nearly buried in a parasitical over-growth of modern speculative doctrine, which passes by the name of Modern Civil Law.   I speak only of that philosophy of jurisprudence, wrought out by the great juridical thinkers of the Antonine age, which may still be partially reproduced from the Pandects of Justinian, a system to which few faults can be attributed except perhaps that it aimed at a higher degree of elegance, certainty, and precision than human affairs will permit to the limits within which human laws seek to confine them.

It is a singular result of that ignorance of Roman law which Englishmen readily confess, and of which they are sometimes not ashamed to boast, that many English writers of note and credit have been led by it to put forward the most untenable of paradoxes concerning the condition of human intellect during the Roman empire.   It has been constantly asserted, as unhesitatingly as if there were no temerity in ad-vancing the proposition, that from the close of the Augustan era to the general awakening of interest on the points of the Christian faith, the mental energies

of the civilised world were smitten with a para-
lysis.   Now there are two subjects of thought—the
only two perhaps with the exception of physical
science—which are able to give employment to all
the powers and capacities which the mind possesses.
One of them is Metaphysical inquiry, which knows no
limits so long as the mind is satisfied to work on
itself ; the other is Law, which is as extensive as the
concerns of mankind.   It happens that, during the
very period indicated, the Greek-speaking provinces
were devoted to one, the Latin-speaking provinces to
the other, of these studies.   I say nothing of the fruits
of speculation in Alexandria and the East, but I confidently affirm that Rome and the West had an occupation in hand fully capable of compensating them
for the absence of every other mental exercise, and I
add that the results achieved, so far as we know
them, were not unworthy of the continuous and exclusive labour bestowed on producing them.   Nobody
except a professional lawyer is perhaps in a position
completely to understand how much of the intellectual
strength of individuals Law is capable of absorbing,
but a layman has no difficulty in comprehending why
it was that an unusual share of the collective intellect
of Rome was engrossed by jurisprudence.   " The
proficiency * of a given community in jurisprudence
depends in the long run on the same conditions as its

* *Cambridge Essays*, 1856.

progress in any other line of inquiry; and the chief of these are the proportion of the national intellect devoted to it, and the length of time during which it is so devoted." Now, a combination of all the causes, direct and indirect, which contribute to the advancing and perfecting of a science continued to operate on the jurisprudence of Rome through the entire space between the Twelve Tables and the severance of the two Empires,—and that not irregularly or at intervals, but in steadily increasing force and constantly augmenting number. We should reflect that the earliest intellectual exercise to which a young nation devotes itself is the study of its laws. As soon as the mind makes its first conscious efforts towards generalisation, the concerns of every-day life are the first to press for inclusion within general rules and comprehensive formulas. The popularity of the pursuit on which all the energies of the young commonwealth are bent is at the outset unbounded; but it ceases in time. The monopoly of mind by law is broken down. The crowd at the morning audience of the great Roman jurisconsult lessens. The students are counted by hundreds instead of thousands in the English Inns of Court. Art, Literature, Science, and Politics, claim their share of the national intellect; and the practice of jurisprudence is confined within the circle of a profession, never indeed limited or insignificant, but attracted

as much by the rewards as by the intrinsic recommendations of their science. This succession
of changes exhibited itself even more strikingly at
Rome than in England. To the close of the Republic
the law was the sole field for all ability except the
special talent of a capacity for generalship. But a
new stage of intellectual progress began with the
Augustan age, as it did with our own Elizabethan
era. We all know what were its achievements in
poetry and prose ; but there are some indications, it
should be remarked, that, besides its efflorescence in
ornamental literature, it was on the eve of throwing
out new aptitudes for conquest in physical science.
Here, however, is the point at which the history of
mind in the Roman States ceases to be parallel to the
routes which mental progress has since then pursued.
The brief span of Roman literature, strictly so called,
was suddenly closed under a variety of influences,
which though they may partially be traced it would
be improper in this place to analyse. Ancient intellect was forcibly thrust back into its old courses, and
law again became no less exclusively the proper
sphere for talent than it had been in the days when
the Romans despised philosophy and poetry as the
toys of a childish race. Of what nature were the external inducements which, during the Imperial period,
tended to draw a man of inherent capacity to the
pursuits of the jurisconsult may best be understood

by considering the option which was practically before him in his choice of a profession.   He might become a teacher of rhetoric, a commander of frontier-posts, or a professional writer of penegyrics.   The only other walk of active life which was open to him was the practice of the law.   Through *that* lay the approach to wealth, to fame, to office, to the council-chamber of the monarch—it may be to the very throne itself.

The premium on the study of jurisprudence was so enormous that there were schools of law in every part of the Empire, even in the very domain of Metaphysics.   But, though the transfer of the seat of empire to Byzantium gave a perceptible impetus to its cultivation in the East, jurisprudence never dethroned the pursuits which there competed with it.   Its language was Latin, an exotic dialect in the Eastern half of the Empire.   It is only of the West that we can lay down that law was not only the mental food of the ambitious and aspiring, but the sole aliment of all intellectual activity.   Greek philosophy had never been more than a transient fashionable taste with the educated class of Rome itself, and when the new Eastern capital had been created, and the Empire subsequently divided into two, the divorce of the Western provinces from Greek speculation, and their exclusive devotion to jurisprudence, became more decided than ever.   As soon then as they ceased to sit at the feet of the Greeks and began to ponder out a theology of their own, the theology proved to be permeated with forensic ideas and couched in a forensic phraseology. It is certain that this substratum of law in Western theology lies exceedingly deep. A new set of Greek theories, the Aristotelian philosophy, made their way afterwards into the West, and almost entirely buried its indigenous doctrines. But when at the Reformation it partially shook itself free from their influence, it instantly supplied their place with Law. It is difficult to say whether the religious system of Calvin or the religious system of the Arminians has the more markedly legal character.

The vast influence of this specific jurisprudence of Contract produced by the Romans upon the corresponding department of modern Law belongs rather to the history of mature jurisprudence than to a treatise like the present. It did not make itself felt till the school of Bologna founded the legal science of modern Europe. But the fact that the Romans, before their Empire fell, had so fully developed the conception of Contract becomes of importance at a much earlier period than this. Feudalism, I have repeatedly asserted, was a compound of archaic barbarian usage with Roman law; no other explanation of it is tenable, or even intelligible. The earliest social forms of the feudal period differ in little from the ordinary associations in which the men of primitive civilisations are everywhere seen united. A Fief was an organically complete brotherhood of associates whose proprietary and personal rights were inextricably blended together. It had much in common with an Indian Village Community and much in common with a Highland clan. But still it presents some phenomena which we never find in the associations which are spontaneously formed by beginners in civilisation. True archaic communities are held together not by express rules, but by sentiment, or, we should perhaps say, by instinct; and new comers into the brotherhood are brought within the range of this instinct by falsely pretending to share in the blood-relationship from which it naturally springs. But the earliest feudal communities were neither bound together by mere sentiment nor recruited by a fiction. The tie which united them was Contract, and they obtained new associates by contracting with them. The relation of the lord to the vassals had originally been settled by express engagement, and a person wishing to engraft himself on the brotherhood by *commendation* or *infeudation* came to a distinct understanding as to the conditions on which he was to be admitted. It is therefore the sphere occupied in them by Contract which principally distinguishes the feudal institutions from the unadulterated usages of primitive races. The lord had many of the characteristics of a patriarchal chieftain, but his prerogative was limited by a variety of settled customs traceable to the express conditions which had been agreed upon when the infeudation took place. Hence flow the chief differences which forbid us to class the feudal societies with true archaic communities. They were much more durable and much more various; more durable, because express rules are less destructible than instinctive habits, and more various, because the contracts on which they were founded were adjusted to the minutest circumstances and wishes of the persons who surrendered or granted away their lands. This last consideration may serve to indicate how greatly the vulgar opinions current among us as to the origin of modern society stand in need of revision. It is often said that the irregular and various contour of modern civilisation is due to the exuberant and erratic genius of the Germanic races, and it is often contrasted with the dull routine of the Roman Empire. The truth is that the Empire bequeathed to modern society the legal conception to which all this irregularity is attributable; if the customs and institutions of barbarians have one characteristic more striking than another, it is their extreme uniformity.

CHAPTER X.

THE EARLY HISTORY OF DELICT AND CRIME.

THE Teutonic Codes, including those of our Anglo-Saxon ancestors, are the only bodies of archaic secular law which have come down to us in such a state that we can form an exact notion of their original dimensions. Although the extant fragments of Roman and Hellenic codes suffice to prove to us their general character, there does not remain enough of them for us to be quite sure of their precise magnitude or of the proportion of their parts to each other. But still on the whole all the known collections of ancient law are characterised by a feature which broadly distinguishes them from systems of mature jurisprudence. The proportion of criminal to civil law is exceedingly different. In the German codes, the civil part of the law has trifling dimensions as compared with the criminal. The traditions which speak of the sanguinary penalties inflicted by the code of Draco seem to indicate that it had the same characteristic. In the Twelve Tables alone, produced by a society of greater legal genius and at first of gentler manners, the civil law has something like its modern precedence; but the relative amount of space given

to the modes of redressing wrong, though not enormous, appears to have been large. It may be laid
down, I think, that the more archaic the code, the
fuller and the minuter is its penal legislation. The
phenomenon has often been observed, and has been
explained, no doubt to a great extent correctly, by
the violence habitual to the communities which for
the first time reduced their laws to writing. The
legislator, it is said, proportioned the divisions of his
work to the frequency of a certain class of incidents
in barbarian life. I imagine, however, that this
account is not quite complete. It should be recollected that the comparative barrenness of civil law
in archaic collections is consistent with those other
characteristics of ancient jurisprudence which have
been discussed in this treatise. Nine-tenths of the
civil part of the law practised by civilised societies
are made up of the Law of Persons, of the Law of
Property and of Inheritance, and of the Law of
Contract. But it is plain that all these provinces
of jurisprudence must shrink within narrower boundaries, the nearer we make our approaches to the
infancy of social brotherhood. The Law of Persons,
which is nothing else than the Law of Status, will
be restricted to the scantiest limits as long as all
forms of status are merged in common subjection to
Paternal Power, as long as the Wife has no rights
against her Husband, the Son none against his

Father, and the infant Ward none against the Agnates who are his Guardians. Similarly, the rules relating to Property and Succession can never be plentiful, so long as land and goods devolve within the family, and, if distributed at all, are distributed inside its circle. But the greatest gap in ancient civil law will always be caused by the absence of Contract, which some archaic codes do not mention at all, while others significantly attest the immaturity of the moral notions on which Contract depends by supplying its place with an elaborate jurisprudence of Oaths. There are no corresponding reasons for the poverty of penal law, and accordingly, even if it be hazardous to pronounce that the childhood of nations is always a period of ungoverned violence, we shall still be able to understand why the modern relation of criminal law to civil should be inverted in ancient codes.

I have spoken of primitive jurisprudence as giving to *criminal* law a priority unknown in a later age. The expression has been used for convenience' sake, but in fact the inspection of ancient codes shows that the law which they exhibit in unusual quantities is not true criminal law. All civilised systems agree in drawing a distinction between offences against the State or Community and offences against the Individual, and the two classes of injuries, thus kept apart, I may here, without pretending that the terms

have always been employed consistently in jurisprudence, call Crimes and Wrongs, *crimina* and *delicta*.
Now the penal Law of ancient communities is not
the law of Crimes; it is the law of Wrongs, or, to
use the English technical word, of Torts. The person
injured proceeds against the wrong-doer by an ordinary civil action, and recovers compensation in the
shape of money-damages if he succeeds. If the
Commentaries of Gaius be opened at the place where
the writer treats of the penal jurisprudence founded
on the Twelve Tables, it will be seen that at the
head of the civil wrongs recognised by the Roman
law stood *Furtum* or *Theft*. Offences which we are
accustomed to regard exclusively as *crimes* are
exclusively treated as *torts*, and not theft only, but
assault and violent robbery, are associated by the
jurisconsult with trespass, libel and slander. All
alike gave rise to an Obligation or *vinculum juris*,
and were all requited by a payment of money. This
peculiarity, however, is most strongly brought out
in the consolidated Laws of the Germanic tribes.
Without an exception, they describe an immense
system of money compensations for homicide, and
with few exceptions, as large a scheme of compensation for minor injuries. " Under Anglo-Saxon law,"
writes Mr. Kemble (*Anglo-Saxons*, i. 177), " a sum
was placed on the life of every free man, according to
his rank, and a corresponding sum on every wound

that could be inflicted on his person, for nearly every injury that could be done to his civil rights, honour or peace; the sum being aggravated according to adventitious circumstances." These compositions are evidently regarded as a valuable source of income; highly complex rules regulate the title to them and the responsibility for them; and, as I have already had occasion to state, they often follow a very peculiar line of devolution, if they have not been acquitted at the decease of the person to whom they belong. If therefore the criterion of a *delict*, *wrong*, or *tort* be that the person who suffers it, and not the State, is conceived to be wronged, it may be asserted that in the infancy of jurisprudence the citizen depends for protection against violence or fraud not on the Law of Crime but on the Law of Tort.

Torts then are copiously enlarged upon in primitive jurisprudence. It must be added that Sins are known to it also. Of the Teutonic codes it is almost unnecessary to make this assertion, because those codes, in the form in which we have received them, were compiled or recast by Christian legislators. But it is also true that non-Christian bodies of archaic law entail penal consequences on certain classes of acts and on certain classes of omissions, as being violations of divine prescriptions and commands. The law administered at Athens by the Senate of

Areopagus was probably a special religious code, and at Rome, apparently from a very early period, the Pontifical jurisprudence punished adultery, sacrilege and perhaps murder. There were therefore in the Athenian and in the Roman States laws punishing *sins*. There were also laws punishing *torts*. The conception of offence against God produced the first class of ordinances; the conception of offence against one's neighbour produced the second; but the idea of offence against the State or aggregate community did not at first produce a true criminal jurisprudence.

Yet it is not to be supposed that a conception so simple and elementary as that of wrong done to the State was wanting in any primitive society. It seems rather that the very distinctness with which this conception is realised is the true cause which at first prevents the growth of a criminal law. At all events, when the Roman community conceived itself to be injured, the analogy of a personal wrong received was carried out to its consequences with absolute literalness, and the State avenged itself by a single act on the individual wrong-doer. The result was that, in the infancy of the commonwealth, every offence vitally touching its security or its interests was punished by a separate enactment of the legislature. And this is the earliest conception of a *crimen* or Crime—an act involving such high issues that the State, instead of leaving its cognisance to the civil tribunal or the religious court, directed a special law or *privilegium* against the perpetrator. Every indictment therefore took the form of a bill of pains and penalties, and the trial of a *criminal* was a proceeding wholly extraordinary, wholly irregular, wholly independent of settled rules and fixed conditions.   Consequently, both for the reason that the tribunal dispensing justice was the sovereign State itself and also for the reason that no classification of the acts prescribed or forbidden was possible, there was not at this epoch any *Law* of crimes, any criminal jurisprudence.   The procedure was identical with the forms of passing an ordinary statute; it was set in motion by the same persons and conducted with precisely the same solemnities. And it is to be observed that, when a regular criminal law with an apparatus of Courts and officers for its administration had afterwards come into being, the old procedure, as might be supposed from its conformity with theory, still in strictness remained practicable; and, much as resort to such an expedient was discredited, the people of Rome always retained the power of punishing by a special law offences against its majesty.   The classical scholar does not require to be reminded that in exactly the same manner the Athenian Bill of Pains and Penalties, or εἰσαγγελία, survived the establishment of regular tribunals.   It is known too that when the freemen of the Teutonic races assembled for legislation, they also claimed authority to punish offences of peculiar blackness or perpetrated by criminals of exalted station. Of this nature was the criminal jurisdiction of the Anglo-Saxon Witenagemot.

It may be thought that the difference which I have asserted to exist between the ancient and modern view of penal law has only a verbal existence. The community, it may be said, besides interposing to punish crimes legislatively, has from the earliest times interfered by its tribunals to compel the wrong-doer to compound for his wrong, and if it does this, it must always have supposed that in some way it was injured through his offence. But, however rigorous this inference may seem to us now-a-days, it is very doubtful whether it was actually drawn by the men of primitive antiquity. How little the notion of injury to the community had to do with the earliest interferences of the State *through its tribunals*, is shown by the curious circumstances that in the original administration of justice, the proceedings were a close imitation of the series of acts which were likely to be gone through in private life by persons who were disputing, but who afterwards suffered their quarrel to be appeased. The magistrate carefully stimulated the demeanour of a private arbitrator casually called in.

In order to show that this statement is not a mere
fanciful conceit, I will produce the evidence on
which it rests.   Very far the most ancient judicial
proceeding known to us is the Legis Actio Sacramenti of the Romans, out of which all the later
Roman Law of Actions may be proved to have
grown.   Gaius carefully describes its ceremonial.
Unmeaning and grotesque as it appears at first
sight, a little attention enables us to decipher and
interpret it.

The subject of litigation is supposed to be in
Court.   If it is moveable, it is actually there.   If it
be immoveable, a fragment or sample of it is brought
in its place; land, for instance, is represented by a
clod, a house by a single brick.   In the example
selected by Gaius, the suit is for a slave.   The proceeding begins by the plaintiff's advancing with a
rod, which, as Gaius expressly tells, symbolised a
spear.   He lays hold of the slave and asserts a right
to him with the words, " *Hunc ego hominem ex Jure
Quiritium meum esse dico secundum suam causam
sicut dixi;*" and then saying, " *Ecce tibi Vindictam im-
posui,*" he touches him with the spear.   The defendant goes through the same series of acts and
gestures.   On this the Prætor intervenes, and bids the
litigants relax their hold, " *Mittite ambo hominem.*"
They obey, and the plaintiff demands from the
defendant the reason of his interference, " *Postulo*

anne dicas quâ ex causâ vindicaveris," a question
which is replied to by a fresh assertion of right,
" *Jus peregi sicut vindictam imposi.*" On this, the
first claimant offers to stake a sum of money, called
a Sacramentum, on the justice of his own case,
" *Quando tu injuriâ provocasti, D æris Sacramento te
provoco*," and the defendant, in the phrase " *Similiter
ego te*," accepts the wager. The subsequent proceedings were no longer of a formal kind, but it is to
be observed that the Prætor took security for the
Sacramentum, which always went into the coffers of
the State.

Such was the necessary preface of every ancient
Roman suit. It is impossible, I think, to refuse
assent to the suggestion of those who see in it a
dramatization of the origin of Justice. Two armed
men are wrangling about some disputed property.
The Prætor, *vir pietate gravis*, happens to be going
by and interposes to stop the contest. The disputants state their case to him, and agree that
he shall arbitrate between them, it being arranged
that the loser, besides resigning the subject of the
quarrel, shall pay a sum of money to the umpire
as remuneration for his trouble and loss of time.
This interpretation would be less plausible than it
is, were it not that, by a surprising coincidence, the
ceremony described by Gaius as the imperative
course of proceeding in a Legis Actio is substantially

the same with one of the two subjects which the
God Hephæstus is described by Homer as moulding
into the First Compartment of the Shield of Achilles.
In the Homeric trial-scene, the dispute, as if expressly intended to bring out the characteristics of
primitive society, is not about property but about
the composition for a homicide. One person asserts
that he has paid it, the other that he has never
received it. The point of detail, however, which
stamps the picture as the counterpart of the archaic
Roman practice is the reward designed for the
judges. Two talents of gold lie in the middle, to
be given to him who shall explain the grounds of the
decision most to the satisfaction of the audience.
The magnitude of this sum as compared with the
trifling amount of the Sacramentum seems to me
indicative of the difference between fluctuating usage
and usage consolidated into law. The scene introduced by the poet as a striking and characteristic,
but still only occasional, feature of city life in the
heroic age has stiffened, at the opening of the history
of civil process, into the regular, ordinary formalities
of a lawsuit. It is natural therefore that in the
Legis Actio the remuneration of the Judge should
be reduced to a reasonable sum, and that, instead
of being adjudged to one of a number of arbitrators
by popular acclamation, it should be paid as a
matter of course to the State which the Prætor

represents. But that the incidents described so
vividly by Homer, and by Gaius with even more
than the usual crudity of technical language, have
substantially the same meaning, I cannot doubt;
and, in confirmation of this view it may be added
that many observers of the earliest judicial usages
of modern Europe have remarked that the fines
inflicted by Courts on offenders were originally
sacramenta. The State did not take from the
defendant a composition for any wrong supposed
to be done to itself, but claimed a share in the
compensation awarded to the plaintiff simply as the
fair price of its time and trouble. Mr. Kemble
expressly assigns this character to the Anglo-Saxon
bannum or *fredum*.

Ancient law furnishes other proofs that the earliest
administrators of justice simulated the probable acts
of persons engaged in a private quarrel. In settling
the damages to be awarded, they took as their guide
the measure of vengeance likely to be exacted by an
aggrieved person under the circumstances of the
case. This is the true explanation of the very different penalties imposed by ancient law on offenders
caught in the act or soon after it and on offenders
detected after considerable delay. Some strange ex-
emplifications of this peculiarity are supplied by the
old Roman law of Theft. The Laws of the Twelve
Tables seem to have divided Thefts into Manifest and

Non-Manifest, and to have allotted extraordinarily different penalties to the offence according as it fell under one head or the other. The Manifest Thief was he who was caught within the house in which he had been pilfering, or who was taken while making off to a place of safety with the stolen goods; the Twelve Tables condemned him to be put to death if he were already a slave, and, if he were a freeman, they made him the bondsman of the owner of the property. The Non-Manifest Thief was he who was detected under any other circumstances than those described; and the old code simply directed that an offender of this sort should refund double the value of what he had stolen. In Gaius's day the excessive severity of the Twelve Tables to the Manifest Thief had naturally been much mitigated, but the law still maintained the old principle by mulcting him in fourfold the value of the stolen goods, while the Non-Manifest Thief still continued to pay merely the double. The ancient lawgiver doubtless considered that the injured proprietor, if left to himself, would inflict a very different punishment when his blood was hot from that with which he would be satisfied when the Thief was detected after a considerable interval; and to this calculation the legal scale of penalties was adjusted. The principle is precisely the same as that followed in the Anglo-Saxon and other Germanic codes, when they suffer a thief chased

down and caught with the booty to be hanged or
decapitated on the spot, while they exact the full
penalties of homicide from anybody who kills him
after the pursuit has been intermitted.   These archaic
distinctions bring home to us very forcibly the
distance of a refined from a rude jurisprudence.
The modern administrator of justice has confessedly
one of his hardest tasks before him when he under-
takes to discriminate between the degrees of criminality which belong to offences falling within the
same technical description.   It is always easy to say
that a man is guilty of manslaughter, larceny, or bi-
gamy, but it is often most difficult to pronounce what
extent of moral guilt he has incurred, and consequently what measure of punishment he has deserved.
There is hardly any perplexity in casuistry, or in the
analysis of motive, which we may not be called upon
to confront, if we attempt to settle such a point with
precision ; and accordingly the law of our day shows
an increasing tendency to abstain as much as possible from laying down positive rules on the subject.
In France, the jury is left to decide whether the
offence which it finds committed has been attended
by extenuating circumstances ; in England, a nearly
unbounded latitude in the selection of punishments is
now allowed to the judge ; while all States have in
reserve an ultimate remedy for the miscarriages of law
in the Prerogative of Pardon, universally lodged with

the Chief Magistrate. It is curious to observe how little the men of primitive times were troubled with these scruples, how completely they were persuaded that the impulses of the injured person were the proper measure of the vengeance he was entitled to exact, and how literally they imitated the probable rise and fall of his passions in fixing their scale of punishment.   I wish it could be said that their method of legislation is quite extinct. There are, however, several modern systems of law which, in cases of graver wrong, admit the fact of the wrong-doer having been taken in the act to be pleaded in justification of inordinate punishment inflicted on him by the sufferer—an indulgence which, though superficially regarded it may seem intelligible, is based, as it seems to me, on a very low morality.

Nothing, I have said, can be simpler than the considerations which ultimately led ancient societies to the formation of a true criminal jurisprudence. The State conceived itself to be wronged, and the Popular Assembly struck straight at the offender with the same movement which accompanied its legislative action. It is further true of the ancient world—though not precisely of the modern, as I shall have occasion to point out—that the earliest criminal tribunals were merely subdivisions, or committees, of the legislature. This, at all events, is the conclusion pointed at by the legal history of the two great states of antiquity, with tolerable clearness in one case, and with absolute distinctness in the other. The primitive penal law of Athens intrusted the castigation of offences partly to the Archons, who seem to have punished them as *torts*, and partly to the Senate of Areopagus, which punished them as *sins*. Both jurisdictions were substantially transferred in the end to the Heliæa, the High Court of Popular Justice, and the functions of the Archons and of the Areopagus became either merely ministerial or quite insignificant. But "Heliæa" is only an old word for assembly; the Heliæa of classical times was simply the Popular Assembly convened for judicial purposes, and the famous Dikasteries of Athens were only its subdivisions or panels. The corresponding changes which occurred at Rome are still more easily interpreted, because the Romans confined their experiments to the penal law, and did not, like the Athenians, construct popular courts with a civil as well as a criminal jurisdiction. The history of Roman criminal jurisprudence begins with the Old Judicia Populi, at which the Kings are said to have presided. These were simply solemn trials of great offenders under legislative forms. It seems, however, that from an early period the Comitia had occasionally delegated its criminal jurisdiction to a Quæstio or Commission, which bore much the same relation to the Assembly which a Committee of the

House of Commons bears to the House itself, except
that the Roman Commissioners or Quæstores did not
merely *report* to the Comitia, but exercised all powers
which that body was itself in the habit of exercising,
even to the passing sentence on the Accused. A
Quæstio of this sort was only appointed to try a particular offender, but there was nothing to prevent
two or three Quæstiones sitting at the same time;
and it is probable that several of them were appointed simultaneously, when several grave cases of
wrong to the community had occurred together.
There are also indications that now and then these
Quæstiones approached the character of our *Standing*
Committees, in that they were appointed periodically, and without waiting for occasion to arise in
the commission of some serious crime. The old
Quæstores Parricidii, who are mentioned in connection with transactions of very ancient date, as being
deputed to try (or, as some take it, to search out
and try) all cases of parricide and murder, seem to
have been appointed regularly every year; and the
Duumviri Perduellionis, or Commission of Two for
trial of violent injury to the Commonwealth, are also
believed by most writers to have been named periodically. The delegations of power to these latter
functionaries bring us some way forwards. Instead
of being appointed *when and as* state-offences were
committed, they had a general, though a temporary

jurisdiction over such as *might* be perpetrated. Our proximity to a regular criminal jurisprudence is also indicated by the general terms "Parricidium" and "Perduellio," which mark the approach to something like a classification of crimes.

The true criminal law did not however come into existence till the year B.C. 149, when L. Calpurnius Piso carried the statute known as the Lex Calpurnia de Repetundis. The law applied to cases Repetundarum Pecuniarum, that is, claims by Provincials to recover monies improperly received by a Governor-General, but the great and permanent importance of this statute arose from its establishing the first Quæstio Perpetua. A Quæstio Perpetua was a *Permanent* Commission as opposed to those which were occasional and to those which were temporary. It was a regular criminal tribunal, whose existence dated from the passing of the statute creating it and continued till another statute should pass abolishing it. Its members were not specially nominated, as were the members of the older Quæstiones, but provision was made in the law constituting it for selecting from particular classes the judges who were to officiate, and for renewing them in conformity with definite rules. The offences of which it took cognisance were also expressly named and defined in this statute, and the new Quæstio had authority to try and sentence all persons in future whose acts should fall under the definitions of crime supplied by the law. It was therefore a regular criminal judicature, administering a true criminal jurisprudence.

The primitive history of criminal law divides itself therefore into four stages. Understanding that the conception of *Crime*, as distinguished from that of *Wrong* or *Tort*, and from that of *Sin*, involves the idea of injury to the State or collective community, we first find that the commonwealth, in literal conformity with the conception, itself interposed directly, and by isolated acts, to avenge itself on the author of the evil which it had suffered. This is the point from which we start; each indictment is now a bill of pains and penalties, a special law naming the criminal and prescribing his punishment. A *second* step is accomplished when the multiplicity of crimes compels the legislature to delegate its powers to particular Quæstiones or Commissions, each of which is deputed to investigate a particular accusation, and if it be proved, to punish the particular offender. Yet *another* movement is made when the legislature, instead of waiting for the alleged commission of a crime as the occasion of appointing a Quæstio, periodically nominates Commissioners like the Quæstores Parricidii and the Duumviri Perduellionis, on the chance of certain classes of crimes being committed, and in the expectation that they *will* be perpetrated. The *last* stage is reached when the Quæstiones

from being periodical or occasional become permanent
Benches or Chambers—when the judges, instead of
being named in the particular law nominating the
Commission, are directed to be chosen through all
future time in a particular way and from a particular
class—and when certain acts are described in general
language and declared to be crimes, to be visited,
in the event of their perpetration, with specified
penalties appropriated to each description.

If the Quæstiones Perpetuæ had had a longer history, they would doubtless have come to be regarded
as a distinct institution, and their relation to the
Comitia would have seemed no closer than the connection of our own Courts of Law with the Sovereign,
who is theoretically the fountain of justice. But the
Imperial despotism destroyed them before their
origin had been completely forgotten, and so long
as they lasted, these Permanent Commissions were
looked upon by the Romans as the mere depositaries
of a delegated power. The cognisance of crimes
was considered a natural attribute of the legislature,
and the mind of the citizen never ceased to be carried
back from the Quæstiones to the Comitia which had
deputed them to put into exercise some of its own
inalienable functions. The view which regarded the
Quæstiones, even when they became permanent,
as mere Committees of the Popular Assembly—as
bodies which only ministered to a higher authority

—had some important legal consequences which left their mark on the criminal law to the very latest period. One immediate result was that the Comitia continued to exercise criminal jurisdiction by way of bill of pains and penalties, long after the Quæstiones had been established. Though the legislature had consented to delegate its powers for the sake of convenience to bodies external to itself, it did not follow that it surrendered them. The Comitia and the Quæstiones went on trying and punishing offenders side by side; and any unusual outburst of popular indignation was sure, until the extinction of the Republic, to call down upon its object an indictment before the Assembly of the Tribes.

One of the most remarkable peculiarities of the institutions of the Republic is also traceable to this dependence of the Quæstiones on the Comitia. The disappearance of the punishment of Death from the penal system of Republican Rome used to be a very favourite topic with the writers of the last century, who were perpetually using it to point some theory of the Roman character or of modern social economy. The reason which can be confidently assigned for it stamps it as purely fortuitous. Of the three forms which the Roman legislature successively assumed, one, it is well known—the Comitia Centuriata —was exclusively taken to represent the State as embodied for military operations. The Assembly of the

Centuries, therefore, had all powers which may be supposed to be properly lodged with a General commanding an army, and, among them, it had authority to subject all offenders to the same correction to which a soldier rendered himself liable by breaches of discipline. The Comitia Centuriata could therefore inflict capital punishment. Not so, however, the Comitia Curiata or Comitia Tributa. They were fettered on this point by the sacredness with which the person of a Roman citizen, inside the walls of the city, was invested by religion and law; and, with respect to the last of them, the Comitia Tributa, we know for certain that it became a fixed principle that the Assembly of the Tribes could at most impose a fine. So long as criminal jurisdiction was confined to the legislature, and so long as the assemblies of the Centuries and of the Tribes continued to exercise co-ordinate powers, it was easy to prefer indictments for graver crimes before the legislative body which dispensed the heavier penalties; but then it happened that the more democratic assembly, that of the Tribes, almost entirely superseded the others, and became the ordinary legislature of the later Republic. Now the decline of the Republic was exactly the period during which the Quæstiones Perpetuæ were established, so that the statutes creating them were all passed by a legislative assembly which itself could not, at its ordinary sittings, punish a criminal with

death.   It followed that the Permanent Judicial Commissions, holding a delegated authority, were circumscribed in their attributes and capacities by the
limits of the powers residing with the body which
deputed them.   They could do nothing which the
Assembly of the tribes could not have done ; and,
as the Assembly could not sentence to death, the
Quæstiones were equally incompetent to award
capital punishment.   The anomaly thus resulting was not viewed in ancient times with anything
like the favour which it has attracted among the
moderns, and indeed, while it is questionable whether
the Roman character was at all the better for it, it is
certain that the Roman Constitution was a great deal
the worse.   Like every other institution which has
accompanied the human race down the current of its
history, the punishment of death is a necessity of
society in certain stages of the civilising process.
There is a time when the attempt to dispense with it
baulks both of the two great instincts which lie at
the root of all penal law.   Without it, the community neither feels that it is sufficiently revenged
on the criminal, nor thinks that the example of
his punishment is adequate to deter others from
imitating him.   The incompetence of the Roman
Tribunals to pass sentence of death led distinctly and
directly to those frightful Revolutionary intervals,
known as the Proscriptions, during which all law was

formally suspended simply because party violence could find no other avenue to the vengeance for which it was thirsting. No cause contributed so powerfully to the decay of political capacity in the Roman people as this periodical abeyance of the laws; and, when it had once been resorted to, we need not hesitate to assert that the ruin of Roman liberty became merely a question of time. If the practice of the Tribunals had afforded an adequate vent for popular passion, the forms of judicial procedure would no doubt have been as flagrantly perverted as with us in the reigns of the later Stuarts, but national character would not have suffered as deeply as it did, nor would the stability of Roman institutions have been as seriously enfeebled.

I will mention two more singularities of the Roman Criminal System which were produced by the same theory of judicial authority. They are, the extreme multiplicity of the Roman criminal tribunals, and the capricious and anomalous classification of crimes which characterised Roman penal jurisprudence throughout its entire history. Every *Quæstio*, it has been said, whether Perpetual or otherwise, had its origin in a distinct statute. From the law which created it, it derived its authority; it rigorously observed the limits which its charter prescribed to it, and touched no form of criminality which that charter did not expressly define. As

then the statutes which constituted the various
Quæstiones were all called forth by particular emer-
gencies, each of them being in fact passed to punish
a class of acts which the circumstances of the time
rendered particularly odious or particularly dangerous, these enactments made not the slightest
reference to each other, and were connected by no
common principle. Twenty or thirty different criminal laws were in existence together, with exactly
the same number of Quæstiones to administer them;
nor was any attempt made during the Republic to
fuse these distinct judicial bodies into one, or to give
symmetry to the provisions of the statutes which
appointed them and defined their duties.   The state
of the Roman criminal jurisdiction at this period,
exhibited some resemblances to the administration of
civil remedies in England at the time when the
English Courts of Common Law had not as yet
introduced those fictitious averments into their writs
which enabled them to trespass on each other's
peculiar province.   Like the Quæstiones, the Courts
of Queen's Bench, Common Pleas, and Exchequer,
were all theoretical emanations from a higher authority, and each entertained a special class of cases
supposed to be committed to it by the fountain of its
jurisdiction; but then the Roman Quæstiones were
many more than three in number, and it was infinitely
less easy to discriminate the acts which fell under

the cognisance of each Quæstio, than to distinguish between the provinces of the three Courts in Westminster Hall. The difficulty of drawing exact lines between the spheres of the different Quæstiones made the multiplicity of Roman tribunals something more than a mere inconvenience; for we read with astonishment that when it was not immediately clear under what general description a man's alleged offences ranged themselves, he might be indicted at once or successively before several different Commissions, on the chance of some one of them declaring itself competent to convict him ; and, although conviction by one Quæstio ousted the jurisdiction of the rest, acquittal by one of them could not be pleaded to an accusation before another. This was directly contrary to the rule of the Roman civil law ; and we may be sure that a people so sensitive as the Romans to anomalies (or, as their significant phrase was, to *inelegancies*) in jurisprudence, would not long have tolerated it, had not the melancholy history of the Quæstiones caused them to be regarded much more as temporary weapons in the hands of factions than as permanent institutions for the correction of crime. The Emperors soon abolished this multiplicity and conflict of jurisdiction ; but it is remarkable that they did not remove another singularity of the criminal law which stands in close connection with the number of the Courts. The classifications of crimes which

are contained even in the Corpus Juris of Justinian
are remarkably capricious. Each Quæstio had, in
fact, confined itself to the crimes committed to its
cognisance by its charter. These crimes, however,
were only classed together in the original statute
because they happened to call simultaneously for
castigation at the moment of passing it. They had
not therefore anything necessarily in common ; but
the fact of their constituting the particular subject-
matter of trials before a particular Quæstio impressed
itself naturally on the public attention, and so inveterate did the association become between the
offences mentioned in the same statute that, even
when formal attempts were made by Sylla and by
the Emperor Augustus to consolidate the Roman
criminal law, the legislator preserved the old grouping. The Statutes of Sylla and Augustus were the
foundation of the penal jurisprudence of the Empire,
and nothing can be more extraordinary than some of
the classifications which they bequeathed to it. I
need only give a single example in the fact that
perjury was always classed with *cutting and wounding*
and with *poisoning*, no doubt because a law of Sylla,
the Lex Cornelia de Sicariis et Veneficis, had given
jurisdiction over all these three forms of crime to the
same Permanent Commission. It seems too that
this capricious grouping of crimes affected the vernacular speech of the Romans. People naturally

fell into the habit of designating all the offences enumerated in one law by the first name on the list,
which doubtless gave its style to the Law Court
deputed to try them all. All the offences tried by
the Quæstio De Adulteriis would thus be called
Adultery.

I have dwelt on the history and characteristics of
the Roman Quæstiones because the formation of a
criminal jurisprudence is nowhere else so instructively exemplified. The last Quæstiones were added
by the Emperor Augustus, and from that time the
Romans may be said to have had a tolerably complete criminal law. Concurrently with its growth,
the analogous process had gone on, which I have
called the conversion of Wrongs into Crimes, for,
though the Roman legislature did not extinguish the
civil remedy for the more heinous offences, it offered
the sufferer a redress which he was sure to prefer.
Still, even after Augustus had completed his legislation, several offences continued to be regarded as
Wrongs, which modern societies look upon exclusively as crimes ; nor did they become criminally
punishable till some late but uncertain date, at
which the law began to take notice of a new description of offences called in the Digest *crimina
extraordinaria*. These were doubtless a class of acts
which the theory of Roman jurisprudence treated
merely as wrongs ; but the growing sense of the

majesty of society revolted from their entailing nothing worse on their perpetrator than the payment
of money damages, and accordingly the injured
person seems to have been permitted, if he pleased,
to pursue them as crimes *extra ordinem*, that is, by a
mode of redress departing in some respect or other
from the ordinary procedure.   From the period at
which these *crimina extraordinaria* were first recognised, the list of crimes in the Roman State must
have been as long as in any community of the
modern world.

It is unnecessary to describe with any minuteness
the mode of administering criminal justice under the
Roman Empire, but it is to be noted that both its
theory and practice have had powerful effect on
modern society.   The Emperors did not immediately
abolish the Quæstiones, and at first they committed
an extensive criminal jurisdiction to the Senate, in
which, however servile it might show itself in fact,
the Emperor was no more nominally than a Senator
like the rest.   But some sort of collateral criminal
jurisdiction had been claimed by the Prince from the
first; and this, as recollections of the free commonwealth decayed, tended steadily to gain at the ex-
pense of the old tribunals.   Gradually the punishment of crimes was transferred to magistrates
directly nominated by the Emperor, and the privileges of the Senate passed to the Imperial Privy

Council, which also became a Court of ultimate criminal appeal. Under these influences the doctrine, familiar to the moderns, insensibly shaped itself that the Sovereign is the fountain of all Justice and the depositary of all Grace. It was not so much the fruit of increasing adulation and servility as of the centralisation of the empire which had by this time perfected itself. The theory of criminal justice had, in fact, worked round almost to the point from which it started. It had begun in the belief that it was the business of the collective community to avenge its own wrongs by its own hand; and it ended in the doctrine that the chastisement of crimes belonged in an especial manner to the Sovereign as representative and mandatory of his people. The new view differed from the old one chiefly in the air of awfulness and majesty which the guardianship of justice appeared to throw around the person of the Sovereign.

This later Roman view of the Sovereign's relation to justice certainly assisted in saving modern societies from the necessity of travelling through the series of changes which I have illustrated by the history of the Quæstiones. In the primitive law of almost all the races which have peopled Western Europe there are vestiges of the archaic notion that the punishment of crimes belongs to the general assembly of freemen; and there are some States—Scotland is

said to be one of them—in which the parentage of
the existing judicature can be traced up to a Committee of the legislative body.   But the development
of the criminal law was universally hastened by two
causes, the memory of the Roman Empire and the
influence of the Church.   On the one hand, traditions
of the majesty of the Cæsars, perpetuated by the
temporary ascendency of the House of Charlemagne,
were surrounding Sovereigns with a prestige which a
mere barbarous chieftain could never otherwise have
acquired, and were communicating to the pettiest
feudal potentate the character of guardian of society and representative of the State.   On the other
hand, the Church, in its anxiety to put a curb on
sanguinary ferocity, sought about for authority to
punish the graver misdeeds, and found it in those
passages of Scripture which speak with approval of
the powers of punishment committed to the civil magistrate.   The New Testament was appealed to as
proving that secular rulers exist for the terror of
evil-doers; the Old Testament, as laying down that
" whoso sheddeth man's blood, by man shall his blood
be shed."   There can be no doubt, I imagine, that
modern ideas on the subject of crime are based upon
two assumptions contended for by the Church in the
Dark Ages—first, that each feudal ruler, in his degree, might be assimilated to the Roman Magistrates
spoken of by Saint Paul; and next, that the offences

which he was to chastise were those selected for prohibition in the Mosaic Commandments, or rather such of them as the Church did not reserve to her own cognisance. Heresy, supposed to be included in the First and Second Commandments, Adultery and Perjury were ecclesiastical offences, and the Church only admitted the co-operation of the secular arm for the purpose of inflicting severer punishment in cases of extraordinary aggravation. At the same time, she taught that murder and robbery, with their various modifications, were under the jurisdiction of civil rulers, not as an accident of their position, but by the express ordinance of God.

There is a passage in the writings of King Alfred (Kemble, ii. 209) which brings out into remarkable clearness the struggle of the various ideas that prevailed in his day as to the origin of criminal jurisdiction. It will be seen that Alfred attributes it partly to the authority of the Church and partly to that of the Witan, while he expressly claims for treason against the lord the same immunity from ordinary rules which the Roman Law of Majestas had assigned to treason against the Cæsar. "After this it happened," he writes, "that many nations received the faith of Christ, and there were many synods assembled throughout the earth, and among the English race also after they had received the faith of Christ, both of holy bishops and of their exalted

Witan.　They then ordained that, out of that mercy which Christ had taught, secular lords, with their leave, might without sin take for every misdeed the *bot* in money which they ordained; except in cases of treason against a lord, to which they dared not assign any mercy because Almighty God adjudged none to them that despised Him, nor did Christ adjudge any to them which sold Him to death; and He commanded that a lord should be loved like Himself."

INDEX.

INDEX.

———

ADOPTION

ADOPTION, fiction of, 130
— influence of the *sacra gentilicia* on the law of, 6, 7, 27
— in Hindoo law, 193
Adprehensio; or assumption of sovereign power in a newly discovered country, 249
Æquitas, the term, 58. See Equity
Æquus, the word, 59
Agnatic and Cognatic relationship, difference between, 59, 146
Agnation described, 147, 148
Agreement, Roman analysis of, 322
Agri vectigales, Roman practice of letting out, 300
— limitrophi of the Romans on the banks of the Rhine and Danube, 502
Alexander the Sixth, Pope, his Bull, 249
Alfred, King, his remarks on criminal jurisdiction, quoted, 398
Alienation of property, ancient difficulties of, 271
— archaic ceremonies of, 272
Allodial property, of the ancient Germans, 228, 281
America, United States of, Declaration of Independence of, 95
Anglo-Saxons, character of their Kingship, 108
— their law of succession, 280
— their penal law, 370, 374, 379
Archon of Athens, office of the, 10
Aristocracies, origin of the rule of, 10
— those of Greece, Italy, and Asia Minor, 10
— difference between those of the East and West, 11
— aristocracies the depositaries and administrators of the law, 11, 12

BURGUNDIANS

Aristocracies, importance of judicial, before the invention of writing, 12
— foundation of aristocracies, 132
Aristotle, his "Treatise on Rhetoric" referred to, 75
Assignees in Bankruptcy, succession of, 180
Athenian wills, 196
Athens, primitive penal law of, 382
Augustus, the Emperor, his alterations in the Roman law, 41, 42
Austin's "Province of Jurisprudence Determined," referred to, 7

BAYLE referred to, 87
Benefices of the invading chiefs of the Roman Empire, 229
— transformation of the Benefice into the hereditary Fief, 230
Bengalee Wills, 197
Bentham, his "Fragment on Government" referred to, 7
— causes of his influence in England, 78
— the Roman counterpart of Benthamism, 79
— his theory of Jurisprudence, 117
— his eulogy of the Bull of Pope Alexander the Sixth, 249
—Bentham and Austin's rules as to the essentials of a contract, 323
Blackstone, Sir William, his theory of the first principles of law, 114
— his justification for the exclusion of the half-blood, 152
— his theory of the origin of property quoted, 251
— his theory criticised, 253
Bonorum Possessio of the Romans, 211
Bracton, his Plagiarisms, 82
Burgundians, the, referred to, 104

CÆSAR

CÆSAR, Julius, his contemplated additions to the Roman Statute Law, 42
Capet, Hugh, character of his sovereignty, 108
Capture in War, sources of the modern International Law of, 246
— ancient Law of, 247
Caracalla, effect of his constitution in enlarging the Patria Potestas, 144
Casuists, the, 350
— comparison of their system with that of Grotius and his school, 351
— origin of Casuistry, 351
— blow struck at Casuistry by Pascal, 352
Cessio in Jure of Property, in Roman and in English Law, 289
Cestui que Trust, special proprietorship created for the, 294
Chancellor, the Lord, compared with a Roman Prætor, 64, 65
Chancery, Court of, in England, remarks on the, 44
— origin of its system, 44, 45
Charlemagne, his claim to universal dominion, 104
— his distribution of Benefices, 229
Children, disinherison of, under the Romans, 215
China, cause of the arrest of progress in, 25
Churches, Eastern and Western, conclusions of the East on theological subjects accepted by the West without dispute or review, 356
— problems of the Western Church, 357
Cicero referred to, 61
— his allusions to the ancient Roman Sacra, 193
Code Napoléon, restraints imposed by it on the testamentary power, 176
Codes, Ancient, 1
— sources of knowledge afforded by the Greek Homeric poems, 2
— Themistes, 4
— Hindoo Laws of Menu, 6
— difference between Case-law and Code-law, 14
— era of Codes, 14
— the Twelve Tables, 1, 2, 14
— the Codes of Solon and Draco, 14
— importance of Codes to ancient societies, 16—19
Co-emption, or higher form of civil marriage of the ancient Romans, 154

CONTRACT

Cognatic relationship described, 146, 147
Co-heirs, rights and duties of, 181
— rights of, under the Roman Law, 227
Coloni of the Romans, 231
— origin and situation of the, 300
Comitia Calata, ancient Roman execution of Wills in the, 199
— end of the, 203
Comitia Centuriata, power of the, 387
— Curiata, powers of the, 318
— Tributa, powers of the, 388
Commentaries of the Roman lawyers, 35
Common law of England, formerly an unwritten law, 13
— difference between Case-law and Code-law, 14
— Case-law and its anomalies, 31
— similarity between English Case-law and the Responsa Prudentum of the Romans, 33
Confarreation, or religious marriage of the ancient Romans, 154
Constantine, the Emperor, his improvements in the Law, 42
— his modification of the Patria Potestas, 143
Contract, movement of societies from Status to, 170
— early history of, 304
— Contract and Political Economy, 305
— Rousseau's doctrine of an original Social Contract, 308, 309
— Montesquieu's apologue of the Troglodytes, 311
— early notions of Contract, 312
— Roman Contracts, 314
— specialising process in ancient law, 316
— historical alliance between Contracts and Conveyances, 317
— changes in the Nexum, 318
— Executory Contracts of Sale, 321
— primitive association of Conveyances and Contracts, 321
— ancient and modern doctrine of Contracts, 323
— the Roman Obligation, 323
— Roman classification of Contracts, 325
— the Verbal Contract, 327
— the Literal or Written Contract, 330
— the Real Contract, 331
— Consensual Contracts, 332
— changes in Contract law, 337

CONTRACT

Contract history of the progress of Contract law, 338
— Quasi-Contracts, 343
— Contract law and Fiefs, 365
Conveyances, relation of Wills to, under the Roman Law, 204
— consequence of this relation, 206
— remedies, 207
— historical alliance between Contracts and Conveyances, 317
Co-ownership of property, amongst the Hindoos, 260, 261
— regarded by the Roman Law as exceptional and momentary, 261
Corporations aggregate, 187
— sole, leading attribute of, 187
"Corpus Juris Civilis" of Justinian, 68
— resorted to by English Chancery judges, 44
Creation, Greek philosophical explanation of the fabric of, 55
Creditors, cause of the extravagant powers given to, by ancient laws, 321
Crimes and Wrongs. See Delict and Crime
Croatia, co-ownership of the villagers of, 267
Curatores of male Orphans under the Roman Law, 161
Curse, inherited, Greek notion of an, 127
Customary Law, 5
— Homeric terms for customs, 5
— origin of customary law, 9
— epoch of customary law and its custody by a privileged order, 13
Cyclops, Homer's account of, quoted, 124

DEATH, disappearance of, from the penal system of republican Rome, 387
— causes for this, 387, 388
— death punishment a necessity in certain stages of society, 389
Debtors, cause of the severity of ancient laws against, 321
Decretals, forged, motives of the author of the, 82
Delict and Crime, early history of, 367
— Penal law in ancient codes, 367
— Crimes and Wrongs, *crimina* and *delicta*, 370

ELPHINSTONE

Delict and Crime, Furtum or Theft of the Roman Law, 370, 379
— Wrongs and Sins both known to primitive jurisprudence, 371
— difference between the ancient and modern conception of Crime, 373
— the Roman Legis Actio Sacramenti, 375
— Homer's description of an ancient law-suit, 377
— primitive penal law of Athens, 382
— old Roman criminal jurisprudence, 382
— the Quæstiones, 382, 383
— Quæstores Parricidii, 383
— Duumviri Perduellionis, 383
— the first true Roman Criminal law, 384
— the primitive history of criminal law, 385
— extreme multiplicity of Roman criminal tribunals, 390
— capricious classification of crimes, 392, 393
— statutes of Sylla and Augustus, 393
— later law of crimes, 394
— crimina extraordinaria, 394
— mode of administering criminal justice under the Roman Empire, 395, 396
— modern history of crimes, 397
— King Alfred on criminal jurisdiction quoted, 398
Discovery, considered as a mode of acquiring dominion, 248
Dominion, its nature, limitation, and mode of securing it, 102
— of the Romans, 317
Dower, the principle of, engrafted on the Customary Law of Western Europe, 224
Draco, rudeness of the Code of, 16
— penal laws of, 367
Dumoulin referred to, 86
Dumont's " Sophismes Anarchiques," remarks, 92
Duumviri Perduellionis, the, 383

EDICT of the Roman Prætor, 41, 57, 63, 64, 66, 209, 293
Egypt, Modern, rule of succession to the throne of, 242
Eldon, Lord, his Chancellorship, 69
Elphinstone's "History of India" quoted, 263

EMPHYTEUSIS

Emphyteusis, system of, 299, *et seq.*
— rights of the Emphyteuta, 301
Emptor Familiæ. See Familiæ Emptor
England, the Land-law of, at the present time, 226
English Common Law, formerly an un-written law, 13
— law, hesitation of our Courts in de-claring principles of, 40
Equality of men, doctrine of the, 92
— as understood by the Roman juris-consults, 93
— its meaning in its modern dress, 93
— ordinance of Louis Hutin quoted, 94
— declaration of American Indepen-dence, 95
— assumption of the Grotian school, 101
Equity, early history of, 25
— equity considered as an agent by which the adaptation of law to so-cial wants is carried on, 28
— meaning of the term equity, 28
— difference between equity and legal fictions, 28
— — between equity and legislation, 28, 29
— remarks on the law of nature and equity, 44, *et seq.*
— the English Court of Chancery, 44
— origin of its system, 44, 45
— the equity of Rome, 45
— origin and history of the term "Equity," 58
— the terms Æquitas and 'Ισότης, 58
— picture presented to the Roman mind by the word "Equity," 60
— the English Chancellor compared with the Roman Prætor, 65
— exhaustion of the power of growth in Roman Equity, 68
— features common to English and Roman Equity, 68, *et seq.*
— distinction between Law and Equity in their conceptions of proprietary right, 293
Ethics, obligations of, to the Roman Law, 347
— the Casuists', 350
— Grotius and his school, 350

FAMILIA, meaning of, in the lan-guage of the ancient Roman Law, 208

FRANCE

Familiæ Emptor, office of the, 205
— rights and duties of the, 206
— remarks on the expression Familiæ Emptor, 208
Family, the, of Archaic society, 133
— disintegration of the Family, 169
— regarded as a corporation, 184
— organisations of elementary commu-nities, 234
— Highland chieftainship, 234
— Families, not Individuals, known to ancient law, 258
— Indian, Russian, Croatian, and Scla-vonian laws respecting the property of Families, 260—269
Feudal view of the ownership of pro-perty, 295
Feudal services, 303
Feudalism, its connection with territo-rial sovereignty, 107
— feudal organisation, 107, 108
— the modern Will an accidental fruit of, 224, 225
— Feudalism and Contract law, 365
Fictions, legal, 21, 23
— early history of, 23
— meaning of *fictio* in old Roman Law, 25
— object of the *fictiones*, 26
— instances cited from the English and Roman Law, 26
— their former importance and modern uselessness, 27, 28
— difference between legal fictions and equity, 28
— and between legal fictions and legis-lation, 29
— instances of legal fictions, 31
— Case-law and its anomalies, 31
Fidei-Commissa, or Bequests in Trust, of the Roman Law, 223
Fiefs, hereditary, gradual transforma-tion of Benefices into, 230
— original tenures, 230, 231
— laws of fiefs, 365
Foreigners, causes of immigration of, into ancient Rome, 46, 47
— exclusion of, under the early Roman republic, 48
France, lawyers and judicial science of, 80, *et seq.*
— effects of the alliance between the lawyers and the kings, on the for-tunes of 80, 81
France, difference between the Pays du

FRANCE

Droit Coutumier and the Pays du Droit Écrit, 84
France, pre-eminence given in France to Natural Law, 85
— Rousseau, 87
— the Revolution, 89
Franks, the, referred to, 104
— Roman institution of the Patria Potestas not known to the, 143
Freewill and Necessity, question of, unknown to the Greeks, 304
Furtum, or Theft, of the Roman Law, 370

GAIUS referred to, 52
— his description of the institution of the Patria Potestas, 133
— his information respecting the Perpetual Tutelage of Women, 153
— on the duplication of proprietary right, referred to, 295
Galatæ, the Patria Potestas of the, 136
Gens, or House, of the Romans compared with the Village Community of India, 264
Gentiles, Roman, their rights in cases of Intestate Succession, 221
German law of Succession, 280
Germans, Wills of the ancient, 196, 198
— penal laws of the, 367
— Patria Potestas of, 143
— primitive property of, 198
— the ancient law of allodial property, 228
" Germany" of Tacitus, its value, 120
— suspicions as to its fidelity, 121
— allodial property of, 281
Greece, aristocracies of, 10
Greek theory of a Law of Nature, 52, 53
Greeks, equality of laws on which they prided themselves, 58
— their tendency to confound law and fact, 75
— their notion of an inherited curse, 127
— assistance afforded by, in the formation of the Roman codes, 15
— limited Patria Potestas of the, 136, 137
— metaphysics of the, 300
— their want of capacity for producing a philosophy of law, 354
Grote, Mr., his " History of Greece," referred to, 5, 9
Grotius, Hugo, and his successors, on International law, 96

HINDOOS

Grotius, his doctrines, 100
— success of his treatise " De Jure Belli et Pacis," 111
— his theory of a Natural State and of a system of principles congenial to it, 114
— his moral philosophy and that of his school, 350
— comparison of his system with that of the Casuists, 351
Guardianship, Perpetual, of Women, under the Roman Law, 153
— amongst the Hindoos, 153
— amongst the Scandinavians, 153

HÆREDITAS, or Inheritance, definition, 181
Hæres or Heir, his rights and duties, 181, 190, 227
Half-blood relationship, 151
— the rule according to the customs of Normandy, 151
Haus-Gesetze of Germany, 232
Heirs, rights of, under the Roman Law, 131, 190, 227
Highland chieftainship hereditary, 234
— form of Primogeniture, 240
Hindoo laws of Menu, 6, 17, 18
— Customary Law, 7
— law of Succession, 280
— difference between Inheritances and Acquisitions, 281
— Perpetual Tutelage of Women amongst the, 153
— right amongst the, to inherit a dead man's property, 191
— the Hindoo sacra, 192
— the Suttee, 193
— the place of Wills amongst the Hindoos occupied by Adoptions, 193
— rights of the first-born son amongst the, 228
— primogeniture of the Hindoos in public office or political power, but not in property, 233
Hindoos, form of Ownership of Property amongst the,—the Village Community, 260
— Co-ownership, 261
— simplest form of the Village Community, 262, 265
— Acquisitions of Property and Inheritances, Hindoo distinction between, 281

HOBBES

Hobbes, his theory of the origin of law, 114
Homer, his account of the Cyclops quoted, 124
— his description of an ancient law-suit, 377
Homeric poems, rudimentary jural ideas afforded by the, 2, 3
— Themis and Themistes, 4, 5
— Homeric words for Custom, 5

INDIA, heroic and aristocratic eras of the races of, 10
— laws of Menu, 6, 17, 18
— Customary law of, 7
— stage beyond which India has not passed, 23
Inheritance a form of universal succession, 177
— Roman definition of an Inheritance, 181
— old Roman law of, 189
— and Acquisition, Hindoo differences between, 281
Injunction of the Court of Chancery, 293
Institutes of the Roman lawyers, 35
International Law, modern confusion between it and Jus Gentium, 53
— function of the Law of Nature in giving birth to modern International Law, 96
— postulates forming the foundation of International Law, 96
— Grotius and his successors, 96
— Dominion, 102
— territorial sovereignty, 103
— the ante-Grotian system of the Law of Nations, 109
— preparation of the public mind for the reception of the Grotian system, 110
— success of the treatise "De Jure Belli et Pacis," 111
— points of junction between modern public law and territorial sovereignty, 112
— sources of the mode in case of Capture in War, 46
Intestacy. See Succession, Intestate
Ἰσότης, the Greek principle of, 58, 61
Italy, aristocracies of, 10
— codes of, 17
— instability of society in ancient, 47

JUS NATURALE

Italy, territorial sovereignty of princes of, 108

JEWS, Wills of the, 197
Julianus, Salvius, the Prætor, his Edict, 64
— effect of his measures on the Prætorian Edicts, 66
Jurisconsults, early Roman, 37—39
— later, 41
— Natural Law of the, 76
Jurisprudence, golden age of Roman, 55
Jurists, Roman, period of, 66, 68
Jus Gentium, origin of, 47, et seq.
— circumstances of the origin of, 50
— how regarded by a Roman, 51
— and by a modern lawyer, 51
— difference between the Jus Gentium and the Jus Naturale, 52, 53
— point of contact between the old Jus Gentium and the Jus Naturale, 58
— difference between the Jus Gentium and the Quiritarian Law, 59
— influence of the, on modern civilisation, 103
Jus Feciale, or International Law of the Romans, 53
Jus Naturale, or Law of Nature, 52
— difference between the Jus Naturale and the Jus Gentium, 53
— Greek conceptions of Nature and her law, 53
— point of contact between the old Jus Gentium and the Law of Nature, 58
— modern history of the Law of Nature, 73
— Natural law of the Roman Jurisconsults, 76
— ancient counterpart of Benthamism, 79
— vastness of the influence of the Law of Nature on modern society, 80
— history of the Law of Nature, 80, et seq.
— pre-eminence given to Natural law in France, 85
— its condition at the middle of the 18th century, 86
— Rousseau, 87
— the French Revolution, 89
— equality of men, 92
— function of the Law of Nature in giving birth to modern International Law, 96

JUS NATURALE

Jus Naturale, sources of the Modern International Law of Capture in War, 246
Justinian's "Institutes" quoted, 46
— referred to, 57
— "Pandects" of, 67
— "Corpus Juris Civilis" of, 68
— his modifications of the Patria Potestas, 143
— his scale of Intestate Succession, 219

KINGS, origin of the doctrine of the divine right of, 346
Kingship, heroic, origin of, 9

LACEDÆMONIAN kings, authority of the, 10
Land-law of England at the present day, 226
Land and goods, English distinction between, 283
Latifundia, Roman mode of cultivating the, 299
Law, social necessities and opinions always in advance of, 24
— agencies by which law is brought into harmony with society, 25
— ancient, 113
— theories of a natural state and of a system congenial to it, 113
— Grotius, Blackstone, Locke, and Hobbes, 114
— theory of Montesquieu, 115
— Bentham, 117
— dissatisfaction with existing theories, 118
— proper mode of inquiry, 119
— the Patriarchal theory, 122
— fiction of Adoption, 130
— the archaic Family, 133
— the Patria Potestas of the Romans, 133
— agnatic and cognatic relationships, 146
— Guardianship of Women, 153
— ancient Roman Marriage, 154
— Master and Slave, 162
Leges Barbarorum, 297
Leges Corneliæ of Sylla, 41, 42
Leges Juliæ of Augustus, 41, 42
Legis Actio Sacramenti of the Romans described, 375
Legislation, era of, 25
— considered as an agent by which the

NATIONS

adaptation of law to the social wants is carried on, 29
Legislation, difference between it and legal fictions, 28, 29
Lex Calpurnia de Repetundis, the first true Roman Criminal Law, 384
Lex Plætoria, purport of the, 161
Lidi of the Germans, 231
Local Contiguity as the condition of community in political functions, 132
Locke, John, referred to, 87
— his theory of the origin of law, 114
Lombards, referred to, 114
Louis Hutin, King of France, his ordinance quoted, 94

MAHOMETAN Law of Succession, 242
Majority and Minority, meaning of the terms in Roman Law, 162
Mancipation, Roman, 50, 204, 278, 317
— mode of giving the effect of Mancipation to a Tradition, 279
Manus of the Romans, 317
Marriage. ancient Roman, 154
— later Roman, 155
Master and Slave, 162
— under the Romans, 163
— in the United States, 163
Menu, Hindoo Laws of, 6, 17, 18
Merovingian kings of the Franks, 104
Metayers, the, of the south of Europe, 301
"Moniteur," the, during the period of the French Revolution, 92
Montesquieu's "Esprit des Lois," remarks on, 86
— his Theory of Jurisprudence, 115
— Apologue of Montesquieu concerning the Troglodytes, in the "Lettres Persanes," 311
Moral doctrines, early, 127
Mortgagor, special proprietorship created by the Court of Chancery for the, 294
Moses, testamentary power not provided for by the Laws of, 197

NAPLES, territorial sovereignty of the monarchs of, 108
Nations, Law of, 96, et seq. See International Law and Jus Gentium

NATURE

Nature and her Law, Greek conceptions of, 53
Nexum of the ancient Romans, 48, 315
— changes in the, 518
Normandy, customs of, referred to, 151
Νόμος, the word not known to the Homeric poems, 5
Nuncupatio, of the Romans, 205

OBLIGATIONS of the Roman Law, 323
— rights and duties of, 324
Occupatio, or Occupancy, of the Roman Law, a "natural mode of acquiring property," 245, 250
— things which never had an owner, 245
— things which have not an owner, 245
— Capture in war, 246
— Discovery, 248
— objections to the popular theory of Occupancy, 256
Ordinance of Louis Hutin quoted, 94
Orphans, Guardianship of male, under the Roman Law, 160

PACTES de Famille of France, 232
Pascal, his "Lettres Provinciales," 352
Paterfamilias in elementary communities, 234, 235
Patria Potestas, the, of the Romans, 133
— of the Galatæ, 136
— of the Greeks, 136, 137
— causes which helped to mitigate the stringency of the father's power over the persons of his children, 141
— liabilities of the Paterfamilias, 145
— unity of person between the Paterfamilias and the Filiusfamilias, 145
— rights and duties of the Paterfamilias, 145, 146, 234, 235
— the Patria Potestas not a durable institution, 146
Patriarchal theory of primeval jurisprudence, 122
— chief points from Scriptural accounts, 123
— Homer's account of the Cyclops, 124
Pays du Droit Écrit and Pays du Droit Coutumier, difference between the, 84
Peculium, the, of the Romans, 142
-- Castrense Peculium, 142
— Quasi-castrense Peculium, 142

PRIMOGENITURE

Penal law in ancient codes, 367
Perjury, how punished by the ancient Romans, 893
Persian monarchy, heroic and aristocratic eras of the races composing the, 11
Persians, the ancient, their veracity, 308
Φύσις of the Greeks, meaning of the, 53
Plebeian Wills of the Romans, 201
— legalised by, at the Twelve Tables, 202
— their influence on the civilisation of the modern world, 203
Political ideas, early, 128
— foundation of aristocracies, 132
Political Economy and Contract, 305
Polygamy, its influence on Primogeniture, 243
Possessory interdicts of the Roman Law, 291
Prætor, origin of the office of, 62
— Edict of the, 41, 57, 63, 66
— the Roman, compared with an English Chancellor, 64, 65
— restraints on the Prætor, 65
— the Prætor the chief equity judge as well as the great common law magistrate, 67
Prætor Peregrinus, office of the, 63
Prætorian Edict of the Romans, 41, 57, 65, 66
— the Edictum Perpetuum, 63
— that of Salvius Julianus, 64, 66
— remedies given by the, 293
Prætorian Will, the, 209
— described, 210
Prescription of Property, history of, 284, *et seq.*
Primogeniture, changes in Law of Succession, caused by, 225
— almost destroyed by the authors of the French code, 225, 226
— results of the French system, 226
— rights of the first-born son amongst the Hindoos, 228
— early history of Primogeniture, 229
— Benefices, 229
— gradual transformation of Benefices into hereditary Fiefs, 230
— the Pactes de Famille of France and the Hauz-Gesetze of Germany, 232
— causes of the diffusion of Primogeniture, 232

PRIMOGENITURE

Primogeniture in public offices or political power amongst the Hindoos, but not in property, 233
— ancient forms of Primogeniture, 235
— why did Primogeniture gradually supersede every other principle of Succession? 235
— earlier and later Primogeniture, 257
— Hindoo rule of the eldest son and of the eldest line also, 239
— Celtic form of Primogeniture, 240
— Mahometan form, 242
— influence of polygamy on Primogeniture, 243
Progress, causes of the arrest of, of the greater part of mankind, 77
Property, early history of, 244
— "natural modes" of acquisition, 244
— Occupancy, 245
— Capture in War, 246
— rule of Discovery, 248
— history of the origin of property, 250
— Blackstone on the theory of Occupancy as the origin of property, 251
— aphorism of Savigny on the origin of property, 254
— objections to the popular theory of Occupancy, 256
— Co-ownership amongst the Hindoos, 260
— the Gens, or House, of the Romans compared with the Village Community of India, 264
— Russian village co-ownership, 266
— Croatian and Sclavonian Laws respecting the property of Families, 269
— ancient difficulties of Alienation, 271
— natural classification of property, 273
— ancient modes of transfer of property, 276
— definition of the Res Mancipi, 277
— tradition of property, 578
— distinction between Res Mancipi and Res nec Mancipi, 279
— Hindoo Law of Inheritances and Acquisitions, 281, 282
— law of moveables and law of land, according to the French codes, 283
— and in England, 283
— Usucapion, or Prescription, 284
— Cessio in Jure, or recovery, in a Court of Law, of property sought to be conveyed, 289

RES MANCIPI

Property, influence of Courts of Law and of their procedure upon Property, 290
— distinction between Property and Possession, 290
— and between Law and Equity in their conceptions of proprietary right, under the Roman and English Law, 293
— feudal view of Ownership, 295
— Roman and barbarian law of Ownership, 296
— Roman system of Tenancy, 299
— the Coloni of the Romans and the Metayers of the South of Europe, 300, 301
— rights of the Emphyteuta, 301
— the Agri Limitrophi of the Rhine and the Danube, 302
Proscriptions, Roman, origin of the, 389
Pupilage or Wardship in modern jurisprudence, 162
— compared with the Guardianship of Orphans under the Roman Law, 162

QUASI-CONTRACT, 343
— meaning of, in Roman Law, 344
Quasi, meaning of the word, in Roman Law, 344
Quæstiones Perpetuæ of the Romans, 384
— theory of the Quæstiones, 386
— results traceable to the Quæstiones, 391
Quæstores Parricidii of the ancient Romans, 383
Querela Inofficiosi Testamenti of the old Roman Law, 215
Quiritarian Law, the, 48
— principles of the, 59
— difference between it and the Jus Gentium, 59

RECOVERIES, collusive, of property in the Roman and English Law, 289
Regency, form of, according to the French custom regulating the succession to the throne, 240
Reipus, the, of Germany, 281
Res Mancipi and Res nec Mancipi, 274, 279
— definition of the Res Mancipi, 277

RES NULLIUS

Res nullius of the Roman Law, 246
Responsa Prudentium of the Romans described, 33
— similarity between them and English Case-law, 33
— decline and extinction of the Responses, 40, 41
Revolution, French, effects of the theory of the state of Nature on the, 91
Rex Sacrorum, or *Rex Sacrificulus*, office of the, 10, 62
Roman Law, 1
— the Twelve Tables, 1, 2, 14, 33
— influence of the *sacra* on the Law of Adoption and of Wills, 6, 7
— class of codes to which the Roman code belongs, 15
— probable assistance afforded by Greeks, 15
— meaning of *fictio*, 25
— instances of *fictiones* cited, 26
— the Responsa Prudentium described, 33
— judicial functions of the Magistrates of Republican Rome, 36
— reasons why the Roman Law was not popularised, 36
— sources of the characteristic excellence of the Roman Law, 38
— decline and extinction of the Responses, 40, 41
— the Prætorian Edict, 41, 57, 63, 66
— the Leges Corneliæ, 41, 42
— later jurisconsults, 41
— remarks on the Statute Law of the Romans, 41—43
— and on the Equity of the Romans, 44, 45
— golden age of Roman jurisprudence, 55
— Roman Equity, 58, 67
— features common to both English and Roman Equity, 68, *et seq.*
— International Law largely indebted to Roman Law, 97
— the Patria Potestas of the Roman Law, 137, *et seq.*
— Agnatic and Cognatic Relationship, 146
— Perpetual Tutelage of Women, 153
— Roman Marriage, 154, 155
— Guardianship of male Orphans, 160
— Law of Persons—Master and Slave. 162
— Testamentary Law, 172, *et seq.*

ROMANS

Roman Law, Wills anciently executed in the Comitia Calata, 199, 201
— ancient Roman Law of Intestate Succession, 199
— Roman Wills described, 201
— the Mancipation, 204
— the Nuncupatio, 205
— the Prætorian Will, 209
— first appearance of Sealing in the history of jurisprudence as a mode of authentication, 210
— Querela Inofficiosi Testamenti, 215
— Disinherison of Children under, 215
— Intestate Succession under, 218
— Fidei-Commissa, or bequests in trust, 223
— rights of Co-heirs, 227
— Occupancy, 245
— Roman distinction between the Law of Persons and the Law of Things, 258
— influence of Roman classifications, 259
— Co-ownership of property regarded by the mature Roman Law as exceptional and momentary, 261
— the Gens of the Romans compared with an Indian Village Community, 264
— Res Mancipi, and Res nec Mancipi, 274, 277
— Mancipation, 278
— Usucapion, or Prescription, 284
— the Cessio in Jure, 289
— distinction between Property and Possession, 290
— Roman and Barbarian Law, 296
— Roman Contracts, 314, *et seq.*
— the Four Contracts, 325
— connection between Theology and Roman Law, 355
— causes of improvement in Roman Law, 361
— Roman Law in the Eastern Empire, 363
— Civil Wrongs of the Roman Law, 370
— the Legis Actio Sacramenti, 375
— old Roman Criminal Jurisprudence, 382
— extreme multiplicity of Roman criminal tribunals, 390
— results traceable to the Quæstiones, 391
Romans, causes of the rapid progress of the Stoical philosophy amongst the, 55

ROMANS

Romans, their progress in legal improvement, 57

Rome, immigration of foreigners into, 46, 47

— exclusion of, under the early Republic, 46

— See of, origin of the tendency to attribute secular superiority to the, 108

— decline of ecclesiastical influence in international questions, 110

— early political ideas of, 130

Rousseau, J. J., influence of his writings, 87

— his doctrine of an original Social Compact, 308, 309

Russian villages, Co-ownership of the occupiers of, 266

SACRA, or Family Rites, of the Romans, 6, 7, 27, 191, 192

— of the Hindoos, 192

Sacramental Action of the Ancient Romans, 48

Salic Law, origin of the, 157

Savigny, on Possession and Property, 290, 291

— his aphorism on the Origin of Property, 254

Scævola, Q. Mucius, his Manual of the Civil Law, 40, 41

Scandinavian nations, their laws respecting the Perpetual Tutelage of Women, 153, 159

Sclavonian laws respecting the property of families, 268

Sealing, first appearance of, in jurisprudence, as a mode of authentication, 210

Sin, mortal and venial, casuistical distinction between, 351

Sins known to primitive jurisprudence, 371

Slavery, ancient, 162

— under the Romans, 163

— in the United States of America, 163

Socage, English law of, 232

Social Compact, Rosseau's doctrine of an original, 308, 309, 345

— Dr. Whewell quoted, 347

Societies, stationary and progressive, 22

— difference between stationary and progressive societies, 23

— agencies by which Law is brought

STOIC PHILOSOPHY

into harmony with Progressive Societies, 25

Societies, perils of early, 75

— primitive, 120

— early moral doctrines, 127

— early political ideas, 128

— fiction of Adoption, 130

— foundation of aristocracies, 132

— principle of Local Contiguity, 132

— the ancient Family, 133

— the Patria Potestas, 133

— agnatic and cognatic relationships, 146

— Guardianship of Women, 153

— ancient Roman Marriage, 154

— Master and Slave, 162

— uniformity of movement of the progressive societies, 168

— disintegration of the Family, 169

— movement of societies from status to contract, 170

— Universal Succession, 177, 179, 181

— primitive society and universal succession, 183

— the ancient family a corporation, 184

Society in primitive times not a collection of individuals, but an aggregation of families, 126

Solon, Attic code of, 16

"Sophismes Anarchiques" of Dumont, remarks on, 92

Sovereign, origin of the doctrine that the monarch is the fountain of justice, 396

Sovereignty, territorial, proposition of International Law on, 102, 103

— Tribe-sovereignty, 104

— Charlemagne and universal dominion, 106

— Territorial sovereignty an offshoot of feudalism, 107

— the See of Rome, 108

— Hugh Capet, 108

— the Anglo-Saxon princes, 108

— Naples, Spain, and Italy, 108

— Venice, 109

— points of junction between territorial sovereignty and modern public law, 112

Spain, territorial sovereignty of the monarchs of, 108

Status, movement of societies from, to contract, 170

Statute Law of the Romans, 41, 45

Stoic philosophy, principles of the, 54

STOIC PHILOSOPHY

Stoic philosophy, its rapid progress in Roman society, 55
— alliance of the Roman lawyers with the Stoics, 55
Succession, rules of, according to the Hindoo Customary Law, 7
— Testamentary, 171
— early history, 171
— influence of the Church in enforcing the sanctity of Wills, 173
— English law of, 173
— qualities necessarily attached to Wills, 174
— natural rights of testation, 175
— restraints imposed by the Code Napoléon, 176
— nature of a Will, 177
— rights and duties of universal successor, 177
— usual Roman definition of an Inheritance, 181
— difference between modern testamentary jurisprudence and the ancient law of Rome, 182
— the Family regarded as a Corporation, 184
— old Roman Law of Inheritance and its notion of a Will, 189
— ancient objects of Wills, 190
— Sacra, or Family Rites, of the Romans, 191
— and of the Hindoos, 191, 192
— the invention of Wills due to Romans, 194
— Roman ideas of Succession, 195
— Testamentary Succession less ancient than Intestate Succession, 195
— primitive operation of Wills, 196
— Wills of the ancient Germans, 196
— Jewish and Bengalee Wills, 197
— mode of execution of ancient Roman Wills, 199
— description of ancient Roman Wills, 201
— influence of ancient Plebeian Wills on the civilisation of the modern world, 203
— the Mancipation, 204
— relation of Wills to conveyances, 204
— the Testament per æs et libram, 204, 213, 214
— consequence of this relation of Testaments to Conveyances, 206
— remedies, 207

TESTAMENTS

Succession, ancient Wills not written, 207
— remarks on the expression Emptor Familiæ, 208
— the Prætorian Will, 209
— the Bonorum Possessio and the Bonorum Possessor, 211
— improvements in the old Will, 212, 213
— ancient and modern ideas respecting Wills and Successors, 215
— Disinherison of Children, 215
— the age of Wills coeval with that of Feudalism, 224
— introduction of the principle of Dower, 224
— rights of Heirs and Co-heirs under the Roman Law, 227
— intestate, 195
— ancient Roman law of, 199, 218
— the Justinianean scale of Intestate Succession, 219
— order of Intestate Succession among the Romans, 220
— horror of intestacy felt by the Romans, 222, 223
— rights of all the children of the deceased under the Roman Law, 227
— Universal, 177, 189
— in what it consists, 179
— the universal successor, 181
— formula of old Roman investiture referred to, 190
Suttee of the Hindoos, 193
Sylla, L. Cornelius, his improvements in the Roman Law, 41, 42

TABLES, the Twelve Decemviral, 1, 2, 14, 33
— collections of opinions interpretative of the, 33
— their legalisation of Plebeian Wills, 202
— Law of the Twelve Tables respecting Testamentary Dispositions, 216
Tablets, laws engraven on, 14
Tacitus, value of his "Germany" as a record of primitive history, 120
— suspicions as to its fidelity, 121
Tarquins, change in the administration of the law after the expulsion of the, 61, 62
Tenancy, Roman system of, 229
Testaments. See Succession, Testamentary

THEFT

Theft, ancient Roman law of, 307, 378, 379
— modern breaches of trust, 307
Themis and Themistes of the Greek Homeric poems, 4, 5, 125
Theology, connection between it and Roman Law, 355
Thirty Years' War, influence of the horrors of the, on the success of the treatise "De Jure Belli et Pacis" of Grotius, 111
Torts, law of, 370
Tradition of property amongst the Romans, 278
— practical effect of a Mancipation given to a Tradition, 278
Transfer of property, ancient modes of, 276
Troglodytes, the, 311
Turkey, rule of succession to the throne of, 242

ULPIAN, his attempt to distinguish between the Jus Naturale and the Jus Gentium, 52
Universatis juris, in what it consists, 178
Usucapion, principle of Roman Law known as, 212
— history of, 284
Usus, or lower form of civil marriage of the ancient Romans, 154

VANDALS, the, referred to, 104
Venetians, their lapse from tribe sovereignty to territorial sovereignty, 109

ZEUS

Village Communities of India, 260, 262, et seq.
Visigoths, the, referred to, 104
Voltaire, referred to, 87

WARFARE, ancient forms of, 247
Wehrgeld, the, of Germany, 281
Whewell, Dr., on original Social Compact, quoted, 347
— his view of Moral Philosophy, 348
Widow's share of her husband's estate, 224
— the reipus, or fine leviable on the remarriage of a widow in Germany, 281
Wills, influence of the Sacra Gentilicia on the law of, 6, 7
— See Succession, Testamentary
Women, laws respecting the status of, 152
— Roman law of the Perpetual Tutelage of, 153
— amongst the Hindoos, 153
— and amongst the Scandinavians, 155
— Guardianship of Women under the Roman Law, 153
— tutelage of, amongst the Hindoos, 153
— tutelage of, amongst the Scandinavians, 153
— ancient Roman Marriage, 154
— later Roman Marriage, 155
— special Proprietorship created by the Court of Chancery for, 295

ZEUS, not a lawmaker, but a judge, 4, 5.